Need I Say More?

Also by Stephen Kessler

POETRY

Where Was I? 2015

Scratch Pegasus 2013

Burning Daylight 2007

Tell It to the Rabbis 2001

After Modigliani 2000

Living Expenses 1980

Beauty Fatigue 1978

Thirteen Ways of Deranging an Angel 1977

Poem to Walt Disney 1976

Nostalgia of the Fortuneteller 1975

TRANSLATION

Forbidden Pleasures (poems by Luis Cernuda) 2015

Poems of Consummation (poems by Vicente Aleixandre) 2013

Desolation of the Chimera (poems by Luis Cernuda) 2009

Eyeseas (poems by Raymond Queneau, translated with Daniela Hurezanu) 2008

Written in Water (prose poems by Luis Cernuda) 2004

Aphorisms (prose by César Vallejo) 2002

Heights of Machu Picchu (poem by Pablo Neruda) 2001

Ode to Typography (poem by Pablo Neruda) 1998

Save Twilight (poems by Julio Cortázar) 1997

From Beirut (poem by Mahmoud Darwish) 1992

Akrílica (poems by Juan Felipe Herrera, translated with Sesshu Foster) 1989

The Funhouse (novel by Fernando Alegría) 1986

Changing Centuries (poems by Fernando Alegría) 1985

Widows (novel by Ariel Dorfman) 1983

Homage to Neruda (poems by eight Chilean poets) 1978

Destruction or Love (poems by Vicente Aleixandre) 1976

FICTION

The Mental Traveler (novel) 2009

NONFICTION

The Tolstoy of the Zulus: On Culture, Arts & Letters (essays) 2011

Moving Targets: On Poets, Poetry & Translation (essays) 2008

EDITOR

The Sonnets by Jorge Luis Borges 2010

Need I Say More?

Portraits, Confessions, Reflections

STEPHEN KESSLER

TO GORDON

STILL ON A ROLL!

El León Literary Arts

Berkeley, California

Most of these pieces originally appeared in the following periodicals, whose editors are gratefully acknowledged: *Catamaran Literary Reader, Coast Weekly, East Bay Express, Mendocino County Outlook, Metro Santa Cruz, Metro Silicon Valley, The Montserrat Review, North Bay Bohemian, phren-Z, Poetry Flash, Quarter After Eight, The Redwood Coast Review, Review of Contemporary Fiction, Santa Cruz Express, Santa Cruz Sentinel, Santa Cruz Weekly, The Sun,* and *Translation Review.*

Need I Say More? is published by El León Literary Arts, a private foundation established to extend the array of voices essential to a democracy's arts and education.

Publisher: Thomas Farber
Managing editor: Kit Duane
Cover design: Andrea Young
Interior design and composition: Peak Services
peakserviceshawaii.com

El León Literary Arts is distributed by
Small Press Distribution, Inc.
800-869-7533
www.spdbooks.org

El León books are also available on Amazon.com

El León web site: www.elleonliteraryarts.org

ISBN 978-0-9891277-1-4

LCCN 2014948149

Contents

Culture & Politics

Writers & Writing

for Walter L. Martin

Preface

For the past forty years I've been writing essays, reviews, columns, interviews, articles and features for alternative newspapers and independent literary journals. Some of those writings have been collected in two previous books, *Moving Targets* and *The Tolstoy of the Zulus*, organized respectively around the general subjects of poetry and cultural criticism. This book picks up where those left off, including pieces on poetry and culture but extending as well into spheres of the personal, the spiritual, the social and the political. I have tried in my selection to eliminate the merely topical and ephemeral, and to include only what may have enduring value and is therefore worth preserving for the record. The reader will decide how well I have succeeded.

I started out as a poet, but journalism has enabled me to write for readers who might never see, much less read, a little magazine, and who are not specialists in literature. In the communities where I've lived, mainly in Northern California, I've tried to offer in print my thoughts and observations on matters of public interest or cultural concern, from presidential inaugurations to erectile dysfunction, from art exhibitions to marijuana legalization, from illegal immigration to literary translation. I consider myself a generalist, and claim as credentials not any authoritative expertise but an alert critical sensibility and an ability to think and write at the same time.

I have never been especially fond of the memoir as a form, nor very comfortable writing about myself and my family, but many of these pieces explore or touch on aspects of my personal history that have informed the ways in which I read the world around me, and in the autobiographical sketches presented I hope to give an honest account of the origins of my particular angle of vision. The kind of commentary and analysis I write is unapologetically subjective, and that subjectivity is influenced not only by my study of the subject, but by my entire formation as a person and as a citizen. I hope that what I share here of my private life proves interesting not only for its own sake, but for the light it sheds on what I have to say about everything else.

Poetry and literature are central to my understanding of almost anything that has ever interested me. For better or worse, I find my apprehension of reality suffused with what I've learned as a poet about paying attention, about listening to the rhythms of language and of experience, about hearing rhymes and seeing patterns and making associations. When a poem works, these elements come together to create a little verbal and musical universe where, while we are reading it, time itself may feel suspended as we immerse ourselves in the small world of its spell. I'd like to think these essays may have a similar effect, while opening into the larger world as well.

—SK

Need I Say More?

A book is nothing but a block
of hot, smoking consciousness.

BORIS PASTERNAK

I know literature cannot save us—it is water,
mercifully, moistening the lips of an
accident victim, before the blackout.

GREG HALL

Lives & Times

With Jack in Seattle

[1991]

"He was as much my father as he was yours."

My uncle Ackie is sitting across the table from me in a lakeside seafood restaurant, treating me to lunch and his recollections of the big brother he idolized. At seventy-two he brims with happy enthusiasm, physically a ringer for my dad at his age, bald except for a thin but untrimmed rim of silver hair, his forehead tanned from driving around all summer in his white Mercedes convertible. Ackie got his name from the way he said "Jack" as a baby—"Ack, Ack"—and he's been Ackie ever since. His comment strikes me as ironic because in some ways Jack was more his father than mine. When I was little he and my mother were consumed with their new business, a swimwear company born about the same time I was, and growing faster. Louise, our housekeeper, my brother Rick and my mother's parents, who lived with us, looked after me day to day. But when Ackie was two and their father took off, leaving their mother with four kids to care for, Jack took over not only as the breadwinner but as the guiding light for his younger siblings. Henry, their other brother, now in his mid-seventies living in LA, was a sensitive brooding introspective boy Jack never could understand, but Ackie's outwardness mirrored his own, and Jack was Ackie's god.

"Everything I am I owe to him," says Ackie. "He was the greatest teacher I ever had. The greatest friend." All his life he solicited Jack's advice on everything, which to him as a kid meant mainly sports, and later business. "I was the jock, and Jack made it possible for me to compete—in basketball, in tennis—he saw that I had the equipment, that I got to the games and the tournaments. He was my coach and he was my mentor. He bought me what I needed, drove me places." I'm getting the picture of a selfless older brother, a lovable guy of sterling character—the kind of description I've heard before, from my mother, from friends at his funeral, and the kind that's to be repeated by practically everyone I speak to in Seattle. A good man, no way around it. Without any evident demons. No darkness, even, for dramatic contrast. A shining example.

It's not that I was looking for my father. I'd found him eight years ago on his deathbed, earlier in fact, his spirit opening gradually in his last years to embrace me after a lengthy stretch of mutual misunderstanding. What I needed now was to talk with people who'd known him in his boyhood. He had a history in this city that he'd scarcely alluded to his whole life. I wanted to hear the story from some eyewitnesses. Whatever was behind his success—he'd built permanent security for his family out of difficult beginnings and modest accomplishment as a salesman, winding up in his mature years running a multimillion-dollar corporation and retiring comfortably to the racetrack—the seeds of that success were bred on the street when he went out at twelve to pull his weight and everybody else's besides. Ackie and his older sister, Doree, were still alive and lucid here close to their roots by Lake Washington, and I had the numbers of a couple of old men, both friends from my father's school days, now in their eighties.

Seattle has changed since then. In the teens and twenties when he was coming up it was a smallish town, a port to the Orient, with an independent western atmosphere charged with the adventurous energies of the fishing and lumber industries. It was a tough town, rugged, home of the original Skid Row, with strong unions, guys who worked with their hands and others who stopped on shore leave or shipped out; traders, hustlers. Skid Row is now an indoor shopping mall, the skyscrapers gleam, their reflections flashing over Puget Sound and across the lake to the suburbs, a city so clean the cops ride around on shiny bicycles giving tourists tickets for jaywalking. Since World War II, with Boeing's arrival as the dominant industry, and the computer boom of the eighties, the city has grown both prosperous and popular. It is more hectic but still feels little enough to find your way around. The people are friendly. I'm staying downtown and walking as much as possible. All I have to do to keep out of trouble is wait for the green light.

"When I was eighteen," says Ackie, "just out of high school, I bought a little cigar store, with Jack's approval. A three-hundred-and-fifty-dollar investment. There was this dice game that customers could play, '26' I think it was called, and the chips were worth twelve-and-a-half cents each, redeemable for merchandise. Well, one day this *slicker* comes in—" Ackie puts extra emphasis on the word, says it with bitter relish—"and in the course of an afternoon wins fifteen dollars worth of chips. This is 1938. Fifteen dollars is a day's receipts. And somehow, since it's such a large amount, this *slicker* talks me into cashing his winnings. Well, I was sick. Heartbroken. I'd never felt so awful. So later, as every night, Jack stops by to ask me how it's going. I'm miserable, of course. I tell him what happened with the slicker. So he says, 'Who was this guy?' And I say, 'Oh I don't know—some schmuck.' And he says, 'Who was the schmuck?'

"I never forgot that," Ackie declares in his tight yet genial nasal voice. "That's the last time I ever called anybody a schmuck."

A classic teaching of the master: Don't blame the other guy for your own stupidity. And an equally important corollary: Stay positive, jettison negativity. That was Henry's problem, too many dark thoughts, doubts. "Henry resented life," says Ackie. "The world wasn't good enough for him. He had all these political ideas; he got so far left he didn't know where he was." Clearly a bad attitude. I see by contrast the glad-handing Ackie, everybody's friend, bantering with the restaurant owner, joking around with the young waiter, signing the back of the check and slipping him a fiver. "Sorry to stiff you, J. T." A generous tipper, just like Jack. A quick smile and a kind heart. No complaints.

Just like Jack. This, he tells me frankly, has been the key to his success: doing as Jack would right down the line. Going into business for himself—sportswear sales, like Jack—instead of working for someone else, even his brother. Making a few good investments. "Now all I have to do is go into the office and read the papers. Open the checks as they come in." Everybody's secure. Whatever's in the papers presumably can't touch the family, thanks to smart planning and prudent living. I reflect that my father read the papers too, and that as far back as I can remember he was a pessimist—"You can always expect the unexpected" was one of his favorite sayings. He anticipated the worst and considered himself lucky to have done as well as he had. Ackie seems instinctively to keep the dark thoughts down. The faithful acolyte has come of age as a happy patriarch: I see him that evening sitting on his porch on the lakefront, blissfully presiding over a family dinner, beaming in the glow of children and grandchildren, living the good life, the city in shadow across the water, sun going down over the lake in a flourish of clouds the color of salmon flesh. This is the fruit of so much work, so many trips to Asia peddling underwear, fruit of an upbeat outlook and a gambling spirit willing to go on guts and horse sense, following Jack's example.

The whole time I'm with Ackie I can't help wondering how he regards me, Jack's youngest, still fighting at forty-four to make it as a writer, the most impractical of professions. I have a history of nonconformity, of challenging authority, raising uncomfortable questions. I've spent my inheritance on profitless publishing ventures, putting out books and magazines and newspapers that couldn't support themselves. I have a companion but no wife or nuclear family, no home of my own anymore, just an apartment in rootless New York City, so little to show for all my efforts but a few heavy cartons of printed matter now in storage in a closet in California. Is my out-of-the-mainstream career, my crankiness, my individuality appreciated by this uncle who measures accomplishment by its material evidence? In his eyes am I a success or a failure for following my own path? Does it even matter to him what I've done with my father's legacy? He doesn't ask me about my life, my work; seems to accept me for what I am—whatever that is. Some kind of thinker, dreamer.

Henry was a dreamer, his sister Doree informs me, not a realist like Jack and Ackie. "Henry had a chip on his shoulder." Doree, white-haired at eighty-three, is tough and earnest yet also somehow dismissive of just about everything. She too went to work as a kid to support her mother and little brothers. She is feared by the whole family for her uncompromising judgments, her temper and her drive to run everyone's lives. She and Henry still clash, according to Ackie. As we talk she appears to be going easy on me, not living up to her terrible reputation, possibly because in her scheme of things I'm not "a going concern" and therefore not worth taking too seriously. She's willing to talk to me about Jack but doesn't have much to say, except to confirm the consensus that he was a fine boy, exemplary, responsible, popular. I ask for specific examples, anecdotes that might illustrate his character, and she waves the question away. "No, I don't have examples, he was just good. You can ask anyone. What are you gonna do with this information?" I tell her I'm not sure, possibly nothing, possibly write a story; I'm trying to satisfy my curiosity. She regards me blankly, puzzled but patient, indulgent of my evident pointlessness. I ask about her father, Sam, the junk purveyor who abandoned them. She says she doesn't remember him, they scarcely saw him even when he was around. From her high-rise apartment we look out over the sound. The port sparkles in afternoon sun, excellent August weather, ferries and freighters plowing the water. Her husband, Charlie, retired fish-packing magnate, pulls out some old photos to show me. One is of my father at twenty-seven or so, holding my oldest brother, Bruce, an infant, on his lap. Bruce has a recognizable scowl on his face, grouchy in the harsh noon light. His own receding forehead shining under the bright sun, Jack is wearing a pinstripe suit, wide-striped three-tone tie and crisp white collar. He has the same half-smile as in the picture taken thirty years later that's the first thing you see on entering Ackie's office. The smile of a modest man. Charlie tells me I can keep the picture.

There's another photo that interests me even more. It shows a banquet table with several young couples relaxing after dinner: my parents, Jack and Nina; Doree and Charlie; Ackie and his wife, Charlette; and Henry and his first wife, Mary. Henry, with his vulnerable lips and dreamy eyes, looks out of place. By the time this picture was taken in the forties he'd given up his writing career—he'd worked for some years as a journalist—and from his wistful expression appears to have resigned himself to a life of commercial drudgery. Amid this group of prosperous or soon to be prosperous merchants, Henry has the face of a lost poet. Which begins to explain his question to me that long-ago Thanksgiving at my folks' house in LA, when I, a young writer, was visiting from my home in the Santa Cruz Mountains:

"What are you doing in this band of cutthroats?"

I last saw Henry a year and a half ago. I'd sold my house in the Soquel hills and was on the way to New York, stopping in Los Angeles to visit family before proceeding east. Henry, the uncle with whom I felt most at ease, would be my first official source of historic gossip about his brother. He and Franki, his wife of many years, invited me to dinner at their favorite neighborhood restaurant, one of those old Italian-American grills that smell like cocktails and slow-cooked meats and high-priced cologne, with black leather booths, red tablecloths and veteran waitresses. Henry concurred that Jack was a most responsible father figure, taking control when the old man disappeared. But he was remote, impatient. He couldn't relate to Henry's inwardness, his moods. "Jack didn't understand me at all. I was too quiet. Too much of a thinker, I guess. I wasn't outgoing like Ackie. Ackie was the one he was close to. You should talk to him."

But Henry, the one who had started out as a writer, who had gone into sportswear sales like his brothers only out of desperation, and who later in life had gone back to school and gotten a degree in history—Henry had a perspective on my father that made room for more complex memories. His low, softly modulated voice was gentle and melancholy. "Sometime after our father left he went to California. He was always moving around. He settled in Oakland and from there he sent for my mother. So we moved to Oakland. It was a horrible time. Ackie and I were out on the street selling papers one night and Ackie got run over by a car. Scared the hell out of me. Luckily he wasn't badly injured. Those were very rough years. Our father would move, so we would move. Oakland, Portland. He'd go away and then come back. Never stayed with us for long. Jack finally brought us back to Seattle. He always took care of us. I remember once I needed some dental work. He made sure I got it. Took me to the dentist himself, and of course paid the bill. But emotionally we were never that close. Not like he was with Ackie."

When Henry was still a teenager their father returned to the family one last time. Emma, their mother, refused to see him. Jack and Doree told Sam to get lost. They never heard from him again. According to family lore he died a few years later in Los Angeles at the bottom of an elevator shaft. Henry's tone as he told the stories was mournful but not evasive or apologetic. He wasn't ashamed. He was able to face the memory of those years with a certain honest regret that I respected. I was secretly relieved to hear him imply that my father had treated him less than ideally, that Jack was not the saintly figure of legend. My occasional clashes with him as I was coming up—over politics, my poetic vocation or my bohemian lifestyle—were evidence of his limited tolerance, but for all I knew that was only where I was concerned. Now Henry was offering a picture that felt more full than much of what I would hear in my Seattle interviews. Jack would have been the first to disavow the notion that he was flawless. In his later life he was well aware of his weak points and mistakes. He liked to say, "I got old too soon and smart too late."

Frail and shrunken, with translucent skin, his voice trailing off, Mort Pinch is a pale shadow of whatever he once was. A stroke and maybe a touch of Alzheimer's have left him, in his wife Louise's words, a little goofy. I'm visiting him in his living room in the university district. The street is quiet and leafy, a settled neighborhood. The big armchair he sits in is draped with towels that are safety-pinned to the arms, back and padded seat of the chair. He loses the thread of the conversation easily, muses aloud, drops non sequiturs, keeps asking me who I am and why I'm here. But he's able to zero in on the old days. He was best man at Jack and Nina's wedding. "Nina saw something in Jack it was hard to figure. She had everything—looks, money—and he had nothing. They were a good team. Nina was the talker. They'd do anything for each other… That bathing suit business, Nina was the crux of it. She ran the business. She *was* the business… You know, he had plenty of chances to shack up with broads—models and all—but he never did. He was pure… Honest to a fault… He took everybody's word for what they said. He was an optimist without any justification… I think he got in over his head and he didn't know it." Mort is referring to the later years when the business nearly went under, but Jack finally managed to sell the company and retire. The problems he had, according to Mort, resulted from his "sloppiness in details, looseness with detail," and from getting involved with a fast crowd, "Los Angeles, Hollywood people. He put his confidence in people… Even when they didn't deserve it."

The boy that Mort remembers "was always laughing, but I think it was more of a nervous laugh than a good-natured one. He hid his problems with laughter. He had that stutter. It made people stop and listen. Damnedest thing… Jack tried everything, he wasn't afraid… But he was loose with details… I think he was in over his head… What are you gonna do, write something about him?… How come you waited this long?… Jack had a brother who was a writer. What was his name?" Henry, I tell him. "Whose brother did you say you were?"

A light mist, barely a drizzle, is falling on Lake Washington as I sit by the southwest shore on Kay Pearl's terrace. He's tall, bald on top. He hasn't shaved; gray stubble grizzles his face, which is long and thin with warm brown eyes. He's wearing casual slacks, an old wool pullover crewneck sweater, his shirt underneath sort of crumpled around the collar. Inside the large modern split-level house his three adult children are puttering. Their mother, Kay's wife, is in the hospital dying. Kay is reflective. He takes his time.

"Jakie had a golden personality," he says. "Even when he was eight he had charisma. You know, he stuttered. But it was a beautiful stutter. People loved him."

I can tell why my father was lifelong friends with this guy. He has that natural earthiness, the lack of pretension Pop appreciated, no doubt because he himself was that way. Kay says he knows why Jakie was such a good kid. "His mother was very kind. Never a bad word. I never met a more pleasant person. A very religious woman. Always welcomed us into her house. The kids get their sweetness from their mother."

But Jakie was also "full of hell," a fiery kid who burned up the playgrounds with his intense competitiveness, ran wild on the streets, snuck into the ballpark to watch the big-leaguers play in the shipyard league during World War I, "took a liking to prizefighters" and became a boxer himself—"he was very clever with his hands, a good fighter"—and at eleven years old would steal his father's 1886 cigars and pass them around to his friends. He thrived on the action at Green's Cigar Store, a hangout for all the hot shots in Seattle. "He played every sport. Jakie means a guy with color, you know. He had a lot of *gutso*. He was always slow, the slowest guy on the team; he was a good hitter, good fielder, but he couldn't run. He had a big ass. We called him Lard Ass. He didn't care. Everybody loved the guy. There was this soccer game in the rain one time, the other team's goalie had a free kick and Jakie dived head-first and blocked it, landed in the mud, but the ball bounced back past the goalie, scored the winning goal. That's what I'd call him, *gutso* with a personality."

Kay savors the recollections. He's enjoying this as much as I am. Maybe it's bringing back some of the life he's losing with his wife.

"He was always a big eater, you know. Ate a bunch of crap. Great appetite. And always worried about constipation. Once I was working in a pharmacy and I gave him some pills I told him would help his digestion. They were really some kind of thing that turned his urine bright blue." Kay chuckles. "Another time this doctor, Dr. Schwellenbach, asked me to watch his apartment for the night, he was going out of town. So I invited Jakie over. We were jumping up and down on the bed—just horsing around—and the bed broke. Oh we were scared. We thought we were in trouble. But the doctor came back and said what the hell, he should have known better than to ask some youngster to watch his apartment. Something about that incident, we always remembered it. The last time we spoke we talked about it. Had a good laugh.

"You know, he didn't have any discipline. That's why he wasn't religious like his mother. In order to be raised religiously you have to have discipline, from your father. Jakie had no discipline, no religion. What he had was courage. He was a gambler. He had that wholesale operation, K & L Distributors, it was very successful, and he left it to start the swimsuit business in Los Angeles. That took courage. Nina was very important in all that. A successful man has to have a wife that's cooperative. He was a great salesman. A great audience—a listener. A great actor, in a way, but sincere. His word was as good as gold. He was a natural. You know, the greatest brains in history are the guys that never went to school. College would have spoiled him. When he was seventeen, eighteen, he was running with guys twenty-five, twenty-six. He always liked the action."

Jake never talked about his father, says Kay, rarely discussed his problems. "His home life was all *shmish*, very confused, but he kept it to himself. But I remember one time, about ten years into his marriage, he was very depressed. He was in a car with my brother and he told him he was thinking about jumping off a bridge. I guess he pulled out of it."

On his deathbed my father lay feeble and lifeless following post-operative radiation treatments. The surgeon hadn't been able to cut the whole tumor out of his brain, so they were blasting him with rays that wasted him away, turned him into a sagging skeleton with a tan. I was visiting him in this condition one afternoon when Kay Pearl telephoned. Suddenly Jack sprang up in bed, a smile flew into his face, he was excited, energized, laughing as they talked. At the end of the call he collapsed again. I tell Kay that I witnessed their last conversation. "Yes," he says. "I remember that. You know what I told him? I said, 'You know, Jake, you were at my birthday party every year and you never brought me a present.'"

Kay made his fortune in real estate and finance, but he has respect for people like me, "an intellect." It's a little hard for me to compare my minor literary accomplishments with those of guys like Pearl and my uncles Ackie and Charlie, "men of substance" who started from scratch or parlayed their resources into sizable holdings, homes, businesses, buildings, money-making machines. My father was one of the most successful of all, yet his perspective was philosophical. "Boy," he'd often tell me toward the end of his life, "you've got a good formula. You're gonna have a lot of fun. You appreciate the true values." He never said exactly what those values were, but they had something to do with knowing what really matters, being your own man, doing what you like doing, not being tricked or impressed or trapped by superficial measures of success.

Kay says, "Jake was proud of you. He admired you. We'd talk on the phone and he'd say to me, 'You should see my son Steve. He writes poetry, he's got a beard out to here, he has a little house in the mountains—he really knows how to live!'"

Good Grief

[1994]

Eleven years ago this month my father died. It was a lucky death in the sense that, though the onset of his illness was sudden and its course debilitating, he had time to be with each of us—my mother and brothers and sister and me—to round things out and say goodbye in peace. After he'd finally expired, surrounded by family, and I remained in the room with my brother as he had signed some papers for the hospital bureaucracy, I remember looking over at the corpse with that dead expression on its face and thinking how strange that this inert object had a few minutes earlier been a living (if barely) and breathing (though feebly) person. It was my first direct encounter with the mystery of death.

A few days later I had the honor of giving the eulogy at his funeral, and was pleased to be able to speak of him in a way I thought he'd have appreciated. Though I felt the loss, I had accepted it as inevitable and easily rose to the occasion, transforming my awe and vexation into a reading from Ecclesiastes and *Song of Myself* and an extemporaneous talk on the kind of person my father had been. It was a valediction and it felt right to be able to say goodbye to the old man in such ceremonial style. Inspiring, in the sense that it confirmed the wholeness and realness of those last days and gave me the strength to grow with his memory.

The next night I was back home in Santa Cruz and went to a local saloon to hear Tracy Nelson. Her blues-based country contralto was as soulfully resonant as ever, and when she broke into "Down So Low," with its desolate refrain—

> *but it's not losin' you*
> *that's got me down so low*
> *I just can't find another man to take your place—*

my floodgates burst and I cried harder and deeper than at any other time in my adult life. Tears cleanse, and those explosive sobs were an immense relief, a release for the grief I'd held clenched in my chest for who knows how long.

My early training in the Marlon Brando school of cool has always made it hard for me to cry, so on the rare occasions when I do it is such a wonderful feeling of liberation that it somehow restores my spirit, strips away the protective layers long enough for some fresh air to blow out some old shit. A deep calm follows, as after an act of love. The body relaxes, satisfied.

I'm not exactly a touchy-feely kind of guy, and I'm not proselytizing for any crying workshops for emotionally constipated middle-aged men. What I'm getting at is the healing power of grief, the physically and psychically restorative force in allowing the whole tragedy of human life to register and make you feel as humbly helpless as you really are, acknowledging that loss will never go away, that the loved one isn't coming back, that we're alone and anything may happen. There's some consolation to be had in action—art, politics, volunteer work, gardening—but death always has the last laugh.

The outside information is bad enough—unbelievable suffering in Haiti, Rwanda, Bosnia, Brentwood, Willits—ordeals whose miseries would drive us mad, set us wailing and tearing our clothes, ripping out our hair and eating dirt, if we could truly let their reality sink in. But it's only electronics that allow us to witness those distant nightmares. They have the primal power of rumor and myth, they evoke pity and terror (but no catharsis), they echo far away in the unconscious, yet their intimacy is somehow synthetic, not as immediate or piercingly painful as the death of a close friend. Whatever their age, everyone dies early. The great philosopher Elias Canetti says there's something shameful about being alive when so many others have perished: How dare we survive in such an unjust order?

But we do, for a while anyway, and even if people didn't die, we'd lose a lot of them just the same. Lives change, intimates separate, people move, things get misplaced or forgotten until something triggers memory and the vortex of nostalgia sucks us in.

Grief is a good thing, an overflow valve, a way to acknowledge our powerlessness, and to deal with it by not "dealing" but accepting. Your lover leaves, your house burns down, your cat gets run over, Jackie Kennedy kicks the bucket, your boat sinks, your business goes under, Ralph Ellison quietly expires—or Bukowski, or Bill Everson, people you've known for years—your nephew OD's, your sister tries to kill herself, your good friend exactly your age is diagnosed with something fatal—or you discover your own days are numbered (as deep down you know they are regardless)—what's not to grieve over, it feels good, there's solace in giving in to it, letting go, letting the waves engulf you, drench you in surrender.

Coming up for air you feel refreshed, the burden lifts for a while, the little obstacles of the day, whatever social obfuscations or interpersonal pettiness, are put in perspective as the minor annoyances they are. A moment of grace—the sight of wildflowers, a team of starlings harassing a hawk, your comrade's face as you sit down to dine together—expands to embrace a universe. You're gifted to be living at all with any of your senses operational to perceive these miraculous events and things and people that compose the ongoing improvisation of your existence.

I miss my father almost every day. Even though we settled with each other before the end, acknowledged our reserved love and saw our differences resolved in mutual affection and respect, there's so much I'd love to have shared with him since—my various fiascos and successes, understandings of his many aphorisms gleaned from the streets, how since his departure I see in myself more of his example all the time. To date, he's the heaviest of my losses, though hardly the only one. It's he of all my dead who returns to me most frequently in dreams.

So grief can be a gift, an opening to life on the other side of the happy-face have-a-nice-day easygoing good-natured social intercourse that's our national ideal. Which is not to say those courtesies are frivolous, only that we can't afford to fall apart weeping in public; you do that one time too many and they call you manic-depressive or something equally reductive, put you on wonder drugs and bang, you're adjusted—back in line. But maybe you've lost that tragic edge that gave you soul.

I don't mean to start a pharmaceutical argument, only to suggest that maybe we're fortunate to have no shortage of sadnesses, of mortality to mourn. This reconciliation with our limits, the boundaries we're born into, can be liberating. "Life's too short," my father used to say when faced with some seemingly big but unimportant conflict. "It's not worth the aggravation." This from someone who faced formidable obstacles, assumed grave responsibilities and overcame daunting circumstances. He didn't have time to indulge in grief, though in the end he opened his heart; he was stoic by experience and disposition. It's me, the one with the luckier, easier life, who grieves for both of us.

An Antinuclear Family

[1989]

Over the past generation there has been a dramatic change in the American family, marked by a huge jump in the number of single people, a soaring rate of divorce and a sharp increase in single-parent families.

THE WASHINGTON POST

My daughter looks more beautiful to me every time I see her. Maybe it's because she lives in San Francisco and I work six days a week in Santa Cruz, so we only get together once a month or so, and she's changed, matured, grown noticeably fuller into the being she is, more independently herself, deepening lately into her eight years. Weekend before last we passed another of our fine days at the Boardwalk, a ritual we've enjoyed recurrently with the summers, strolling, snacking on the trashy food, riding a few of the not-too-scary rides and admiring the wild faces of families and roving bands of adolescents on the loose for a few hours.

Holding Claire's hand and letting her lead the way, part of my personal history that I thought lost is restored—adventurous afternoons at Ocean Park with pals and those violent, nauseating, exciting rides and the sticky lyrics of pop songs heard over the radios of cruising Chevys. Claire's mom drives a Chevy, a little silver station wagon with a rack on top for their camping trips and travels around the country or down the coast. Our family is antinuclear and we like it that way despite the obstacles—never married, never divorced, there's no bitterness, no lingering ill will over disillusioned love, only the honest friendship of slightly eccentric people growing gradually to know each other in time. We are comfortable together or apart, accepting the reality of separation.

This natural understanding of our circumstances enables my daughter and me to appreciate each other as autonomous individuals bonded by earned affection as well as blood. We know we've missed a certain continuity inherent in other family situations, but we've established a rhythm of our own destined to improve with age. Through gentle touches and subtle words laced with ironic edges we share a matter-of-fact intimacy no distance can completely undo.

I've known some fathers who've tried to control their daughters, manipulating the levers of money or instruction, but of course that's a vain exercise. Girls will be girls, experimenting with living, learning for themselves as they go along. Once you show by example that physical safety makes sense and that it's right to tell the truth, how much can you do to control their conduct? A little respect goes a long way toward earning theirs. If you listen, they listen back. There's no cause for coercion.

It's funny how some people still think only one kind of family is acceptable: the imaginary Ozzie-and-Harriet model from the fifties or its psychic equivalent. Surely it's possible for couples to stay together all their lives, cultivating their comradeship and raising kids in contented domesticity, but most of the families I've known that looked unshakable from the outside eventually gave way to breakups or breakdowns that permanently split their façade. Children suffer far more from their parents' hypocrisy than from the honest strains of day-to-day wear and tear. There are so many good ways to grow up with kids—or to let them grow up without you—that it's useless to pretend one pattern fits all. Some of the finest people I know developed their self-reliance and their gift for friendship thanks to a laissez-faire policy on the part of a warm, wise mom.

In Claire's case, her mother plays an active role in the evolution of her kid's consciousness by engaging her each day as a credible human being—talking about everything, explaining, discussing, playing games as well as declaring limits. The seriousness of their fun and the fun of their seriousness show me a great relationship in progress, and one I credit for the earthiness and security of this eight-year-old. Nobody knows the correct formula except by trial and error, and admitting that you're improvising rather than following a script imparts, I believe, a creative sense of adventure as long as there's a larger pattern of reliability.

But what do I know about parenthood-—I'm a part-time pop with hardly an opportunity to share a few days in a row with my own daughter. I don't know the wholesome agony of sleepless feverish nights and the ongoing closeness that borders on claustrophobia. It will be a while before I have the pleasure of watching her drive off with some teenage boy to who knows what kind of father-defying experience. We haven't yet had the soul-searching dialogues that sooner or later we may have to explore her origins and our unconventional history.

Still, I feel like we're blazing some kind of trail through increasingly common but as yet unsettled territory, a land where moms and dads and sons and daughters have to find ways of staying together across miles and years of circumstantial separateness, inventing new instruments of emotional navigation that keep us beamed in to the guiding tone of our love.

Past-life Regression

[1994]

Last month I attended my thirty-year high school reunion. Every ten years I perform this ritual despite the fact I have few positive memories of that period of my adolescence. High school for me was zits, angst-riddled insecurity, social competition, conformity, indoctrination in cynicism, glandular overload and girls too tall for me to kiss. It was the end of my athletic career and the beginning of my literary vocation. Going from jockdom to poethood was painful, a wrenching departure from everyone's expectations, including mine.

Still, I had my share of good times, I suppose, or so it seems from this distance. Cruising the LA streets with rock and roll on the radio, letting the rhythms spill through me in waves of sexual electricity, bantering sarcastically with my so-called friends intent on keeping each other edgy through an ordeal of nonstop mean-spirited wit, transcendent moments on the baseball field or making out on the couch—such typical experiences for better or worse left their mark on my developing self. And going back further, I lived in the same house from the age of three until I left for college back East, so some of my former high school classmates are people I've known since kindergarten. Seeing any one of them now is primal déjà vu with deep associations.

So once a decade when I'm sent word of the get-together, I go, just to see who else will show up and what kinds of encounters will occur. Seeing some of those faces, exchanging greetings and recollections, is strangely touching—not nostalgic exactly but nonetheless evocative of a sense of loss. I have no desire to live through high school again, my luck has steadily improved since then, but somehow this casual contact with the past drives home how old I am, how far I've traveled yet also how much I still share at some level with these aging strangers.

Take David Mann for example. As we caught each other's eye across the rustic grounds of the gathering, our natural rapport of nearly four decades immediately kicked in: we exchanged a cool yet affectionate greeting and picked up an ancient conversation, inquiring about family, casually accounting for current activities. "Still hanging out with criminals?" I asked, alluding to his longtime practice as a public defender. "Almost exclusively," he said.

Dave was student body president, most likely to succeed, an easygoing friendly guy, good athlete, smart—kind of a Bill Clinton type, I guess, without the omnivorous ambition. At the end of our sophomore year in college—he at Stanford, I at UCLA—we traveled through Europe together, discovering among other things some of our personal differences. A few years later, when I was in graduate school flipping out and he was studying law, I found myself in the psycho ward at San Francisco General with no identification, and when asked who I was I answered, "David Mann." Part of my reply was no doubt generic—a way of saying Everyman—but another part must have arisen from an impossibly ironic identification with my former (even then) friend. At some level maybe I wanted to be him—a regular guy, popular, tall, from a seemingly perfect All-American family, a golden boy. The Manns had one of those 1950s father-knows-best façades; I admired their apparent solidarity even as I rejected that unreal model of happiness. Perhaps the appeal of being "David Mann" was a sense of belonging just when I felt most exiled and alienated from my own relations.

Anyway there was this recognition between us the other night, just a flash or submerged glow of comfortable familiarity, of some hopefully remembered or imagined home. And yet after schmoozing for a few minutes we moved on, making the rounds of the swirl of other faces, talking, swapping news, trading condensed stories. Dave and I didn't even exchange addresses, as if this was as close as we were likely to get at this point, so why push it. We know we can find each other if we want to.

There were dozens of such collisions that night, though only a few so poignant. One of those was with Alan Meyer, a prosperous bank consultant, about to retire at forty-eight. Poor Meyer looked perplexed, his sensitive brown eyes bewildered not only at this Fellini-dream carnival of lost-and-found characters but at the puzzling prospect of what to do with himself now that he's sold his business and can afford to coast into old age. I felt his gentle kindness, his sincerity, and yet there was some gaping gulf between us—thirty years of vastly different experience. When we were twelve he was the outstanding athlete among my peers, but like me he had bad knees and never grew enough to compete with the bigger, faster, meaner guys. Now he looked exactly as I remembered him—unmistakably the same old Meyer. He said to me, "You look just like your father."

Beyond that, there wasn't much else for us to say.

Then there were those I hadn't liked in high school—lots of them—whom I saw no reason to get chummy with now. And those I hardly knew in high school, who now seemed fine and likable folks. One woman struck up a conversation that appeared to be fueled by Prozac: I'd never known her to be so friendly and self-assured. Others seemed shy or paranoid—or maybe I was projecting. Randy Holland, who I remember as a clownish wildboy with the socks of his Little League uniform flopping and his shirttail flapping, is now an on-the-rise documentary filmmaker and an animated yakker with a radical take on the LA riots. Bigtime Bay Area restaurateur Mike Dellar recited to me my lyrics to our senior song among other youthful compositions I thought I'd succeeded in forgetting. Hot-shot entertainment agent Jimmy Wiatt waxed enthusiastic about a beach house of my parents' on Point Dume where we used to party—long since replaced by a mansion inhabited by some other Hollywood honcho.

And of course there were the missing persons, the famous who shall remain unnamed, and various shady entrepreneurs ashamed to show their faces. Not to mention the dead and the prematurely defeated and those who couldn't afford to spring for the seventy-dollar dinner and the ones who admitted to themselves up front that they wanted nothing to do with useless adolescent flashbacks.

Some faces I saw looked so familiar and went so far back with me that all we had to do was nod and grin from a distance, as if having a conversation would be superfluous; what really mattered was the mere recognition that the other still existed. Ten years from now we'll check in again to see if we're still alive. I realize now that though those years were not necessarily happy, they're the only ones we had at the time, and with any luck they opened into a larger and better life—so as part of the passage from there to here they are to be regarded with some gratitude.

But maybe the strangest encounter of the whole evening for me occurred shortly after I arrived. A small blonde woman approached me and introduced herself as Susie Williams. I could swear I had never seen her before in my life. But she had in her hands a stack of pictures—those collective class photos from grammar school—and proceeded to share with me the amazing faces of kids with whom I'd gone through grades one to four (Nicky Nayfack, Jeffrey Fine, Nicky Diggs!), some of them here tonight and looking recognizably the same. But who was Susie Williams? Could I have sat in classrooms with her during those formative years and never even registered an impression? Could she have made herself so invisible as to vanish from memory's radar screen completely? And now, with these perfectly preserved photos, she was literally the bearer of memory, even though I had no idea who she was.

I believe it was Simone Signoret who said nostalgia isn't what it used to be. And I confess that reminiscence has its limits. But I'm glad I went to the reunion because I got a glimpse of the cute little guy I was for a while before becoming a screwed-up teenage boy. And I was glad to be reminded of the teenage boy because the mere fact that I'm no longer him seems to me an encouraging sign of progress. Getting old may have its disadvantages, but it sure beats being in high school.

Smoke Damage

[1999]

Sometimes I wonder what I might have amounted to if I hadn't become a pothead thirty years ago, when I was in graduate school, and pretty much remained one ever since. If not for marijuana, by now I'd probably be securely tenured in some English department, and my mother would be able to brag to her friends about her son the doctor of philosophy. I'd be fluent in Academese, a respectable specialist in some form of critical theory, a teacher admired by his brightest students, a defeated imaginative writer, and a wretchedly unhappy and neurotic person. This, at least, is how I envisioned the path I was on at the time and where it must inevitably lead. Luckily, marijuana intervened.

Getting high, for me, in 1969, at the age of twenty-two, provided a vitally helpful perspective on the pettiness and irrelevance of an academic career to the creative vocation I felt was calling me. Following an acute psychotic episode—usefully assisted by psychedelic drugs, which triggered the explosion of all my internal conflicts and contradictions—I left the doctoral program and its generous fellowship for the full-time pursuit of my first love, poetry. This may not have been possible without a small but steady independent income that enabled me to live without a "real" job, but that financial independence was also existential in that the freedom it afforded left me no excuses for not doing what I claimed to want to do, which was to write. Smoking marijuana gave me courage, at the time, to follow my deepest imaginative instincts, not only in the actual writing of poems but in the larger arena of making decisions about my life and how I wished to live it. Contrary to conventional wisdom, my judgment felt to me more fundamentally sound when I was stoned than straight.

Encouraged by the permission I felt to write without parental or professorial approval, I set out on the slow, uncertain, and mostly thankless path of the young poet, laboring over less-than-brilliant lines, writing, revising, sending the finished works to magazines, occasionally publishing, more often collecting rejections. Through most of this artistic apprenticeship I was accompanied by the sweet smell of burning hemp, whose presence surrounding my efforts seemed to expand the atmosphere of creative possibility, enhancing my sense of heroic romance on the seas of the blank page, that heady journey into the unknown. Frequently stoned as I indulged my imagination, I knew I was learning something about poetry, about writing, and about myself.

From there it was a slippery slope into the harder stuff: translation, criticism, journalism, editing and publishing. In the years since my earliest days as a dropout hippie poet I've managed to make a working life for myself in these various branches of literary practice, and while I wouldn't presume to credit pot for anything I've managed to accomplish, I do believe its companionship has helped me to maintain a certain equanimity amid the myriad distractions, confusions and aggravations of the surrounding world, enabling me to focus on what matters most, or what I most enjoy. If anything, marijuana has tempered my ambition, relaxing the compulsion to overachieve and giving license to play.

It is this sense of permission—or permissiveness, as the virtue-pushers would have it—that makes the forbidden herb, for me, a useful antidote to the various societal prohibitions against, for example, "doing nothing." Pot reinforces my instinctive Taoism. Maybe that's why it's considered by some to be a dangerous drug: if everyone used it, nothing would get done. But paradoxical as it may seem, it is precisely when "doing nothing" that I tend to get the most accomplished as an artist. Or the deep involvement, the timelessness, experienced in the flow of creation may feel so aimless or effortless that it might as well be nothing, except for the fact that when I resume more consciously purposeful activity I often find persuasive evidence that I was doing something after all: a written text or other crafty artifact, a rack of freshly washed dishes, a stack of firewood, a pile of paid bills whose checks were written while listening to music or some radio show.

Stoned or straight, I find these kinds of meditative activities to be a means of grounding myself in the mundane patterns and rhythms out of which imagination rises. The content, style and quality of what I write are not, I've found, especially affected by whether or not I've been smoking, but I am aware, when high, of more intimate sensuous relations with the language, with the rhythm and texture of lines and sentences, with a kind of musical understanding not always readily evident to my more rational and sober self. The mild psychosis induced by this subtle alteration of consciousness may provide a different angle of vision, or revision, that can be of use in making esthetic decisions—what works and what doesn't, how to refine some detail, trim out the excess or develop some incomplete idea.

Obviously such working habits are more dependent on the mind and skill of the individual than they are on what drugs he may or may not be taking. An idiot on marijuana is still an idiot, possibly more so. And one's response to pot may vary greatly, depending on personality and circumstances. The health effects of smoking anything cannot be entirely positive, and I've seen enough stupid people in herbally induced stupors to be disabused of any evangelical notion of marijuana as a panacea. Like any other substance—food, tobacco, caffeine, alcohol, television—its abuse can be toxic and destructive. But unlike these ordinary and often insidious additives to daily life, pot remains not only legally prohibited but even now, at the turn of the millennium, socially stigmatized in a way that, say, coffee (a truly mind-altering substance) is not.

Among my friends, some smoke and some don't, for reasons of their own—just as I don't drink coffee because it makes my stomach jumpy—but the ones who do are just as productive in their lives and work and social contributions as are the abstainers. Anecdotally, I've seen no correlation one way or another between marijuana use and creativity, citizenship, ethics or character. What I have noticed when smoking with friends is a ritual affirmation of time out, a refreshing pause in the everyday onslaught, a moment of quiet dialogue to savor, an island of sanity in the rush of events. Different people have different ways of relaxing, but those who habitually watch TV—whether in the lethargy of their own living rooms or in the noise and convivial drunkenness of a bar with ballgames blaring—seem to me far more at risk for various psychopathologies than those who routinely prefer a few tokes of pot.

While I don't exactly take pride in my own habit, I don't consider it a major vice. A couple of puffs in mid-afternoon, following a late lunch, or at the end of a longish day, in the cocktail hour, or in the evening while listening to music, strikes me as an eminently civilized way of decompressing the psyche. Whenever I find myself using it more than feels healthy—when I wake up in the morning foggy-headed, or feel a strain on my respiratory system—I may take a break for a few weeks as a way to remind myself of the drug's potentially negative effects and to refresh my appreciation of its positive ones. I wouldn't recommend it to anyone, especially children (I'm content with the knowledge that my eighteen-year-old daughter doesn't use it), but neither would I discourage the curious from trying it in a conscious, responsible way.

Partner, collaborator, accomplice, friend, companion—marijuana, over the years, has woven itself gently into the pattern of my life in a way that may have prevented me from pushing myself above and beyond whatever I've done as a writer. Without the benign corruption of pot, who knows, I might have been a contender. Instead, up to now, in my early fifties, I've managed to maintain my physical and mental health, create a few works I hope may be worth saving, cultivate many lasting friendships, and contribute what I could to my communities. For someone of alternately competitive and contemplative tendencies, the path I've taken, accompanied by the herbal reality-check of marijuana, feels to me thus far to have been a reasonable compromise.

As my father used to say, "Everything in moderation."

Manhattan Panorama

[1989]

New York is such a charmingly provincial town. There's so much going on at all times, so many people moving around in the streets, so much high and low cultural activity, so many nationalities mingling that the rest of the world seems to exist only as ingredients in the cosmic stew of the city. Manhattan Island hums, growls and vibrates continuously, its World-Trade-Empire-State-class social and financial grandeur and depravity radiating from the rock itself, which is artfully carved into Byzantine tunnels where hundreds of trains are racing day and night. As in Steinberg's famous *New Yorker* cover, from the heart of the city one doesn't perceive much detail beyond the Hudson River. New York is impersonal but intimate, a universe unto itself.

I recently returned from ten days there, my first visit in nearly a decade. The air was crisp and dry for most of my stay, scarcely falling below 30 degrees, so the streets were completely walkable—touring the island on foot with no particular itinerary remains the greatest way to experience the place in all its gruesome splendor—and I was able to connect with a few friends, eat a pleasing diversity of authentic ethnic cuisines, hear a little music, see some new movies, catch two or three museum exhibitions and gossip with colleagues in the publishing profession.

New York's cultural arrogance has a lot to do with the fact that it's home to so many publishers and publications; just as Hollywood is our imagery capital, projecting into the caverns of the national psyche the illusions by which Americans measure each other and themselves, the New York publishing industry dominates public and literary discourse—not to mention advertisingese—establishing the standards of meaning and imagination. A visiting writer feels a curious blend of intoxication and repulsion faced with Manhattan's publishing monstrosities, the exciting prospect of plugging into that power and reaching millions of people combined with a sickening mistrust of the costs of big-league success and commodification.

But publishing on any scale is a powerful tool, as I was reminded New Year's Day at The Jewish Museum where I walked through an exhibit called *A People in Print: Jewish Journalism in America.* The show was a historical survey of the hundreds of Jewish newspapers that served that particular immigrant community in various cities around the country from the earliest days of the Republic until 1948, when Israel was founded. Beyond the glass-encased display of so many pages from so many papers—including full-page ads in *The New York Times* at the height of the Holocaust imploring Americans to wake up and do something—what touched me most deeply was the life-size portrait (artist unknown) of one of my heroes, Abraham Cahan, longtime editor of the *Jewish Daily Forward*, a legendary journal of the Lower East Side during the great waves of Jewish immigration after the turn of the century. Under Cahan's direction the *Forward* served as a secular guidebook, debating platform, philosophy seminar, news medium, political lookout and people's university for the millions of emigrants fresh from Eastern Europe who found themselves in the New World. Cahan's paper, like many others of its kind produced by and for minority cultures in the United States, was a voice, or chorus of voices, for the voiceless.

But museums in New York, however remarkable and moving their exhibits, are retreats from the street, islands of social control and cultural propriety, of artificial sanity, shelters from the city's cacophonous intensity, and as such cannot be trusted any more than temples of worship to show you reality whole. My visit to the Metropolitan for the Georgia O'Keefe and Edgar Degas shows evoked more claustrophobia than edification, the mobs of muffled spectators plugged into their headsets for the guided tour somehow out of sync with the spirit of art. For relief I negotiated my way through several centuries of European painting to rediscover Jackson Pollock's *Autumn Rhythm*, a gloriously wild yet harmonious field of sweeping drips that never ceases to astonish me with its beauty. What Pollock and his fellow Abstract Expressionists started to accomplish—before they became momentary gods of art and therefore expensive commodities—was to reveal the canvas as a field of action rather than contemplation, to rescue art from the spectator syndrome so evident in galleries and museums where all the average visitor can do is gawk. Gawking at Pollock's accomplishment, I felt my creative reservoirs recharged.

New York itself is so rich with cultural resources that a sensitive consumer runs the risk of turning into a walking culture sponge, soaked—overwhelmed, immobilized—with the volume of works in every medium to which one is exposed. The Abstract Expressionist painters, breakthrough poets and jazz musicians of the fifties in New York were transforming the overload into energetic expression-in-motion, and today the sounds of subway trains, taxicabs, jackhammers and saxophones layering the city's noisescape can either paralyze the listener or inspire, John Cage or Coltrane-wise, the creation of one's own music. Those who close out the urban onslaught by cranking up the sound on their Walkman may be doing so in self-defense but they're missing the constant and amazing messages delivered at every opening of the senses.

To live in New York and survive as an imaginative being, you have to know when to stop being a spectator. A tourist has no such problem, knowing that time and money will soon run out and you'll return home, jolted by the voltage of the city's colossal energy, the density of its impressions, the complexity and contrasts and contradictions of its many simultaneous levels of life. The hivelike busyness and inhumane hardness of the rockscape are matched by moments of startling intimacy—a conversation in a café, a meal in some tiny restaurant, a drink in a friend's apartment, a street corner where a stranger asks directions, a subway car where a beggar shares his personal tragedy. Exposed to the cold realities and costs of survival in their city, New Yorkers display a matter-of-fact acceptance of—or resignation to—the misery so visible in their midst: homeless people curled up on subway platforms or making their way through the trains soliciting change, the blind, the lame, the strung-out, the enterprising hustlers running their myriad scams. Yet out of the stoicism cultivated in the presence of so much suffering and scrambling, flashes of compassion come—in the way one young man, obviously poor, drops a dollar bill into the paper cup of another.

Of all the environments in which I moved during my ten days in Manhattan, none evoked more response from me than the subway—both for its miracle of speedy transit and for its unrelenting human drama. Staying at my sister's place on the Upper East Side and drawn downtown on business or pleasure daily, and often nightly, I found myself taking the number 6 train of the Lexington Avenue line for frequent round trips of hundreds of blocks, rocking alongside and across the car from and mashed up against all manner of humanity, wrapped in overcoats and gloves and scarves and hats and furs and rags, clutching newspapers and books and magazines and cassette tapes piped through headsets, most of the riders trying to remain oblivious of each other—eye contact is taboo—but fearless and foolish witnesses like me taking the opportunity to study faces and finding that these faces, cruel or beautiful or hideous or indifferent, seemed to me the esthetic equal of any painting in the Metropolitan.

The borderline brutality of urban civilization, whether by atmosphere alone or the actual pain imprinted in the flesh of the people who endure it daily, leaves extraordinary signs of character in the visages of those it touches. Despite the hostility and paranoia, the aggressiveness and impatience, people remain the most organic element in the cityscape and as such are like flowers sprouting through the concrete, the anomalous loveliness and vulnerability poignant reminders of our tender neglected selves.

Looking at so many solitary faces, each with its individual

history and personal path of tears and laughter leading back to its cell in the immense hive, can be emotionally devastating. García Lorca's *Poet in New York* expresses as well as anything the existential terror of a sensitive being colliding head-on with its own demons as seen in the alienated masses of Manhattan, even as far back as the late 1920s. But Lorca's book, like so many masterworks hatched on the same hostile soil, is ultimately a triumphant celebration of the human power to transform horror into the heroic redemption of great art. Not everyone sees the city as a nightmare—Walt Whitman and Henry Miller, Hart Crane and Frank O'Hara, to name some favorite lyrical examples, manage to reveal the humor, awe and wonder implicit in such a setting, unfolding personal myths to meet the impossible anonymity of the metropolis—and, again, the visitor has the advantage of knowing which way is out and is therefore primed to relish the encounter with rootlessness and confusion.

Probably the highlight of this whole trip was the walk I took to Brooklyn and back one sunny chilly morning and afternoon. Of all the architectural marvels of New York, for my money nothing surpasses the Brooklyn Bridge. The way the cables fan out diagonally like the strings of some angelic instrument and the old stone towers rise with such dignity out of the East River, the bridge is a gorgeous and functional achievement in visionary design and engineering. With automobile traffic on the lower deck, and the upper deck, a wooden walkway, designated for bicycles and pedestrians, the gently arched span was an inviting path as I set out on foot in search of the Arab delis of Atlantic Avenue. The wind was blowing, my nose was running, I kept having to pull my cap down over my ears, but as I walked I admired the intricate structure of the bridge and through a thick web of safety netting watched the workmen high overhead painting and doing repairs. Runners puffed past, sweating in their athletic underwear, seemingly indifferent to the tremendous view of the harbor and Liberty, the awesome Manhattan skyline, the string of other bridges linking the island to the boroughs, the industrial wilderness of Brooklyn itself whose gateway is the Jehovah's Witness *Watchtower* factory.

Out in the middle of the bridge, if you stand still for a moment and look around—airplanes and helicopters groaning overhead in every direction and at all altitudes, trucks and autos whizzing by both ways under your feet, barges moving up and down the river below that, and beneath the river itself the rumbling subways—you may feel a liberating humility akin to the speechlessness felt before the Grand Canyon.

Returning to lower Manhattan after lunch in a Moroccan restaurant, I notice the strange way the Empire State Building alternately looms gigantic in your face or disappears into the skyline depending on the angle at which you approach the island. King Kong himself could get lost in that jungle, just another big lug hung up on a blonde. Some kids have sprayed graffiti at various points along the bridge: *YUPPICIDE.* A boy who looks about twelve years old struts by with his little sister, explaining to her something about "anarchy, the freedom to do whatever you want whenever the hell you want to." Political science aside, there *is* a great feeling of freedom on the bridge, a sense of wide-openness to the world that's seldom granted in the city itself. Suspended above the river on a structure that's barely a century old but seems somehow prehistoric, the lightness of your utter insignificance renders all deadlines irrelevant, all personal ambitions absurd, all bonds dissolved in the monumental space around you.

Night and the City

[1993]

It was Saturday night, a little past eleven, and I'd already caught one set at Birdland—the Jimmy Heath Quartet—and had stepped out on Broadway to get some air and decided I might as well buy the Sunday *Times* and bring it home. My beloved was in California, Humboldt County, reporting a story on pot growers, so I was on my own, and it was still early, so after setting the *Times*' tonnage on the kitchen table and taking a pee I decided I wasn't tired and went back out.

My hand was still stamped and I could get into the club for the last set, maybe more, savor those sounds, breathe that noxious alcoholic atmosphere urbane with cancerous intoxication. It was cool out, early November, and the night air braced me as I shoved open the building's wrought-iron-and-plate-glass door and went down the stone steps to the sidewalk.

At one end of the block, to the south, was the Buddhist Church with its 15-foot bronze statue of Shinran Shonin, the itinerant monk whose likeness had survived Hiroshima and been brought back intact to New York after the war. At the other end, to my right, was 106th Street, Duke Ellington Boulevard, with its bigger buildings and 6-foot Haitian security guards in their cop-like uniforms, armed with cellular telephones. The safer street was106th, wider and better lit, but between these guys and the city's finest from the 24th Precinct, that stretch of Riverside never seemed especially threatening to me, even though I'd seen car-radio thieves at their trade and homeless crackheads getting high in the bushes and scavengers rummaging through the garbage and the occasional crazy person smashing bottles against a lamppost or sharpening a fork on the cement. So at the bottom of the stairs I turned left toward 105th and the church. Birdland was two blocks east.

From the shadows in front of the statue two forms emerged as I approached, two shapes in hooded sweatshirts with the hoods pulled over their baseball caps were coming toward me, space opening between them as they came. As we neared each other the tall one, to my left, pulled a sleek handgun—its weight was palpable—out of his sweatshirt, pointed it at me and declared, "This is a stick. Give us the money and nobody gets hurt."

No problem. Nothing to fear. No need for heroics. I reached for my wallet and the little one approached, the big one holding the gun at a discreet distance. He said, "Hurry up!" as I was pulling out my forty-two dollars and handing it to his partner. The kid, up close, couldn't have been more than nineteen, scared shitless, almost shy. The gunman was nervous too, and not much older.

"Relax," I said, cool as a kosher dill. I was cooperating. The scene was under control. If these punks could chill and just take the cash, we'd all be okay. They could go score their drugs and I could get back to the club. But they were jumpy.

"There's more!" said Gun Boy, and I spread the empty flaps of my wallet to show him it wasn't true. Junior believed me, he could see I wasn't holding anything back. "That's it," he said to his friend. The friend said to me, "Just keep walking," slipping the gun back into his waist as they passed me headed toward 106th. I strode past Shinran Shonin, standing there with his staff and his big hat, seeing no evil.

As I turned the corner I looked back, just as my muggers were glancing back at me, the big one going for the gun, or making as if, as they took off; I carelessly ignored which way because I had begun running toward the nearest doorman, across the street. "Call the cops," I said, "I just got robbed." He said he had no telephone, so I loped up to the pay phone at 105th and West End and punched 911.

By now my legs were spaghetti, I was short of breath as I reported the particulars, the adrenaline had kicked in and the realization had registered that I might have been, like so many others you read about every day in the metro pages, just another puddle on the sidewalk. By the time the cops arrived—a couple of squad cars and two flatfoots, one of them female—I'd calmed down, and spent the next twenty minutes cruising in the backseat scanning the streets for the culprits.

The bad guys got away. The cops were professional enough but less than inspiring, barely competent youths not a whole lot more together than the robbers. They had more guns, cars, two-way radios, crisp blue uniforms, but they wore them without style, without grace, without confidence. The hoods had been shakier but no less imposing.

Anyway, I was alive. I still had my watch, my wallet, my leather jacket, the joint (I suddenly remembered) in one of the pockets. The boys in the blue cruiser took me to 24th Precinct to show me some pictures, none of which looked familiar, then drove me back and dropped me off at home. I paused for a second on the front steps, then turned for Birdland, where there might be time to catch the end of the last set.

Spirits in the Dark

[1985]

Driving home after midnight in a torrential downpour, my car conked out on a dark street on the east side of town. Luckily I was able to coast into a closed gas station, there was a public telephone, and I had a couple of dimes to call the auto club. It was Sunday night, the first full-blown storm of a precocious winter, nobody out but fools in broken-down roadsters with leaky convertible tops looking gloomily down deserted streets for a sign of sympathetic life.

I had just come from reading, live on the radio, an essay by Emma Goldman on "The Philosophy of Atheism," and as I stood soaking under the sheets of rain I reflected that maybe the crazy gods were giving me something to think about while I waited for the tow truck to arrive. My automobile's problem was obviously electrical—the most spiritual component, the ghost in the machine, the force that shines the guiding light on winding mountain roads and keeps the windshield wipers flipping in the fiercest weather—and I felt the primitive urge to invent some tricky spirits to explain my plight.

"The conception of gods originated in fear and curiosity," according to Red Emma. "Primitive man, unable to understand the phenomena of nature and harassed by them, saw in every terrifying manifestation some sinister force expressly directed against him; and as ignorance and fear are the parents of all superstition, the troubled fancy of primitive man wove the God idea."

Were these fictitious powers, so sensibly scorned by Goldman and regarded by me as the raw material for the mental blocks of organized religion, trying to tell me something I was loath to believe? Had God died laughing at human credulity, as Nietzsche claimed, or was the joke on me? Miles removed from any ordinary faith, my skepticism is riddled with mystical suspicions, which inform my respect for natural phenomena even while shrugging off god-fearing fog. Yet here I was being shown by the elements the true dimensions of my puniness, and I secretly longed to hold someone responsible for what I knew to be a meaningless mishap.

Clearly the Biblical Big Daddy supposedly responsible for the cosmic *kreplach* would hardly have time to go out of his way to drench one unbeliever. Delusions of "chosenness" aside—including the notion of personalized punishment for unrighteous acts—such divine high jinks would be unworthy of any self-respecting Jahweh. My theo-illogical ruminations were eventually interrupted by the arrival of a St. Christopher figure, who carried my car across the waters.

Now, having had my battery recharged and my alternator replaced, I ask myself by what leaps of faith my spirit has made it this far without a god. Oh, I know that "the gods" exist, in the way of mythic heroes, and that goddesses are unnervingly omnipresent. As Robert Graves has pointed out, poets through the ages have been stricken with the affliction of inspiration delivered by a muse who assumes the form of a gorgeous woman (or a beautiful man, I suppose, in some revisionist twist of the myth). But grace in the flesh has been known to make itself felt independent of any divinity.

My faith is with a way that allows for what can't be explained, that eschews the supernatural for earthy paths winding ever more mysteriously into unknown zones of ongoing realization. God is the great improviser inventing itself by way of everything else, an epic anarchy of contradictions no dogma can begin to contain. Religion may be a major industry but spiritual life has less to do with churches and all their trappings than it does with the progress of a raindrop sliding down a schoolroom window observed by a squirmy boy who can't wait to get out and play football in the mud.

Isn't that where our imaginary forebears allegedly originated anyway? Adam and Eve and the first amoeba all crawled out of the mud, correct? And that's why the world is such a mess—crawling, no less, with metaphysicians who claim they can clean it up with supreme fictions. The social potency of popes, grand rebbes and ayatollahs is no less chillingly irrational than the power of any political leader who claims to have a hot line to Hades.

History proves, however, that people would rather submit to a higher authority than take responsibility for composing their own prayers. Individuals or groups who dare to dissent from prevailing religious prejudices have traditionally been burnt at the stake or otherwise purged from the ranks of the righteous. Evangelical Christians, if I understand their *spiel,* are sold on their own salvation and more than happy to slam its doors eternally on all the poor devils that didn't see the light in time.

But "the Hell of dead gods," as H. L. Mencken wrote, "is as crowded as the Presbyterian Hell for babies." So those of us doomed to such a destiny will at least have the pleasure of hob-nobbing with a multitude of deities whose omnipotence, omniscience and immortality burned out like so many light bulbs. Since common sense and comparative religion assure us that all gods are created equal, we can safely expect to meet the Maker of our choice regardless of how bad we may have been.

Without any credible Supreme Being, what is there for people to believe in? Surely the State, which traditional hard-core commies elevate to more-or-less almighty status, is a far-from-holy ghost to most of us. Secular humanism, which scares the hell out of right-wing salvation-slingers, isn't such a bad idea if it weren't for the fact that humans are constantly screwing up. Any standard of absolute value ought to have a better track record than humanity.

Some folks believe in the 49ers, faithfully worshipping at the Church of Football. The soap-opera gods on the covers of supermarket magazines also throw their weight around in the temple of popular unconsciousness. The less contact people have with the natural world, the more credence they're prone to put in such quasi-cultural fabrications.

Art, of course, is worshipped by those who can afford to invest in its appreciation. And artists themselves have been known to believe they were saving their souls and praising the Lord with every stroke of their own making. In this realm it is musicians (especially certain saxophone players) whose work aspires to pure spirit by virtue not only of its being invisible but of its integration with living breath.

As I stood in the rain the other night awaiting St. Christopher's coming, I decided my dilemma was a natural disaster rather than an act of God. The amazing and largely ungraspable fact of creation need not be attributed to some cosmic clockmaker or census-taker in the sky in order to inspire our awe and humility. Respect for life in its infinite forms, an irreverent love for this stormy world, requires no higher cause.

I Didn't Know What Year It Was

[1982]

There's something reassuring about the solstice. From here on, for a while, the days will stretch out and time will seem a little easier on us, the brilliant January light sharpening our sense of the present as it climbs into the clear sky of spring. Pieces of the last year fall none too neatly into the collage of our past lives, saved for savoring in the memory buds of the mind's eye, which in turn work overtime in the dark months to see some meaning, some redeeming evidence that what little we've come to know isn't a total loss.

As the old year closes and the new one begins I always feel a little stronger, perhaps because astrologically my sign is in sight—or maybe because the effort required to keep warm tones the firewood-splitting limbs to a toughness unknown since last year at this time, when the same chores told us to take the cold seriously and make ourselves at home under the storms.

I am astonished continually at the increasing swiftness with which the years race through our flesh leaving their deepening traces, age filling us with a strange sweetness even as it burns away what we were. The keen, evergreen smells, the crisp stars, the flying smoke are us also, all disappearing and returning eternally with the turning earth somewhere this side of the inevitable. Yes, as we live we die, everything-in-its-time, and time can be kind if we stay alive to its changes as they overtake us, our songs shuttling through space long after liftoff, outlasting the hardware cluttering the stars.

"What are years?" asked Marianne Moore. Unable to answer, surrendering to the limits of a life, she heard eternity in the mortal singing of a bird; heard its pure joy, though captive, transcend mere freedom and transient satisfaction. Oceans and poets, singing in their chains, keep the birds' music in motion, reaching into the air with a fine spray that touches our faces, tearlike, as we stand vanishing at the edge of years.

Maybe it's escapist to muse on mortality while politics eats us alive. Maybe the trees this page would be if it weren't for all these words would be better off standing on some mountainside than stacked by the doors of shops the day after an overwrought holiday only to be picked up by exhausted shoppers, skimmed and thrown away. Or perhaps events are not as current as we presumed. Even our representatives are resting, numbed by the numbers battering their sad brains.

Sometimes there is less to admire in a line of legislation than in a wedge of cormorants skimming the bay lightly at the last minute before oil is struck and the black platforms appear to pollute the view. Even if industry can be prevented from poisoning the sea, its blue luminousness just before dusk always feels final, as if this indescribable shining—an illusion of silver rising to the surface—were its farewell flourish before a bottomless dark.

This is for those of you who know how futile journalism is in representing the real. I'm kissing the year goodbye the only way I know how, trying to touch on what has escaped me all these months and will continue to, however lovingly I embrace it now. The faces staring out from postage stamps will never be as sweet to my tongue as yours: I drink to the look in your eyes, toasting our time together.

Nothing is newsworthy in this equation. The tickertape is swallowing my knees as I speak yet I refuse to recognize its currency. No year is so unique as to warrant a blow-by-blow recapitulation of its casualties, its crashes and wars and earth-shaking eruptions. Look back, scrambling your calendars, and find historic headlines multiplied to the last power, identically tragic and untouchable. Now let those lie as you taste your own findings and losses over the last months, everything shredded by the days' blades and strewn into the future to be recollected.

As the pivotal midnight approaches, Champagne foaming, we desperately and tenderly celebrate our survival. Before the confetti hits the floor, each of us is rescued by a child.

What is time, and what are you doing about it? Apart from or within its physical dimension—the way its transformations register in everything—our intimate concept of its workings helps determine what it does to us and how we use are or used by the notions of time we harbor in our minds. Can time, for example, be "wasted"? Can it "pass us by" or bear down on us like some kind of mythic vehicle—a winged chariot or speeding taxicab?

If you feel time running you over, then that's what it's probably doing. If you see it ticking away numerically on your split-second digital watch, chances are your psyche has been colonized by the same industrial drones that drove the shadow out of business. People imprisoned in the workaday clock relish the weekend as someplace temporarily beyond time, but even then there's rarely enough time to "make up for lost time."

Organic gardeners, whose every plant is time realized or realizing itself, have a far more reliable sense of time than almost everyone else. As the shoots sprout and the fruits bud, we gain a rhythmic wisdom that no amount of stimulants can improve upon. The earth is in no hurry, and as we tune in to the subtleties of its tempo we feel the steady force of its green creation moving through us as well. We are like lucky seeds on whom the compost of the past has fallen.

Seen and felt and lived as a fertile gift, time ceases to be the thief depriving us of everything we had and becomes instead the future's gushing source into which we can plunge or dip at our own risk. Conceived as an opening opportunity, time is a field whose cultivation is ours for the digging.

Forgive me for waxing purple, or Emersonian, but the ends of years always seem to trigger a flurry of such reflections. More than personal birthdays, the "dead of winter" awakens in me the desire to record what I can never know—how all these days, lived solitarily or shared with loved ones or collectively constructed in some visionary tower of incomprehensible historic babble, continue to echo and recur in our lives even after they've gone.

Going Bald

[1994]

I'm going bald.

It's been happening for quite a while now, but faster every year as I near fifty. First it was the hairline in the upper corners of my high forehead gradually creeping back, and the little hole toward the back of my head where the yarmulke should have been, a hole slowly expanding, enlarging, spreading, opening into a shiny surface of skin over naked skull, a "bald spot." These surfaces have recently converged, the retreating line in front and the advancing line in back, so that on top of my head a kind of bush remains, a finely textured tuft of hairs high up in front surrounded by bare skin, a little island of hair in a rising tide of baldness. It is not the baldness itself that bothers me—my father was bald by the time he was half my age, my uncles are splendidly bald, my brothers are bald, lots of the greatest Pablos (Picasso, Casals, Neruda) were brilliantly bald—it is the agonizing slowness of the process, the absurdity of my little island of hair, which, when cut to what I consider normal length, waves like the funny little plume atop a quail or, as a friend observed, like the topknot of a Kewpie doll.

Sometimes I see ads or hear commercials for various techniques of hair restoration, drugs, surgery, implantations—rugs that look more real than a real head of hair. I saw a former classmate at my thirty-year high school reunion who was wearing one of these, and it didn't look that bad except for the fact that I'd seen him bald at the twenty-year reunion, so to me he looked ridiculous, vainly attempting to deny the course of nature. Then there's my former brother-in-law, whom I see every so often at family functions, with that spectacularly tacky toupee masking his dome, and it's all I can do to keep from laughing in his otherwise earnest face. And of course there are those who stylishly deploy their baseball caps or golf caps or fedoras or berets not just for shade or insulation, but as a form of cosmetic cover-up, a helmet against the inevitable. These desperate efforts at disguise may be no more foolish than the traditional ruses females resort to in the course of resisting gravity and the other inexorable laws of time, but somehow on men they appear to me more comical. Perhaps I'm laboring under the sexist delusion that men, don't ask me why, should be less vain than women. When in fact men, with their evolutionary rooster instincts, obviously suffer no shortage of vanity.

What I need is a drug or anointment or technique that doesn't delay or reverse or conceal the balding process but accelerates it. I don't mean radiation treatments or chemotherapy or even the freak case of alopecia an auto upholsterer in Glendale explained to me as the reason for his unearthly absence of hair. And shaving the head à la Mr. Clean—a tactic that several balding men I know have resorted to—strikes me as the kind of defiantly macho gesture, an act of manly self-assertion, I can't really relate to. A shaven head looks to me like some sort of overcompensation, like a buffed-out physique, as if all those muscles or that radically scraped skull were covering for a fear of weakness or, paradoxically, baldness. I believe one should go bald gracefully, naturally, with a certain nonchalance, a casual dignity. But dignity is difficult when you look as ludicrous as I do with my half a head of hair. So at the suggestion of a friend I've lately traded in my wispy Kewpie-doll look for a close-cropped military haircut, or that of a gay Italian racecar driver. It looks no less absurd than my previous 'do, but it's less unruly and requires almost no maintenance.

Now when I look in the mirror, instead of seeing an aging balding version of the handsome young man I used to be, I see an aging balding version of the little boy who at the age of six or seven had his first flattop. I wonder what kind of regression I'm undergoing, and if when my head is truly bald (as I wish it would get already) I'll resemble the six-month-old baby looking alarmedly into the camera in the photo I have on my wall, a baby (me) as distressed at having his picture taken as I am now when I must face my face in the mornings of middle age. If I squint my eyes a little I can discern an almost Mohawkian punkishness latent in my otherwise adult demeanor; if I were to snarl a little and stick a few nails and rings through my lips and nostrils and eyebrows, and perhaps dye a DayGlo green or chartreuse stripe along the rim of my graying sidewalls, I could pass for an ancient imitation of a post-alienated adolescent. This could be considered a second adolescence, an awkward interlude between the accomplished confidence of adulthood and the serenity of true maturity, when baldness is borne as a badge of distinction.

What's called for, then, is not a cure for baldness but a cure for my impatience-to-be-bald. I have to cultivate the equanimity, the composure to live at peace with the shrinking island of silly hair I see on top of my head when I catch my reflection in a passing window, a gratuitous patch of bodily excrescence which serves as, say, a clown nose would in the middle of my face to keep me from taking myself too seriously. Yes, this is surely an opportunity to abandon vanity and reach a more spiritual stage of self-realization, a stage where the way one looks no longer matters and what's inside the head counts for more than what's on top. I remember twenty-five or so years ago arguing with my father about my beard and uncut tresses—how just because I might look like Charlie Manson, that didn't make me a criminal, how looks were deceptive, how judging people by the volume of their hair was as illusory as drawing conclusions from (as in my old man's case) their lack of it. I must now allow this hippie wisdom to percolate through my consciousness to some deeper understanding. If hair is handsome and bald is beautiful, I can learn to live for a few more years in this twilight zone, this no-man's land, this tonsorial purgatory, this half-baked mortification of the pate.

The Tao of Gossip

1 [1989]

At day's end, when I get together with the one I love to cleanse myself of the mundane corruptions, distractions and exhaustion attendant to working in the noble yet dirty business of journalism and in the world of business with its colorful cutthroat drama, we customarily greet each other with the tender question, "Hear any good gossip?"

I—a reputedly serious individual, editor of a major metropolitan weekly, explainer of important political issues, crusader for truth and justice, critic of culture, man of ideas—thrive on gossip. It's true. Gossip is a great pleasure. It is comic relief for those of us who risk taking the world and ourselves too seriously. It is a bonding ritual for comrades, who can say things candidly to one another that they would never say among strangers—an exercise in the discreet charm of knowing who can be trusted. It is one element in the intimacy that weaves lovers together.

In a larger sense and in mysterious ways, gossip brings the community together. When people talk about each other to others the common knowledge, even if untrue, allows them to share in a public secret. It creates networks of shared stories, sometimes circulated via the media but more often and more satisfyingly spread by word of mouth, stories embellished by each teller, with facts and fictions added and subtracted, until little myths and legends are created, legends limited only by the imaginations of their propagators. People who hear new gossip are like journalists getting a scoop—excited to have the inside word on what's happening and drunk with the power to pass it on.

Journalists in fact are in many ways professional gossips. Such eminent scribes as *The New Yorker*'s Janet Malcolm and radical polemicist Alexander Cockburn in his book *Corruptions of Empire* have written with eloquence of the journalistic impulse to extract secrets from an unwitting subject and expose them in the often unflattering light of public scrutiny. When the gossip is reliable and concerns powerful people—sexually promiscuous politicians, for example—it can provide valuable insights into who these characters are, or if they have any. In the case of more obscure figures, the journalist-as-gossip can, if the story is good enough, make them celebrities and therefore interesting to people who have never heard of them before.

But celebrity gossip is fundamentally different from down-home personal gossip about your own friends and acquaintances. Celebrities, especially movie stars and politicians, are a dime a dozen and so overexposed that the latest factoid about their sex lives or eating habits is inherently tinged with absurd shades of irrelevance. My favorite column in the *San Jose Mercury News* is Jim Jeffress's "People," in which the writer relishes with wicked irony the folly, not of the famous and not-so-famous figures whose usually frivolous or silly tales he picks up off the wires, but of the reader who could care about such things. Jeffress's droll perspective is a refreshing antidote to the more prevalent gossipmongers who seem to think what the rich and renowned are doing actually matters.

Gossip is like soap opera, a delightful or dopey entertainment, and the more entertaining the closer it gets to home. If I were to spill the beans about some friends of mine, it probably wouldn't mean much to you unless you knew who they were or knew them personally. If you know the people, there's something vaguely titillating about what's allegedly transpiring in their private lives. In a strange way, gossip keeps people interested in each other; it enables us to compare our most intimate melodrama with others' and, when the story is not so happy, to experience a kind of catharsis, a relieved gratitude it didn't happen to us. As with the catharsis of classic tragedy, however moved we are by the performance, it's vital to remember that gossip is also fiction.

I know this because, as a longtime small-town resident and reluctant player on the local stage, I'm constantly hearing things about myself that are fascinating (at least to me and maybe a handful of friends and enemies) but fanciful. Not famous or notorious enough to be scandalized or annoyed but such inventions, in a perversely literary way I actually enjoy the spectacle of experiences, embarrassments and adventures I never had.

When someone like Bob Dylan says derisively to an interviewer, "Gossip is king," he speaks as a famous victim of its vampirism. People whose lives are not particularly interesting can attain a certain vicarious rush experiencing, millions of times removed, whatever is rumored to be happening to the star. To be the host of millions of such parasites must indeed be draining. But gossip *is* king—it sells magazines, commands prime TV time in the name of exposés, gives history itself a run for its money, at least for a little while. Biographies tend to be fun to read not necessarily because they're true but because they are epic exercises in gossip: the biographer ransacks available documents or interviews as many acquaintances of the subject as possible and, reorganizing the quotes as suits the author's purposes, repeats what he or she has been told.

Self-made mythmakers like Dylan have the last laugh, however, when they keep on making up the story of their lives more amazingly than their fans or spectators can imagine. The person whose life is so unremarkable as never to generate a little gossip, even among an intimate circle of friends, is either unusually pure of heart and therefore above it all or is missing one of the little thrills of social pathology, one of the poisons that inoculates us against larger evils.

For gossip is petty, and often mean, and endlessly interesting despite our desire to ignore its nasty but tasty little morsels. It is the essence of "human interest," the candid account of what we're not supposed to know. It was eating the fruit of the tree of gossip that drove our proto-parents from the garden and gave our species a devilish sense of humor, the capacity to laugh at falls from grace, beginning with our own.

When my partner and I are cooking dinner, or riding our bicycles after work, or caught in traffic in the car together, or sipping a beverage in our favorite café, or lounging in bed on a Saturday morning, a good piece of gossip can cheer us up like some great song heard unexpectedly on the radio. Birds gossip and it too sounds like music. The streets are live with the sounds of gossip. Listen.

2 [1994]

A friend called recently while I was out and left a message that she had some good gossip for me. Of course I returned the call as soon as I could. "So what's the gossip?" I asked up front. "Not so fast," she replied. "You think I'm going to tell you just like that?" We proceeded to have a rambling conversation, exchanging reports on current events in our mundanely interesting or routinely exciting lives, until about twenty minutes into our chat I asked again, "So what's the gossip already?"

What she told me was worth waiting for, but I doubt it would interest you, because it concerns people you don't know. But the ritual of conversational foreplay we performed, building up to the choice revelation, is part of the joy of gossip—the little ceremonies we share with friends in the course of trading news and rumors and confidences and secrets. It set me thinking on the nature of gossip and why everyone loves it so much and how it exerts such a powerful pull on our social imaginations. For while on the surface gossip may often seem petty or trivial, at a deeper level I believe it satisfies primal narrative and psychic needs. People love stories, and when the protagonists are friends and acquaintances, that makes the stories all the more engrossing.

But any serious philosophy of gossip has to begin from an understanding of the differences among the three main gossip groups: mass gossip, local gossip and intimate gossip. True, the boundaries between these categories sometimes blur, but it's vital to acknowledge the distinctions before we can appreciate how and when they merge.

Mass or public gossip can be found every day in the papers, on the TV news, the supermarket magazine rack, even NPR. It's widely and freely available and therefore cheap, even though in a case like that of what's-his-name, the football player, every meaningless morsel of information is feverishly consumed as fast as it's exposed. Celebrity gossip sells tons of magazines because people appear to need the distraction from the boredom of their private lives. The problems of some famous stranger are low-risk drama, and often their fame makes us feel we "know" them even though we don't have a clue who they really are. Unless they're "really" fulltime celebrities, in which case their public persona is their whole identity.

Anyway, mass gossip is cheap because it's so plentiful. And unless you're a media addict chances are that if your own life is halfway interesting, hearing what O. J. had for breakfast won't make or break your day. Biography takes our natural curiosity about the famous one step further: reading a few hundred pages about a person who fascinates us can at least provide an approximation of scholarship. However prurient our interest may be in the sordid or gorgeous details of some historic character's sex life, we can take comfort in the fact that we're sort of *learning* something. One person's trivia is another's history.

Local gossip is much more personal, usually involving people familiar to the gossipers. In relatively small communities like those of the Mendocino Coast, everyone who's not a recluse is hearing stories all the time about their friends and neighbors and acquaintances and enemies and the local players on the public stage who through their very visibility set themselves up as popular gossip objects. In a strange way this kind of gossip actually brings the community together, the shared stories and public secrets acting as a bonding agent. This is the oral tradition at work, and while events are inevitably fictionalized one step further from the facts with every telling, these rumorous fictions can shade into legend and myth, giving their subjects larger- (or sometimes smaller-) than-life dimensions in the minds of their contemporaries and thereby serving a paraliterary purpose as well as a psychosocial one.

Small-town (or big-city) in-person soap opera thus seems harmless enough to me, as long as its auditors and spectators acknowledge its distortions, especially when you're receiving something second- or third- or thirteenth-hand. In my tumultuous public and private life I've often enjoyed or been vaguely amused by some of the tales I've heard about myself, even when they don't resemble what I know as my experience. After all, it's almost an honor to be gossiped about; it shows that people care in one way or another how destiny's treating you.

Gossip can also be a provider of tragic or comic relief. Hearing of others' fiascos and triumphs, problems and scandalous scenes can give us new perspectives on our own. Our gratitude, relief, envy or jealousy—however we react to the information—can tell us, if we're paying attention, something about ourselves. But it can also take us out of ourselves long enough to get a fresh look at our situation and realize it could be worse—or better, as the case may be.

My favorite kind of gossip is the intimate kind, the sort shared only between the closest friends. This private gossip is a measure of mutual trust, the sharing of closely held information creating implicit pacts of confidence. You aren't going to take your choicest tidbits and priceless interpretive commentary and spill them to someone who's going to turn around and blab them all over the place. No, you save your best stuff for those who mean the most to you, who won't be promiscuous with the scoop—and who will reciprocate with juicy morsels of their own. These kinds of conversations, when they occur, are sexy not just because the subject matter often has to do with sex but because the intimacy of the transaction brings the participants closer together, interweaves their personal mythologies, deepens their connection as comrades.

There are no gossip police to enforce truth-in-gossip guidelines, no ethical standards by which to measure gossip's moral equivalent, only the integrity and sincerity of the source. Gossip from the lips of a known liar is not worth the breath that speaks it, even though the tale may be entertaining, whereas gossip uttered by a faithful confidante is priceless. The longer you hold on to such a secret, the more valuable it becomes.

Which brings me back to that telephone call and what my friend had to tell me. Obviously I can't repeat it here.

Dining Alone at Home

[1997]

Everyone knows, or ought to, that having dinner with a lover, friend or friends is one of the simplest and richest gifts of existence. The convivial exchange of news and gossip, the sharing of food and drink, the meandering conversations that can ramble aimlessly around the table adding a certain social or intellectual seasoning to the sights and smells and flavors of the meal—these are the kinds of things that can revive one's faded faith in civilization. Sometimes these choice hours are passed in restaurants, and such public settings may have their own ambient charm—my favorite scenes in almost any Woody Allen movie tend to take place in New York eateries which always seem to have a special warmth otherwise absent from the director's cranky sensibility—but for me a big table in somebody's kitchen is the ideal place to enjoy a friendly feast.

As it happens, in most of our lives the occasion for such an encounter is a rare and treasured event. Between work obligations, family duties and the general rush and press of everyday distraction and its attendant fatigue, the opportunity to pause and dine at leisure may arise only at intervals. When children are factored into the equation, the idea of a low- or no-stress meal becomes even more exotic; cute and amusing as they can be, kids are not always the ideal dining companions. But some of us with no resident offspring may also have no partner, mate or spouse with whom to share the regular ritual of dinner, and while that may be a source of regret or lonesome longing for those who'd rather be coupled, even the solo monk or monkette may find great pleasure in this nightly rite without having to invite company. If you can find an hour or two in the familiar comfort of home at dusk, you can turn that primal time into a savory and satisfying experience.

A sensuous monk myself, I work at home and like to cook, and after enough hours at the desk or doing household chores I find the act of preparing and eating dinner to be one of the day's more restorative projects. As those streaks in the early evening sky are turning from pink to purple and the ambient indigo darkens into a spacescape sizzling with stars that look like bits of garlic in a black skillet, the thrift-shop gourmet cum gourmand in me begins to get inspired. I live in the country now but I remember neighborhoods where this time of day brought out the most amazing aromatic evocations of eternity, a stream of olfactory associations flowing all the way back to childhood and its archetypal pork chops or roasts or simmering stews and soups whose smells are somehow always and everywhere the same. Even in the absence of those specific smells, the minutes just after sundown when I start to cook commonly give me that sense of domestic wellbeing, possibly nostalgic, even melancholy or sentimental, but with a Keatsian poignancy I don't mind indulging. I pour a glass of red wine, light a couple of candles on the kitchen table, put on some music to suit my mood and cleanse the psyche of whatever residue may remain of the evening news, and set to work intently at the butcher block.

Order, as far as I'm concerned, is one of the keys to creativity. Rimbaud's derangement of the senses, and its more pedestrian manifestations of messy chaos, only depresses and confuses me. Whether I'm writing a poem or tossing a salad, I need to have my tools and materials immediately at hand, I need to know where everything is so I can reach for it, like a percussionist, at precisely the timely extemporaneous moment. I have to arrange the ingredients, selecting whatever happens to be left in the classically empty bachelor refrigerator along with what I may have just picked from the shaggy late-winter garden, lining up half an onion, a head of garlic, some broccoli stalks, kale leaves, a piece of leftover chicken from last night's restaurant meal, and for an uptown touch the bottom of a jar of sun-dried tomatoes in olive oil. Thus organized for the entrée, I turn my attention to the slightly slug-maimed leaves of romaine and whatever remains of a store-bought organic red-leaf lettuce and a handful or arugula salvaged from the bolted plants fallen over out back—arugula, most distinctive of salad greens, with its spicy zing, wild sprays of it volunteering profusely in unforeseen places, another gift of winter. Washed and dripping in the colander, these greens are the opening movement in a musical composition that seems to rhyme with the overlapping layers of Bill Evans's thirty fingers improvising harmonies on *Conversations with Myself.* I toast his sound with the house red.

A few quick rhythmic strokes against the butcher's steel and my favorite knife is smiling. I press down the flat of the

8-inch stainless blade on a garlic cove: the tough skin splits and slips off, the flesh is crushed, pungent juice spurts out, seasoning the wood of the cutting board. Chopped fine, this clove is dropped into a jar where I've poured a wristful of extra-virgin olive oil, a splash of balsamic vinegar, juice of half a lemon and a dash of soy sauce, the mixture sprinkled with pinches of basil, rosemary, thyme and oregano, the jar lid tightened and the dressing shaken, then set down to brew for a few minutes while the salad is assembled. The simplest salad is for me the most eloquent introduction to the entrée; I tear the leaves one by one, editing out the funky spots as I alternate arugula, red leaf and romaine, and drop them into the chipped white restaurant plate, scored for a quarter at a rummage sale, that will serve for both courses of this basic meal. The plain white plate with its high glaze makes an elegant setting for the light and dark and red-tinged green of the leaves. What's left of the loaf of Italian bread I bought the other day isn't quite fresh, so I slice off a thick piece, sprinkle a bit of tap water on it and slip it in the oven for a few minutes. By the time Bill Evans gives way to Ben Webster, or Coltrane's *Ballads*, or Billie Holiday, the bread is warm and moist and the crust is crisp. Another shake of the jar, the salad is dressed and I sit down.

Different evenings, different moods, different reading matter or none at all. Even though I'm up to here with news, sometimes I can't get enough, so I may prop a section of *The New York Times* against the book stand and browse the op-ed page or the obituaries to see whose eventful life is being summarized as I take the first bites of the rest of mine. Or maybe I'll dive into the highbrow discourse of some essay in the *New York Review* or, in a lighter vein, catch up on the latest poetic gossip in Joyce Jenkins's column in *Poetry Flash.* Or else, content with the sounds coming out of the speakers, I'll simply savor the taste of the salad while Lady Day serenades me; the singular beauty and grace of that voice feeds and seasons the soul. Between the music and the printed matter many conversations may be generated, reflections multiplied in the blue light of "Easy to Remember," thoughts of new projects advanced in the imagination, works in progress clarified. The evening opens before me, empty and pregnant with possibility. The appetite awakens. Mysterious juices circulate in the brain.

The salad finished and the last of the dressing matched with the last bite of bread and a sip of wine, I fill a pot with fresh cold water and set it to boil on the stove. The 12-inch cast-iron skillet clangs into place on the adjacent burner and the wrist resumes its dance with the knife, slicing the chicken from the cold bone (and setting aside a few scraps for Jackson the cat), crushing, peeling and chopping more garlic, cutting the half-onion into vertical crescents, trimming the tough stems from the kale and broccoli. The water comes to a boil, flame is ignited under the other pan, a bit of olive oil anoints the black surface, linguine goes into the pot with a surge of roiling bubbles, the oil spreads in the pan and then, like a clash of cymbals, the onions are introduced with a sizzling flourish, followed by the shredded bits of chicken, sun-dried tomatoes and the rest of the chopped greens, all stirred a few times with the wooden spatula, the flame turned down to a low simmer and the glass lid put in place on the skillet to seal in the flavor and moisture even as streams of steam escape and perfume the kitchen with a luscious blend of Mediterranean aromas.

I dip a fork into the boiling pasta, lift out one long strand

and wind it around the tines for a texture test: it's done. I shut off the burner and the water settles, then pour out the contents of the pot into the empty colander in the sink, stir the contents of the skillet once more before shutting off the flame and mixing in the steaming linguine. I fold the pasta over several times in the pan for maximum absorption of ambient oils and flavors, add salt and pepper, and slide the food onto the empty plate last occupied by the salad. This dish has taken maybe fifteen minutes to make, enough time for the appetite to be re-aroused by the smells, for the wine to be replenished in the glass, for the music to be changed as I sit back down for the main course.

Food is a famously ephemeral art form, but even a plate of pasta can look beautiful. Jackson Pollock could not have improved on this composition. Before digging in with fork and tablespoon I feast my eyes on the design, just in case I should decide to paint it later. But no, this is for eating—that strange necessity shared by humans and other animals alike, though we have more ways of embellishing and abusing the act than they do. Somewhere between the omniphagic excesses of the perpetual junk-munchers and fast-fooders and face-stuffers, on the one hand, and the gourmet gastronomes whose mandarin preciosity fetishizes their own estheticism on the other, there is a range of reasonable responses to dinner, and one is to note how easy it is to raise this mundane experience out of the everyday even as you celebrate its mundanity. I understand why some people pause and say grace, for grace is needed to acknowledge such a routine sacrament. As you slow down and savor what's in front of you—the way you might read a favorite poem or study the uniqueness of your lover's face—that attention can be a model for bringing full consciousness to other areas of the ordinary.

After finishing the last forkfuls and the last few swallows of wine, followed by a few sips of fizz-water, I clear the table, set the dirty dishes on the counter beside the sink, and turn toward the pantry where a chunk of pure dark chocolate and a packet of Dutch tobacco beckon, promising a dangerously delicious finish, a ritual so civilized it carries a whiff of decadence: fine bittersweet chocolate, the oral equivalent of orgasm, followed by a hand-rolled smoke on the back porch—sitting down, letting the linguine settle, marveling at the mystery of the cocoa bean, alternating deep drafts of cool night air with puffs of good-tasting tobacco. Just one cigarette a day, after lunch or dinner, is enough for me. But that one is lingered over as a rounding-off, a meditative reverie that calms and refreshes as it ravages.

The final meditation is cleaning up, which when you're just one person is seldom overwhelming; even a couple days' dishes hardly amount to much. Gathering the few plates and utensils in the sink, I squirt some soap in there and run hot water and next thing I know there's a rack of just-washed dishes handsomely stacked on the side, as pleasing to the eye as a mountain range, mist rising from the ridges. Hot water only on the cast iron, you have to preserve the cure; I rinse the skillet and place it back on the stove, where the heat of the metal evaporates the water as you watch, even without turning on a burner. A few strokes of the sponge over the wet tiles, the butcher block and the table, where droplets of olive oil may have fallen between the newspapers, and the kitchen looks more beautiful than ever, a temple of monastic sensuality. Now

I'm ready to sit by the fire and read a book, or write a letter, almost unaware of what a pleasure it's been to have had myself over for dinner.

Next time I may have to invite friends.

What's Wrong with Romance and Why Pursuing Happiness Won't Help

[1995]

When my beloved and I split up a couple of years ago I thought I'd die of sexual deprivation. It wasn't just the jealousy attacks—the knowledge that she was trying out a series of new suitors—but the understanding that we'd never again share the bliss of erotic union, the oneness of intense connection that marked the highest and deepest hours of our love.

I wondered how or where I might ever again find such perfect intimacy and despaired of how unlikely it was that I, already well into my forties, would encounter such exquisite chemistry in any available woman. After six years together it was hard to get used to sleeping solo, and every throbbing signal in the surrounding culture bombarded me with messages of mating.

Though our numbers in this country are larger than ever, people who live alone are often regarded by our paired peers—and often regard ourselves—as somehow defective, subnormal, less than complete. One look at *People* magazine proves that the only Beautiful People who count are the ones who are currently coupling (or uncoupling). More than just sex, which in the present moral climate is looked on with some suspicion, joining forces with a partner gives one a certain respectability, gives others the impression that you must be...well, *together*, no matter how miserable you actually are.

It was in fact the unbearable unhappiness of most of our days together those last couple of years--the fights, the rivalries, the jealousies, the resentments--that finally drove my love and me apart. Still, it's hard to get over not only the loss of a companion but the redemptive notion that somewhere, somehow, the ideal mate will save us from ourselves.

Classical Agonies & Romantic Myths

The idea of love as consolation for the difficulties of existence was not invented by Smokey Robinson. The fatuous longings of popular song, the aches and pains of romance and the imaginary happy endings of movie comedies can be traced back in our collective consciousness to eras way before Shakespeare's.

Denis de Rougement in his illuminating study *Love in the Western World* identifies the source of our romantic obsessions in a medieval religious cult called the Cathars who worshipped the Virgin Mary as an object of spiritual desire. Out of the Cathars came the troubadours and the conventions of courtly love, and from the troubadours evolved the Romantic poets, and from the Romantics eventually came the blues, and so on through rock and roll up to the present.

Desire is biological not literary, but culture being what it is, one step removed from nature, it's in the written record that we find the most eloquent testimony to desire's power. In the poets of the *Greek Anthology*, who predate the Cathars by more than a thousand years, and especially in the fragments of Sappho, who wrote in the sixth century BCE, the pleasures of sexual love and the agonies of its absence are pervasive. *With his venom*, writes Sappho (in Mary Barnard's version),

Irresistible
and bittersweet

that loosener
of limbs, Love

reptile-like
strikes me down

Sappho wasn't looking to get married—she was the original Lesbian, attracted not only to a great range of lovely girls but also to beautiful young men—yet the aching need for sexual connection, the yearning and hunting for the ultimate erotic embrace recorded in her poems are among the pinnacle poetic expressions of pure lust.

If love is consolation for the sufferings of life, Sappho's lyrics are balm for the wounds of love. The only voice I can compare with Sappho's in its power to express this feeling is Billie Holiday's. These forms of singing persist, alongside the myths of romantic happiness, because we need their solace for the disappointments those very myths make inevitable.

The Pursuit of Happiness

Jefferson really opened a can of worms when he wrote in the Declaration of Independence of our "unalienable rights" to "Life, Liberty and the pursuit of Happiness." Is there any other culture on the planet where happiness is proposed as a realistic ambition for human beings? Maybe that's what's great about the United States, the notion that happiness is attainable, which may account in part for Americans' historically optimistic outlook as well as for our epidemic anxieties. Happiness is that endlessly receding promise just ahead that keeps us hustling.

As historian Page Smith has pointed out, this somewhat abstract quest was early translated into the pursuit of money, a more concrete and therefore achievable proposition. Money as a means to material security remains a primary motivator in US culture, a principle most vividly epitomized by the waves of immigrants continually arriving in search of economic opportunity.

But for many Americans since the prosperous 1950s and 60s, money and all the goodies it brings with it—the cars and the clothes and the high-tech toys, and even the homes and the immigrant help who assist in raising the kids—don't quite add up to happiness. Indeed the pursuit of material security for most people doesn't mean entrepreneurial adventure in the great American open-frontier tradition but the heartless demands of a job that affords very little time for what Jefferson called Life.

For those unyoked to the full-time work of family, or who as single parents would like some relief from that nonstop responsibility, it isn't money but love that often embodies the slippery notion of happiness. The personals section of any newspaper pulses with the desperation of happiness-seekers in search of the lover who'll provide what's missing. I wonder how many of these earnest searchers realize that happiness is as elusive as a mirage and that love as often as not creates more problems than it solves.

It seems as if half the psychotherapy industry is sustained by the romantic unhappiness of single people, and the other half by the unhappiness of couples. Yet the expectation that we can or should be happy in any abiding way is pure homegrown and media-reinforced mythic American fantasy. If we aren't happy we feel there must be something wrong with us, and that makes us even more depressed, and for depression there are various treatments ranging from compulsive consumerism to pharmaceutical chemistry, each "cure" bringing with it a whole new syndrome of problems.

Renunciation of desire, including the desire for happiness, is taught by many religious traditions as a step toward wisdom or enlightenment. Jefferson, who personified the eighteenth-century Enlightenment in its American manifestation, would have made a lousy Buddhist.

A Befuddled Bachelor

Benjamin, a successful software engineer, has rediscovered religion after many years of a rather bohemian young manhood. He tells me now that he wants to be married but just hasn't found the right woman. He envisions a wife and family as a path to spiritual union, a way of getting closer to God and living a righteous life.

Meanwhile he's "dating," which, at forty, isn't so much fun. He meets women through his temple, through his professional associations, and has even taken out personals ads and answered a few. But not one woman he's gone out with thus far feels to him like wife material. Whenever we get together he complains of how ridiculous it is for a man in his position to be going through these transient emotional skirmishes with women equally eager to find a man but obviously not compatible with him. He knows he can't just settle for anyone who happens to be nice and Jewish; she has to be a person of impeccable character, spiritual depth, psychological self-awareness and intellectual substance--and naturally it wouldn't hurt if she was really good-looking.

"I set out on a devotional quest," Ben said to me recently, "but I feel like I'm stuck in a Woody Allen movie."

"Maybe," I suggested, "God is trying to tell you something."

A Biological Time Bomb

Grace, a friend and former lover of mine, is an alluring woman in her mid-thirties. For reasons I'm not sure even her shrink could explain, she remains unmarried despite the fact there's nothing she wants more ardently than to fall in love and settle down and have babies.

Gorgeous, intelligent, professionally accomplished, financially stable, witty and a great kisser, Grace mysteriously hasn't yet met the man with whom she would ride off into the sunset. She keeps on having these half-baked affairs with the most ridiculous characters--noncommittal self-involved academics, married men she meets through her corporate job, adoring suitors who fail to provide the brilliant banter that turns her on, quick-witted jokers who lack the moral character she requires--while she grows increasingly desperate to find the special one with whom she might procreate.

What Grace doesn't seem to realize is that the perfect man does not exist, so she may never find one who measures up to her exacting standards. I fear that her ovulational volatility may drive her into a marriage she'll regret. In her desperation to plunge into the bliss of domesticity the odds are that she'll end up, a few years hence, divorced from some schmuck who'll refuse to pay child support because she can afford to raise the kids herself.

Legendary Marriages

Great marriages are definitely possible. I've known a few couples who met when young, formed permanent amorous unions and stayed together all their lives as if the gods intended it that way. These are the exceptional models most of us imagine as ideal. They seem effortlessly harmonious, less a matter of work than of perfect chemistry, intuitive understanding, sympathy and mutual support.

Other good marriages start later, after a divorce or two, or after each person has come into their own professionally and is able to bring to the other a wholeness, a centered maturity that provides balance. The couples I know who aren't yet old but whose marriages seem most rich are paradoxically the same ones whose lives are overloaded, utterly driven by children and/or work, so that they rarely have a spare moment to savor what's supposed to be Happiness.

In letters and conversations with my friends in such fulfilling partnerships I'm always hearing lots of moans and groans about how they wish they had just a little time free of the relentless everyday demands. They vicariously enjoy or vaguely envy the Liberty of those of us who have remained independent, just as we may admire from a safe distance the frenzied but fertile chaos of their family lives.

There is no "having it all." The choices we make require sacrifices. Whatever we do, we're always missing something.

The key to not feeling cheated is to settle for less than everything while making the most of what's in front of us. This may be what the much-divorced Saul Bellow meant when he wrote, in *The Adventures of Augie March*, of "the refusal to live a disappointed life."

Self-Loathing & the Single Woman

Rachel, who has an interesting if necessarily stressful job, wonderful friends and a rewarding spiritual practice, confesses to being hung-up on a guy who will never commit to her. Every so often she gives him an ultimatum but he always ignores it, so she calls it quits, can handle being without him for a while, then can't stand it anymore, so they get together, go to bed, and the cycle starts all over again.

Like Grace, the biological time bomb, Rachel wants a baby and can feel the demands of her body to find a mate. She also says she feels a certain contempt for herself as some kind of loser when she's alone. Of course when she lets her boyfriend come and go at will she feels lousy about that too.

Janet, an artist, was celibate for four years before she got together with Walt, whom she recently married. She told me the secret of her ability to remain sola and sane for those four sexless years was to channel her energy into creative work. By cultivating her self and her individual vision through painting and sculpture she found a kind of erotic fulfillment that kept her sexuality alive even while its carnal manifestation remained dormant.

There's something in art that enables its practitioners—I think of Emily Dickinson, Joseph Cornell, Marianne Moore, Glenn Gould and other solitary eccentrics—to harness erotic energy for esthetic purposes, returning to the artist not only a sense of beauty and embodied mystery but also dignity and self-respect. However lonely and miserable you may be as a poet or painter or musician, you can always pour your soul into the work and it gives you back something akin to the reflected radiance of a lover.

The Joy of Celibacy

One of my favorite philosophers, Lin Yutang, calls celibacy "a freak of civilization." Dr. Lin is neither the first nor the last to assert the supremacy of marriage and family life over the dubious pleasures of autonomy. Social historian Christopher Lasch, in his great book *The Culture of Narcissism*, excoriated a whole generation of Americans for abandoning the commitment to home and family and community as concentric centers of the universe, and as far as I know Lasch wasn't even a Confucian, much less a Republican.

But some of my friends who have chosen the path of celibacy—not out of principle but just because that's the way things have evolved in their personal relations—appear to be far less angst-riddled than either their uncoupled peers still hunting for a mate or the happily married parents whose lives are virtually controlled by their kids.

My own parents didn't have that problem; they were out building their business while I was growing up, so they weren't around too much, and maybe that, for better or worse, is the source of my self-reliance. I wouldn't exactly call myself celibate—I'm more of a sensuous monk, monogamous when I have a lover but more often, since being single, doing without—but during those periods when I'm unattached I relish the freedom of my eccentricities, all those quirks and habits that can so easily annoy or alienate a partner.

Veronica, a graphic designer and organic gardener, has told me she's far happier since she quit a difficult relationship and decided to be herself without the intervention of a man. Her life is no longer at the mercy of her hormones, and she feels emotionally liberated, free to focus on things that give her a steadier kind of pleasure.

Jackson, a handsome entrepreneur and reformed ladies' man who finally realized he didn't want to marry his six-year sweetheart--so she left him--reports that despite the presence in his life of a number of attractive women, for now he much prefers the peace of sleeping alone to the complications of emotional entanglement.

The chosen bonds of mutual commitment can be wonderful, but so can the openness and clarity of being wholly your own person. Good sex feels great, and combined with love can make for the profoundest alliances, but I've witnessed enough desperate and temporary pairings to recognize the limits of the mating instinct. The people I know who proceed with reserve, resisting rather than seeking romance, seem to me much more grounded in a reliable reality.

The Drug of Love

Everyone knows that being "in love" is one of the all-time highs. Endocrinologists tell us that the endorphins released by vigorous exercise, presumably including sex, are what pump our minds and bodies full of those euphoric feelings.

When the initial high wears off, however, love can be as dangerous as any other drug in its revelation of what it succeeded in masking or suppressing for a while—not just the dreaded Human Condition but those nasty interpersonal incompatibilities and insecurities our sexual pleasure seemed to render irrelevant. Surely sex is an excellent cement for holding lovers together, but without the sustaining presence of other essential adhesives one can expect a crashing letdown.

Lewis, divorced for a couple of years and hungry for sexual fulfillment, fell in love with a woman who was raising two teenagers by herself. He wanted to sleep with her every night, so he moved out of his tidy little cottage, where he had the tranquility to pursue his work as a poet, and into the more complex dynamics of her larger home.

Every so often, when Lewis and I get together for lunch or a beer, he laments the difficulty of doing his writing amid the demands of his lover's kids, and of her own need for attention and her lack of comprehension of *his* need for periods of peace and quiet. Yet he craves the intimacy he has with this woman who gives him the sexual sustenance he also needs.

I wonder how he'll be able to resolve these irreconcilable addictions.

Is Sex Necessary?

Marriage was described by Immanuel Kant, another titan of the Enlightenment, as "the union of two persons of different sexes for the purpose of lifelong mutual possession of their sexual organs." More recently and only a bit less cynically, Charles Bukowski wrote, in his grueling novel *Women*, "Sex is like money. It seems more important when you don't have any."

The underlying theme of both these witticisms is their shared understanding of the insecurity most of us feel when we're without a steady sexual partner. Marriage is like an insurance policy that guarantees we'll get laid--even though things don't always work out that way.

Last spring, when I was visiting New York, two casually dressed middle-aged couples were sitting near my table in a restaurant. One of the couples was clearly having problems; the woman was very upset with her mate and kept getting up as if to leave. After gently persuading her to stay, the other man put his arm around his wife and said reassuringly to his companions across the table, "We may not have the best sex life in the world, but I love her." To which his wife added cheerfully, "You know what? I'm not even interested in sex anymore."

Then they all ordered another round of drinks.

Contentment & Its Discontents

Some years ago Maria married her best friend, a guy who couldn't be more reliable, accommodating, devoted, compatible, securely employed, sensitive, intelligent, kind--the sort of person any girl's mother would love for a son-in-law. And for a while there, Maria felt she'd found the right formula for the balance of companionship and independence she required. Her work as a veterinarian received the unconditional support of Eugene, her understanding husband, and their life together seemed a model partnership of equals.

But after four years Maria began to become uneasy with the smoothness of their domestic life; something was wrong, or missing, some essential tension, not necessarily conflict but *energy*. She needed more resistance than she was getting, more give-and-take. Contentment, the perfect marriage, was not exactly constricting but it was dull.

Since moving to her own apartment a few months ago Maria has perked up, life seems interesting again, not because of any desire to pursue some new and exciting romance—she remains close friends with Eugene and has no lover—but because the boundaries of her situation are not so clearly defined. I wouldn't go so far as to say she's happy—Maria cultivates a certain tragic resignation—but she's evidently less miserable than when she was happily married.

The Happiest Man I Know

Ray, a retired high-school Spanish teacher, is in his early seventies but looks about fifty and is one of the most vitally energetic people I've ever met. Gay, unattached, fit and still sexy, when asked how he is he invariably answers, "Terrific!"

I have no way of knowing how sexually active he is, but he has plenty of friends, both gay and straight, and a busy social life as well as a continuing interest in books and ideas and politics. But what seems to give Ray the most satisfaction is service: he volunteers as a courthouse interpreter, he works with homeless people at a community garden, and he takes care of men who are dying of AIDS, cooking for them and delivering meals as well as being present as a companion.

Because he comes from a line of long-lived ancestors, Ray is sure he's going to live to be at least a hundred, and so, despite his senior-citizen status, maintains the forward-looking enthusiasm of someone in his twenties.

He's told me of one great love in his life, a handsome dancer who, after their years together in San Francisco, eventually returned to his native Spain. Whatever suffering this breakup may have caused him at the time, Ray now seems anything but nostalgic about the relationship. The photos of Emilio on his wall, alongside pictures of more recent boyfriends, appear to be points of personal reference not to love lost but life gained, happy reminders of a richness even time, the great eradicator, can't negate.

The Love of Comrades

In my experience sex has served as a beautiful bonding agent between long-term or even one-time lovers who gradually evolve into friends, or as a tantalizingly flirtatious possibility between friends who never get sexually intimate, maintaining a certain erotic tension that charges the friendship to a higher voltage of affectionate intensity, as if not having sex were sexier than having it.

If not quite *agape*--the famously chaste Christian brotherly/sisterly love--perhaps this is something like what Walt Whitman meant by "the dear love of comrades," that adhesive longing, consummated or not, that draws companions together. Kenneth Rexroth used to speak of "erotic comradeship," an anarcho-utopian concept of sacred sex not to be confused with the so-called "free love" of the 1960s and 70s; comradeship implying solidarity, an ongoing spiritual and practical affinity that is neither the randy randomness of indiscriminate intercourse nor the Super-Glue bondedness of wedlock.

Friendship, as I've known it, is a far more reliable and lasting form of interpersonal relations than romantic attachment. Those I've loved most dearly and longest, male and female, carnal lovers and platonic sidekicks alike, are almost without exception individuals I wouldn't want to live with.

Happiness Happens

While I subscribe to the Nietzschean notion that we create our lives and are responsible for how we live them, I doubt that any self-respecting existentialist would buy the idea that happiness can be had.

What happens with happiness is, *it has us*, whenever and for however long it likes. A colleague compares it to the unexpected current of warm water one may sometimes move through for a few pleasant seconds while snorkeling. We can't even plan for its presence, much less possess it.

Etymologically speaking, the word means luck, chance, happenstance. When, in "My Last Affair," Billie Holiday sings *My happiness is misery* in an incongruously perky tone of voice, the ambiguity of the line resounds in the heart that knows how the feeling can cut both ways: the strangely delicious misery of losing the happiness one had in the rapture of romantic passion, and the perverse happiness some thinkers thrive on, that immersion in sorrow out of which the deepest truths of existence may be lifted.

The catharsis of tragedy, the terrible encounter with our human limits revealed at best through the beauty of art, the fact of our inevitable losses transformed into something that gives pleasure even as it lays bare our desolation—like Lady Day singing of ruined love, or van Gogh painting a tormented landscape, or Thelonious Monk seducing a piano, or Sophocles putting Oedipus through the wringer--these are the gifts of misery that somehow make happiness possible.

When I behold such a work, or am given a glimpse of a hawk on the coast or a flash of human grace in the urban landscape, or am lucky enough to pull from my self and reveal on paper some private grief that's been eating me––like the loss of a lover whose body and soul I had hoped to hold forever despite the pain of our relations––I have a taste of that serendipity no self-help manual can teach.

As William Blake so neatly put it in a four-line poem he called "Eternity":

> *He who binds himself to a joy*
> *Does the winged life destroy;*
> *But he who kisses the joy as it flies*
> *Lives in eternity's sun rise.*

Hard Sell

[1998]

As we grow older, men are prone to suffer from the ravages of both vanity and gravity. To our distress, our youthful beauty withers, and parts of our bodies once perkily erect by nature begin to droop and sag. Women have been dealing with these irresistible forces in various ways for ages, and now it appears to be men's turn to fight back for their so-called potency: the power to carry out certain mechanical acts even when the body may prefer not to.

Among the redeeming aspects of male maturity is that one's sex organ seems to grow a brain. Instead of being perpetually primed to shoot its juice into any available receptacle, as it was when younger, the penis becomes selective. Only certain people, under certain circumstances, are likely to turn us on. For some men this feels like a setback, a blow against full-time on-duty virility, especially if they conceive of manhood as a virtue defined by the stiffness of one's tool.

Impotence—or erectile dysfunction, as it is now more sensitively designated—is no joke. I speak from experience. In 1967, when the so-called Sexual Revolution was revving up in earnest, I was a twenty-year-old college junior with the normally rampant libidinal energies of any other guy that age. (According to urologist Sherman Silber, the male libido gradually declines from its peak around age eighteen.)

A nasty case of gastroenteritis, complicated by a combination of personal, historical and academic stresses, landed me in the hospital. Among the medications prescribed to calm my hyperactive colon was Thorazine, which I continued to take for a while that summer following my recovery.

No doctor bothered to tell me that Thorazine, a heavy-duty depressant, was likely to have as a side effect the suppression of my sexual capability. So when I went to bed for the first time with my favorite girlfriend, a young woman with whom I felt a wonderful affinity, for reasons unknown to either of us my cock would not cooperate. In our youth and ignorance and inexperience, both of us were so distraught by this traumatic event that it murdered our budding romance.

As sex expert William H. Masters, of Masters and Johnson fame, points out: "Regardless of why or under what circumstances the male fails to achieve or maintain an erection the first time, the greatest cause of continued sexual dysfunction thereafter is his fear of nonperformance."

For the next few years, with the exception of the familiar lover who had been my high-school sweetheart, I was terrified of trying to have sex with anyone for fear I would once again fail to live up to what I assumed were my manly duties. It was especially depressing and humiliating to be caught in this vortex of erotic dread amid the expectations of the time to "do it" with any available lover whenever you had the chance. Though I've since learned that mine was a textbook case of what Dr. Masters was talking about, the thought of the agony I went through then still makes me feel a little sick.

Gradually, thanks to the patience of someone who was to become a longtime lover, companion and friend, my confidence was restored and I became as recklessly promiscuous as anyone else of my generation, spreading my semen freely, as Allen Ginsberg famously put it, "to whomever come who may."

Since then, in the tumultuous intervening years of my mostly single or serially monogamous life, there have been numerous occasions when for one reason or another—insufficient chemistry, first-time shyness, circumstantial misgivings, subconscious revulsion—I haven't had an erection when I thought I wanted one. If there is promise of a real connection, patience can cure this temporary setback and eventually all will be well.

But if there's something wrong with the encounter, I've found, some bad faith or fundamental lack of trust, the "failure" is really the body's way of saying, "Whoa, maybe we should reconsider." Freud, personifying the penis as a fellow with a mind of his own, wisely counseled men to pay attention to what *he* is trying to tell you.

From anecdotal evidence and conventional medical wisdom on the subject, it appears that my experiences—the occasionally droopy or recalcitrant member asked to rise to the occasion under the wrong circumstances—are classic examples of the psyche's sexual sensitivity and nothing to worry about.

As Franklin Roosevelt astutely observed in another context, the only thing we have to fear is fear itself.

Surely fear—fear of failure, fear of intimacy, fear of losing control, fear of emotional exposure, fear of the other person—is one of the powerful forces driving the demand for a pill that will make it easier for men to fuck.

Is Sex Show Biz?

Easily the creepiest metaphor dominating the discourse around erections is the concept of sex as "performance." Are lovers really supposed to be performers attempting to impress an audience? Or are they more like spiritual pilgrims seeking dissolution of the ego?

In his classic work of religious existentialism *I and Thou*, Martin Buber distinguishes between "experience" and "relation": the former implying perception, distance, control and manipulation between a person and the world he or she inhabits—all necessary aspects of a functional existence—and the latter suggesting oneness, a mystical union with the other in which individuality is obliterated.

Sex at its best, as I have known it, is more relation than experience. Whatever conscious delight one may take in the sensory pleasures of lovemaking, where love is involved the richness of intimacy is taken to another level. You forget who you are and become one with your lover, bodies and souls and spirits intertwined, a bond that with luck and cultivation may carry over into the more practical partnership of common everyday experience.

When the act of love is conceived as a performance, no wonder it's a source of anxiety. Whatever ego gratification may ensue from a successful display of sexual prowess, a sense of deep connection is sacrificed. Failure to live up to some Hollywood model of expected studliness further exacerbates what was already an absence of intimacy, and the would-be lady-killer (a disturbingly telling term) is left even more isolated than before.

Oneness, the I-and-Thou relation that is sexual love in its most fulfilled form, temporarily annihilates the performing self. The power that is shared between two people is bigger than both of you, and therefore humbling. The gratitude I've felt in my lover's embrace flows not just from the bliss of our fused bodies but from the healing immersion in a vast and mysterious universe.

It's hard to believe that any "potency" medication, operating at an essentially mechanical level, could begin to open the valves that truly matter—those of the soul.

Sorrows of Priapus

Priapus, the Greek god of fertility, is usually depicted (in the *Columbia Encyclopedia*'s succinct description) as "a grotesque little man with an enormous phallus." Priapism, the painful medical condition, is an erection that won't go away. Priapic, used as an adjective, generally refers to the kind of man whose behavior is driven by sexual desire—a man whose cock is incorrigible.

As any teenage boy can tell you, this is not a happy state of affairs. When compulsively boner-driven conduct extends into adulthood, as it does for many men, the results can be personally and interpersonally calamitous—just ask President Clinton. Priapic appetites and the problems they engender have long been a theme of literature. In our time Isaac Bashevis Singer, Milan Kundera and Philip Roth have been among the more eloquent investigators of the agonies brought on by men's inability to keep their peckers in check.

Perhaps the foremost exponent of this tortured genre is Henry Miller, whose work has been widely misinterpreted by feminist critics and macho admirers alike as somehow glorifying sexual athleticism, when on closer reading it's clear that Miller is presenting himself (or his fictional persona) as a rather wretched sexual buffoon.

Even Miller's great friend and champion Lawrence Durrell was repelled by *Sexus*, the excruciating and immensely funny first volume of Miller's trilogy *The Rosy Crucifixion*; this is the book that ends with the perpetually horny narrator dreaming that he's a little barking dog. An appalled Durrell advised Miller in a letter to withdraw and revise the book—which he calls vulgar, obscene and "painfully disgusting"—lest it ruin the author's reputation.

In Miller's patient and lengthy reply he explains, "If I were a braggart and an egotist I might have written more gloriously. There is a poverty and sterility I tried to capture which few men have known…That life of 'senseless activity,' which the sages have ever condemned as death—that was what I set out to record."

Unfortunately the idea of the sexual athlete, the dude who planks as many babes as possible, remains for some people the model of true manhood. Even within the sanctity of a tired marriage, a readiness to go at it is not always reciprocated, and the arrival of Viagra, while it may improve some couples' sex lives, may ultimately stir up more aggravation than satisfaction.

Most women, unlike most men, are not fixated on the penis as the main source of sexual pleasure. A lot can be done with a nimble tongue applied to a tender button. Disappointing as it might be for certain women under certain conditions, men need to learn that it's okay *not* to have an erection. The absence of one in some cases could save them and their partners a world of suffering.

One female friend of mine insists that Viagra will only further destabilize already shaky relationships; using this drug, she says, "is like erecting a flagpole on a condemned building."

Dangerous Drugs

I haven't tried Viagra and I don't intend to, even if it might come in handy on an off night or otherwise "enhance" my so-called performance. Side effects aside, the idea of inserting such a substance into the intimate interaction between me and a lover gives me the creeps.

But evidently a lot of men have no such reservations. Persuaded by the powerful marketing cum media crusade of the drug's manufacturer, Pfizer, guys of all kinds (45 percent of whom are under sixty, according to the latest market research) are gulping the pills at ten bucks a throw, with or without insurance coverage, sparing no expense in pursuit of a better hard-on. This is not to mention the international black market, where in some places Viagra is more expensive than heroin.

Other pharmaceutical companies are pressing ahead with competitive medications. Very big bucks are at stake: Viagra, *Time* magazine tells us, "could reach $2 billion in sales by the year 2000." I can see the ad campaigns now: "Get hard quicker and stay harder longer with Phalluxo! Outperforms Viagra in four out of five clinical copulations!" As the Godfather used to say, it's only business.

In a recent book entitled *Bitter Pills: Inside the Hazardous World of Legal Drugs*, journalist Stephen Fried shows that in the rush to approve new drugs and get them on the market, pharmaceutical companies and the FDA often forgo additional tests that might reduce the risks. The manufacturers and marketers argue that it's a matter of supply and demand: Americans want more drugs, new drugs, and they want them now.

Almost everyone has a horror story of a bad reaction to some medicine, and that's not counting the people who drop dead. *The New York Times* recently reported on a study in the *Journal of the American Medical Association* revealing that "adverse reactions to medications" are "one of the leading causes of death in this country," killing more than one hundred thousand people a year.

These accidental deaths, according to JAMA and the *Times*, "are not due to mistakes by doctors in prescribing drugs or by patients using them. Rather, drug reactions occur because virtually all medications can have bad side effects in some people, even when taken in proper doses." All drugs, says Dr. Bruce Pomeranz, one of the authors of the JAMA article, "have a toxic component."

A range of unpleasant side effects, from headaches to heart attacks, have already been documented in connection with the use of Viagra—especially in combination with other drugs. It seems a pretty high risk to run for the sake of getting laid.

Erection on Demand?

Pfizer and its fellow corporate drug dealers would have you believe that erectile difficulties are mostly physical and thus subject to correction by their products. With all due sympathy for those who suffer from diabetes, prostate problems and other illnesses, most medical opinion I've seen on the subject—ranging from Masters and Johnson to alternative health guru Andrew Weil—registers a more nuanced diagnosis.

Obesity, depression, alcohol and cigarette addiction, stress, fatigue, financial anxieties and—most significant from a marketing standpoint—the natural aging process are other factors that may contribute to diminished sexual responsiveness. "No one has done studies on how Viagra affects normal men," *The Washington Post* reports. "But several urologists said any man over fifty would likely get a boost from Viagra—physically and psychologically." *Time* notes that no less than "79 million boomers have begun to turn 50 at the rate of one every eight seconds or so," and the drug industry has done the math.

But erection on demand—the insidious and oppressive notion that any man at any age ought to be able to get it up and get it on at a moment's notice—has little to do with the art of making love. Whatever our athletic limitations, older men are commonly known to be better lovers than our younger selves. Experience counts for something. And the occasional slowness of our erectile action may give us the leisure to explore other paths of love play, thus prolonging the act and increasing the pleasure of everyone's gratification.

As Dr. Silber the urologist declares repeatedly in his book *The Male*, the most important sex organ is the brain. How interestingly erotic it might be to cultivate other forms of closeness than the grinding together of groins. Thoughtful reflection and verbal communication cost nothing and are vital to intimacy.

Sex at best can be the highest state of human communion. It can be prayer, rescue, shelter, consolation, power, surrender, relief, clean fun, dirty fun and lots more besides. But love is what gives it its transcendent supremacy as an exalted way of being.

What Tennessee Williams told *Playboy* twenty-five years ago may well be true of many aging men who need more than Viagra: “I can’t get it up without love.”

The Poets of Auto Row

[1993]

The ritual of shopping for a pickup truck is probably akin to spending a day at some kind of wild man retreat. As you scrutinize the merchandise preparing to part with a sizable hunk of cash, your masculine juices start to percolate, your mechanical aptitude intuitively rises and the bargaining instincts of the poker player surface for the first time since you last gambled. Only instead of bonding with some New Age guru, you find yourself getting emotionally entangled with a car salesman.

Little as I imagined this happening to me, it did last weekend as I hunted for a tough utility vehicle for hauling stuff to the dump. Ordinarily an auto plaza is the last place I'd want to spend a Sunday, but the practical demands of country living can lead you along strange paths. While I might have preferred to be working in the garden or puttering around my desk, instead I found myself browsing among the Chevys and Fords and Toyotas and Jeeps and Nissans and Mitsubishis on a vast slab of paved-over farmland in the automotive soul of Santa Rosa.

It was the second straight day of decent weather, also the

second day of spring, in an otherwise interminably soggy season, so naturally people in need of new wheels were out in substantial numbers. My companion and I were one of many couples cruising the lot, and swarms of eager-to-be-of-service salesman were also lurking, it seemed, behind every fender. Pregnant women hung with their husbands as the men talked power trains and warranties. Windshields, paint jobs and bumpers gleamed in the sun. The smells of new-car vinyl and rubber evoked archetypal showroom associations.

We were admiring a shiny white shortbed that fit our desired profile and budget when a sales rep swooped into view. Balding, well tanned, Buddha-bellied, sixtyish, he introduced himself as Dave Kiefer. A genial easygoing auto-sales veteran, he'd spent twenty-one years in the business, a dozen at this dealership alone, with a break to run a related franchise in Reno. Dave was a pro, cordially explaining the features and virtues of the truck we were coveting. He proudly showed us the service department, a vast immaculate hangar—"This is as filthy as it gets," he said—before turning us loose for a test drive. When he saw the coastal address on my driver's license he launched into a lyrical oration on the elk herds of Tomales Bay; an amateur photographer, he'd been there just last weekend shooting pictures.

The truck ran strong and solid, a hummingly clean machine, and by the time we returned to the lot I was ready to sign. A thousand down, sixty months to pay, a little more debt on the books—the prospect made me feel like a real American. Dave didn't need to persuade me; the vehicle sold itself. Back in his office, writing up the contract, he took down my credit information. When I gave my occupation as a writer his face lit up as if he'd spotted an elk. "Do you mind if I shake your hand?" he said, practically leaping out of his seat. "You're my first writer. It's a pleasure."

Dave, it turns out, was a writer too—a poet, no less, if only as a hobby—a lover of Whitman and Shelley and Lao Tzu, three of my personal favorites. No wonder we'd hit it off from the outset. What are the odds, I marveled, of my finding a poet to sell me a pickup truck? He had to contain his literary passions in order to keep his mind on the business at hand; first the contract had to be completed and sent to the finance manager. After the transaction we could talk poetry.

A few minutes later I sat across the desk from the finance manager, a chunky well-groomed middle-aged fellow whose agile fingers danced at his computer keyboard. He too remarked on my profession. "When I was in college I wanted to be a writer. I read Kerouac and Kesey and all those guys. I thought that would be an interesting way to live: go around having experiences and writing about them. There was a poet up in Washington named Theodore Roethke. Great poet, beautiful poems. But he died an alcoholic. It seemed like they all had to suffer so much. I decided to do something practical."

As I signed my name a few dozen times on the stack of financial documents, I mused with amazement at this commercial wizard with a weakness for Theodore Roethke. What kind of dealership was this anyway, where the two presumably hardheaded dudes with whom I was doing business were, underneath everything, sensitive souls infected with the poetry virus.

Back at Dave's desk, with the deal closed, we spoke of our poetic affinities. "I write two or three poems a week," he said.

"For me it's a way of getting at the essence of things. I mean, a scientist can describe an eagle, the measurement of its wing-span, its weight, diet, habitat, all the facts, but when Tennyson says, 'He clasps the crag with crooked hands…' you *see* the eagle. The finest biologist can't capture that essence. A poem reads between the facts. That's what I love about poetry."

And listening to this man rave, I realized, is one of the things I love about my truck.

A Used Car Named Desire

[1993]

My urban half in LA works as a free lance and had just filed a story for the *Weekly* on "the culture of paranoia"—epitomized in that city by The Club, a simple heavy-duty piece of hardware you clamp to your steering wheel to keep your car from being stolen. I was visiting from the remote north where I live amid marauding raccoons and marijuana poachers but few auto thieves to speak of. My *camarada* and I had just returned from a good meal in our favorite Spanish restaurant, parked our Mazda a few feet from her front door and retired. I was to fly out of Burbank in the morning.

One problem: when we opened the door in the morning the car was gone.

Staring at the empty space by the curb where the Mazda should have been I felt strangely detached, as I had after the Loma Prieta earthquake while surveying the rubble of my trashed house. So your material world is shaken, you feel violated but big deal, it's nothing personal, just your turn on the wheel of misfortune, a minor inconvenience compared to more life-threatening or everyday-degrading urban calamities.

Two weeks later I'm waiting in line at the Glendale office of the DMV registering our new used wheels. The Mazda never turned up, the insurance settlement was shockingly fair, so we'd been driving around for five days in my nephew's Honda shopping for a replacement. It was the hottest week of the year, smoggy as hell, and while up north my winter lettuce was trying to sprout I was cruising freeways I never knew existed in 100-degree heat in search of a vehicle both reliable and personable, your car in LA being not only vital to getting around but a stylistic statement of personal identity. As it turns out we scored a way cool low-priced BMW sedan, old and funky yet elegantly stylish with a rebuilt engine and character to spare.

In those five days I discovered Glendale, recently highrised yet still maintaining the backwater charm of any American small town, a place where the faces are mostly pale rather than the more colorful mixture you find on the other side of the Los Angeles River. Yet the white men of Glendale that I encountered—neatly dressed bums hitting you up for change, chain-smoking car salesmen with poison suntans from too much time on the lot, a guitar-playing pool-shooting auto upholsterer whose hair had all of a sudden fallen out, a furniture salesman so meek and defeated I felt like giving him a hug for encouragement—were not the omnipotent monsters of Catherine MacKinnon's fantasies (though who knows what they did when they got home) but powerless aging ciphers barely scraping by.

And Glendale isn't the half of it. We hit Silver Lake, Culver City, West LA, Brentwood, Van Nuys, the outer limits of Pasadena, meeting people whose autobiographies unfolded before us as they recounted the histories of their cars. We met Neecy the nurse, whose 79 BMW she says she seized from her no-good brother and restored, Neecy whose street-tough South Central style reminds me of a poet I know; she drives to survive, has too many cars, has sunk thousands "up under the hood" in this one and wants to unload. And Leslie the blonde fastidious jockette whose Saab we test-drove through Beverly Hills—the second you pass that city's sign going east on Sunset a motorcycle cop is parked there pointing his radar gun in your face, very impressive. And Dawn the English nanny and her husband Peter whose dinner we interrupted for a drive in the dark; it was awkward barging in on their pasta in front of the TV but this was the only time they were available, and as Peter assured us, "That's why microwaves are for." And Gary the middle-aged surfer with a trunk full of crushed Bud cans and a strong smell of gasoline everywhere, a smell his cigarettes evidently screened because, as he innocently put it, "I don't smell anything."

And John the ad man from Foote, Cone & Belding, and Mike who works the late shift at CBS, and Wendell with the ancient Volvo who speaks on the phone as if he's too stoned to drive, and Lee the young grad-student mathematician ("We don't use numbers") who'd rather ride his bike to UCLA. The *Recycler*, where we found their ads among others, abounds with stories like theirs—a chain of classified haiku encoded in carspeak, highly condensed occult narratives, a number-studded epic like the financial pages, daunting but decipherable, crawling with real lives.

Just a few months ago I was purchasing a pickup in Santa Rosa for hauling horseshit on the North Coast. Now I'm bopping around El Lay trying to scope some clean, affordably stylish transportation. Last time I did this I met a couple of closet poets cleverly disguised as car dealers who confessed to me their literary leanings after the deal was done. This is a more grueling and complex mission. The smog is thicker, the temperature higher, the traffic heavier, the selection of vehicles vaster, which naturally increases my existential anxiety. Sweat sticks my back to the seat of the Honda, open sunroof baking my bald spot. This is the LA millions have fled and millions more dream of leaving, the horizontal inferno, noxious tar pit of commuterdom, an atmospheric swamp of ozone and toxic particulate and carbon monoxide.

Reward and antidote for our ordeal my last night in town is the late show at the Nuart of a limited run of the restored director's cut of *A Streetcar Named Desire*. As Stanley Kowalski, one of the great prefeminist wild men, Brando is scary yet charmingly animalistic. As Blanche Dubois the burnt-out Southern belle, Vivian Leigh is fragilely, campily tragic. Elia Kazan's direction is fine, but what carries the film is Tennessee Williams's pungent language, lines of dialogue that pierce the heart with their sad wit. Stanley's a vulnerable out-of-control working guy; Blanche has seen brighter times, has lost everything including her mind, but somehow keeps on.

Both in their way resemble the men of Glendale.

Notes on a Return to My Native Land

[2012]

On a recent visit to Los Angeles I rolled into town around 9 pm and thought I might catch a movie before checking in at my Westside hotel. The Nuart Theater, conveniently located just off the 405, was showing the new Juliette Binoche film, *Elles*, an unrated contemporary Franco-Polish drama whose explicit sexual content guarantees limited circulation in the United States. The movie's brief run was ending in the next couple of days, Binoche is my favorite actress—for her subtle intelligence as well as her beauty, which only deepens with age—and I had nothing else to do, so I pulled off the freeway at Santa Monica Boulevard, parked around the corner from the theater and prepared to voyeurize some Parisian eroticism for the next couple of hours.

The movie didn't start for another forty-five minutes, so I took the time to browse in a secondhand bookstore on Sawtelle, a shop I hadn't visited for fifteen or twenty years. In the

1970s I found there a copy of a rare collection of Henry Miller watercolors, and I recalled many interesting hours spent in its narrow aisles over my years as a native and recurrent visitor to the city. As soon as I entered the old building I noticed something different: instead of the cluttered, abundantly overstocked and dusty bookshop of memory, the collection was pared down, with shelf space to spare, and as I scanned the titles it struck me that each book seemed to have been selected by a highly literate and discerning sensibility. For me it was an extraordinary and encouraging rediscovery, and I was heartened to be told by the fellow at the desk (there was no counter or cash register and the owner wasn't present) that the store, now called Alias Books, was doing very well and had been in business in this new incarnation for more than a decade.

I found, among other unexpected things, a copy of Camus's *Notebooks 1951–1959*, the third and final volume of the author's private musings, translated by Ryan Bloom and issued in a handsome trade paperback by Ivan R. Dee, an independent publisher in Chicago, as recently as 2010. It was a book I had never seen before, and in light of Justin O'Brien's earlier version of the *Notebooks 1942–1951* (originally published by Knopf in 1965 and reissued in paperback thirty years later by another obscure American publisher, Marlowe & Company), I was happy to get my hands on this one. Camus is, for my money, one of the deepest and wisest thinkers of the twentieth century, and in his notebooks he reveals himself (at the time to himself alone) to be a touchingly vulnerable human work-in-progress, dealing with his own growing fame as a writer as well as with big ideas and private doubts. The notebooks of such a mind at work, jotting down thoughts for essays or novels, tossing off incidental epigrams ("Naturalness is not a virtue that one has: it is acquired." "The opposite of reaction is not revolution, but creation."), observing the behavior of contemporaries, remarking on their character, acknowledging rivalries, reflecting on politics, sorting out for himself how best to live, make for provocative and thrilling reading.

And how synchronistic to find this book by this great French-language writer during a brief interlude before watching a seriously sexy French-language film. Binoche plays a middle-aged bourgeois journalist with a businessman husband and two school-age sons who is finishing an article for *Elle* magazine based on interviews with a couple of young women who are paying for their college education by freelancing as prostitutes. As Binoche's character, Anne, taps away at her laptop under a looming deadline, she visualizes scenes her subjects have described to her of encounters with their clients—dramatized onscreen in unusually graphic yet not gratuitous terms—and she becomes increasingly unsettled by the contrast between these girls' assertion of their sexual power and independence and the constraints and frustrations of her own respectable family life.

It is a very good film, and Binoche as usual is excellent in her embodiment of the complex inner conflicts of her character. It is also a strikingly erotic film, yet neither romantic nor exploitive in its exploration of female sexuality and male sexual need. In American hands such themes would surely have been sensationalized, but the female Polish director of *Elles*, thirty-nine-year-old Malgorzata Szumowska, manages to create a broodingly intelligent investigation of the crosscurrents between desperation, desire, economic necessity and familial obligation. You could watch it, if you were so inclined, just for the sexy parts but you would be missing the deeper and more interesting existential questions it raises—about love, about work, about marriage—so beautifully enacted by the great Binoche.

Camus and Binoche, what a dream couple. They have everything: great looks, cool demeanor, creative accomplishment, star power, both of them extremely nuanced practitioners of their respective arts. It was a stroke of luck to begin my visit to my old hometown in their illustrious company. For me, such good companionship, experienced through books or movies, paintings or music, provides the kind of inspiration that sharpens perception, enhances appreciation of the fleeting phenomena of ordinary life, especially when one is outside the routine surroundings of home. Colored by the company of these artists, Los Angeles, with all its smog and traffic and commercial cacophony of billboard flash and non-stop razzle-dazzle, came intimately alive for me, thanks in part to these brilliant and handsome imaginary friends, as a landscape brimming with not just the usual urban aggravations but with vivid dramatic reality.

The meals and conversations I enjoyed while there with family and select friends were complemented by time I had alone to explore the city and county, from the wilds of Malibu's Decker Canyon and the nature preserve on Point Dume at the northwest tip of Santa Monica Bay to a charmingly civilized French bistro a few doors down from Skylight Books on Vermont and across from the post office in the Los Feliz district where I had lunch one afternoon and, just like an old-school tourist in some exotic locale, took time while sipping a leisurely espresso to pen a letter to a far-off friend and then slip it into the slot across the street.

Another significant touristic stop was a visit to the La Brea Tar Pits on Wilshire Boulevard's Miracle Mile where I marveled that the ancient dinosaur graveyard, now surrounded by a safety fence and a grassy park next door to the LA County Museum of Art, was more or less the same black swamp it was in the fifties. The anagrammatic rhyme of art and tar suggested to me the curious coincidence that both have a way of preserving evidence of ancient existences: the mammoth fossils long since recovered from the gooey ooze by industrious paleontologists, and now represented by lifelike scale models rising out of the pits to catch the attention of passersby, are oddly analogous to the artifacts displayed in the adjacent museum complex, the artists' creations outlasting their buried bones.

During these leisurely afternoons I gave myself permission to do nothing, and that sense of aimlessness moved me somehow to follow my random instincts and revisit parts of a city utterly changed since I was growing up there more than half a century ago. Favorite old drive-ins and hot-dog stands, drugstores and bookstores and movie houses, landmarks of my childhood redolent of popcorn and French fries (again the French), are gone or transformed, replaced by high-rise office towers or turned into luxury shopping malls, the landscape of the past too lost for even a Proust to recapture.

Sipping a margarita in a Mexican restaurant over a meal with my nephew Mike (a freelance journalist who has eclipsed my dubious example by becoming a first-rate investigative reporter) or having a Kingfisher beer with my old friend Bart (whom I first met when we were students at UCLA in 1965 and who is now a Talmud scholar and lawyer specializing in mediation) at his favorite Indian eatery, I can almost remember everything I left when I fled this city so long ago, everything that's too late to recollect now yet paradoxically lingers in the mind, the psyche, the soul somehow shaped for better or worse by this often exasperating environment. The LA climate, its soft desert air, is part of my pores; its vast grid of streets an infinitely associative map of my formative years; its culture of accelerated striving and glittery glamour something I hope to have escaped and yet remains embedded in my tarry heart like the fang of a sabertooth tiger; its ring of beaches spread thickly with sand poured through the waist of some mythic hourglass of time forever running out.

And yet one thing has remained the same: The Apple Pan, that charming little diner on Pico near Westwood, just around the corner from my hotel; a greasy spoon with a U-shaped counter and two or three dozen stools and a minimal menu of burgers and fries, coffee and apple pie still served by the same old guys in their little white hats and soiled aprons and perfunctory manners—a time warp like some Hopper painting where night owls gather to be alone together in the darkness of some existential eternity. And who is that cool-looking couple on the far side of the grill smoking and speaking low over their coffee cups?

The Sun Also Goes Down

[2009]

It was hard not to take the earthquake personally. That October Tuesday, my newspaper, *The Sun*, which I had started three years earlier in a surge of journalistic urgency and entrepreneurial folly, was on deadline, preparing to go to press the following morning. That week we were running a dining feature and were trying out some new food writers, including the editor (me), who contributed a short piece on the pleasures of cooking with olive oil, garlic and onion. But I was distracted by less-appetizing realities: our business manager, Cherie Maitland, had informed me earlier in the day that we, as a business, were broke. We didn't have enough money in the bank to cover payroll.

As publisher and principal shareholder in the corporation I had founded and raised the capital to launch, and as the one who had gone back again and again to investors in search of additional operating funds, I was in despair as to how our staff of fifteen was going to receive, as due on Friday, paychecks that wouldn't bounce. As an employer, I couldn't imagine a more distressing scenario than to leave my company's workers up a creek. It was a horrible feeling, and I had no idea what more could be done about it.

How had I gotten into such a mess?

When I returned to Santa Cruz in 1972, after being away for a year following grad school at UCSC, I discovered *Sundaze*, an investigative yet also highly imaginative underground newspaper that included among other things in its weekly format a full page of poetry. *Sundaze* was a great read because, in addition to doing the serious work of snooping out and exposing corruption in the body politic, it was also funny and unpredictable in its experimental journalism. This was a moment in the larger culture when a lot of conventional assumptions were being called into question, and the *Sundaze* gang, led by publisher Lee Swanson and editor Patrick Fox, was taking a local newspaper into zones of daring reportage and creativity previously unknown in Santa Cruz. As a rebellious young poet I was smitten with what *Sundaze* was doing, and soon I was publishing poems in there and contributing satirical prose under pen names like R. D. Pickle and The Champagne King.

The *Sundaze* sank in 1976, and that summer the *Independent* took its place. The Indy had some of the spirit of its predecessor, and some of the same people, but it resembled a more recognizable kind of radical newspaper, and appeared to have more of a normal business model. I started writing book reviews for the Indy, and the arts editor, Buz Bezore, liked my writing and soon had me doing a weekly column called Words. When editor Richard Cole departed, Buz's domain moved to the front of the paper, and he immediately installed me as an op-ed columnist with instructions to write about whatever interested me.

After initially resisting such a weighty assignment, soon enough I was hooked, and when, a few years later, the Indy folded and was succeeded in 1981 by the *Express* with Buz at the helm, I was on board from the beginning. Five years after that, with the *Express* in a deathward spiral due to problems with the IRS among other pathologies, I—having put up my little Soquel Valley farmhouse as collateral for a loan to buy new typesetting equipment—was called in by the board of directors to try to rescue the business. The board removed the current management and installed me as editor/publisher, but too late, and in a matter of weeks we had to put the paper out of its misery.

By then I had discovered that making a newspaper was serious fun, and at that time—before the Internet and its myriad digital gizmos—the printed word in a lightweight, disposable (or recyclable) form was by far the most vital medium for information and community dialogue on everything from politics and culture to entertainment and food, from arts and ideas to gardening and health. By 1986 Santa Cruz, having been transformed over the preceding couple of decades from a sleepy conservative out-of-the-way town to a vortex of progressive politics and offbeat artistic activity and University-fueled intellectual vigor, had shown that it needed a paper like the *Express* as an alternative to the *Sentinel* on one hand, with its sclerotic Republicanism, and the *Good Times* on the other, with its "lighter than air" philosophy of publishing nothing that might trouble a potential advertiser. The *Express* had been a paper you could actually enjoy *reading* because Buz's genius as an editor was to find good writers and turn them loose to write.

Now what would we do, writers and readers alike, without the *Express*? Having saved my house from foreclosure by paying off that loan, I should have had the good sense to retire from the newspaper business and go back to being a poet. But I was in too deep; like most of my colleagues, I was addicted to newspapering. Immediately a group of ex-*Express* staffers began conspiring to create the incarnation of Santa Cruz's next alternative weekly. Somehow I got it in my head that if the new paper was adequately capitalized, organized and run like a real business rather than some kind of clubhouse, it might actually have a chance of succeeding—that is, surviving.

And so, *The Sun* was born. We published our first issue on September 11, 1986, just a few months after the *Express* had gone down, and we'd taken over the lease of its offices upstairs at the corner of Cedar and Union streets, above what is now Caffé Bene. From my corner desk I had a fine view of the passing show outside, and as I slammed out editorials on my 1974 Adler manual portable (the same machine on which I am typing this) I could watch the parade of local characters enacting their daily dramas. I loved the job despite the stresses of losing money week after week, and not being able to afford a health plan for the employees, and having to put up with angry politicians and activists and merchants who regularly complained that our agenda wasn't in line with theirs, and the various other aggravations of running a small business. In addition to writing and editing I was the boss, and therefore the rabbi in residence, the house shrink, the authority figure, the mediator, the person on whose desk every crisis landed.

On October 17, 1989, the crisis was that we were out of money. Only a *deus ex machina* could save my ass—or whip it definitively.

That afternoon our ace reporter and managing editor, Elizabeth Kadetsky, had asked me to pick up the prints of some photos she needed for a story she was finishing. At 5:04 I was standing at the counter of Bay Photo Lab in Soquel when the shaking started. As a California native who had experienced many earthquakes, including the Northridge tremor of 1971 that jolted me out of my bed in Malibu, I was accustomed to taking them in stride, but this time the agitation was violent and prolonged enough to send the half-dozen people in the shop darting out into the parking lot to avoid being hit by falling objects. I stood there as the ground was rocking and rolling—not knowing the epicenter was just a few miles away in Nisene Marks State Park—then had to crouch into a four-point position to keep from being knocked off my feet.

When the shaking finally stopped after what felt like minutes, my first impulse was to re-enter Bay Photo and ask for the prints—we were still on deadline—but the manager said no way: their equipment was all on the floor. Driving back into town, as I approached Santa Cruz I could see pillars of smoke rising here and there. Highway 1 northbound was closed past the fish hook, so I took the Ocean Street exit and was surprised at how many plate-glass windows had shattered. Clouds of whitish dust were hovering over the Pacific Garden Mall, and by the time I made it back to the office it was clear that what had just happened was not your average earthquake.

Inside the office the worst thing was that the water cooler had fallen over and Brooke Towne, our office manager, had cut herself on the broken glass. Otherwise everyone was in one piece, if acutely rattled. Elizabeth—with whom I was living at the time because, after working at adjacent desks for a year, we had fallen in love—had of course instinctively dashed out into the chaos of Pacific Avenue with her notebook and pen to report the story. The power was out, buildings had collapsed, parts of town were burning, everyone was spooked and we were obviously not going to make our deadline, so we called it a day and, rather than seek her out on the battlefield, I awaited the return of my reporter-inamorata.

She turned up as the sun was going down, and we tried to drive home to our place in Soquel Valley, but roads were closed and we had to take a detour up Highway 17 and then across various back routes through the mountains over to Old San Jose Road. When we finally made it to our house on Hoover Road—a mile-long private lane with some dozen families in residence—we found a domestic disaster: the Gold Rush-era redwood farmhouse, the one that had withstood the quake of 1906 and various storms and floods in the years since, had been knocked askew from its wooden foundation and appeared, in the dimming twilight, to be slightly tilted.

The floor was far enough out of level that I could barely force open the kitchen door, and we beheld on entry a gaping void in the center of the house where the granite fireplace had stood. The chimney had plunged through the living room floor and was now a pile of masonry in the basement. An acrid smell of charred brick, spilled kerosene, dead ashes and mortar dust pervaded everything. My library was mostly on the floor, or in the basement among the fireplace stones, pictures had flown off the walls, and from the kitchen shelves dishes and glasses and food had been flung all over the room. Dusk could be discerned through the big hole in the ceiling.

I felt oddly calm, beyond shock or distress, as if floating above the catastrophe.

With dead wires everywhere and telephones out, we didn't go to work the next day, but Thursday I posted a note on the office door calling for a meeting Friday morning. It was clear to me the paper could not survive this cataclysm: aside from our own fiscal problems, our downtown advertising base had been devastated, so even if we'd had the means to make it through the immediate aftermath, the businesses we depended on for cash flow had crises of their own to cope with. So I broke the news to the staff that we would put out one last issue and call it quits. I asked each of our writers to cover the earthquake from a personal angle, geared to their particular beat, and told our regular visual artists to give me images of their own visions.

Over the course of the next five days we put together *The Sun*'s best issue ever, a document that in its unabashed subjectivity—each contributor offering a unique perspective on what had happened—caught in words and pictures a true-to-life account of the city's most apocalyptic event since the 1955 flood. I'm still proud of that issue, which I recently reread to find completely gripping in its immediacy, and of the team of writers and illustrators and ad designers and salespeople who rose heroically to the occasion, despite whatever personal trauma they had experienced (and, during production, re-experienced whenever the building trembled with an aftershock).

Elizabeth wrote the feature, a diary-like account of the days immediately following the quake; Geoffrey Dunn turned in an op-ed piece on the people of Santa Cruz as its resilient heart and soul; Venise Wagner, our bilingual South County correspondent, reported on the damage, and people's responses to it, in Watsonville; Roz Spafford critiqued the media for their ghoulish pursuit of the story of the two workers, Shawn McCormick and Robin Ortiz, killed under the collapsed walls of the Coffee Roasting Company across the street from our offices; Robin (Somers) Schirmer examined the psycho-emotional fallout of the event; I wrote in my column about the hit my home had taken and the strange relief I felt about losing my business; Rob Brezsny, in addition to his usual astrology column, wrote a dreamlike account of a temblor in the collective unconscious; and arts editor Mark Zepezauer reported on the earthquake's cultural repercussions.

Artists Futzie Nutzle, Tim Eagan, Elizabeth Williams, Karl Vidstrand and Diana Moll, and photographers Chip Scheuer, Holger Leue and David Alexander delivered some of their most arresting images. Our art director, Mott Jordan, made a witty adjustment to our banner so that the final N in SUN was knocked off-kilter, and Kevin Jewell and Scott Dunn, our ad and editorial designers, dealt elegantly with the larger-than-usual thirty-six-page issue, which our sales staff—Diana Mayo, Kathy Edwards, Jeff Howitt, Pablo Reiter and Yvette Cadeaux—had made possible against all odds. Traffic coordinator Elisa Pederson coolly managed the hectic flow between the advertising and art departments. Perhaps most remarkable, our typesetter, Rosemary Balsley, swiftly transcribed the text of the entire issue with scarcely a single typo.

We also had nearly three full pages of letters, some reflecting on the quake, some responding to stories in recent issues, some lamenting the news—already going around—that this would be the last our readers would see of *The Sun*. We ran twenty-one letters in all, evidence of our key role as, among other things, a community bulletin board.

In my full-page editorial, headlined "The Sun Also Rises," I tried to downplay the loss of our newspaper, putting it in perspective next to the greater tragedy of lives lost and the millions of dollars in physical destruction suffered by so many, and by the economy as a whole. I also optimistically invoked the history of local weeklies that had arisen one after another over the previous twenty years, assuring our readers that sooner or later another paper would take the place of *The Sun*. But in trying to contain my own sorrow and disappointment over my failure as a publisher, and to console our readers who had avidly picked us up each week and appreciated our sharply distinctive take on the news and the life of the community, I wrongly compared the loss of *The Sun* to that of the several cafés that had been flattened, suggesting that a newspaper, like any other cultural institution or public venue, was an important gathering place but not an irreplaceable one.

The truth is, almost any newspaper, even now—perhaps especially now that the printed medium is being eclipsed by various virtual info-delivery systems—plays an essentially vital role in the life of a community, and the loss of such a publication gravely wounds that community's political, cultural and intellectual health. I had come out of the peaceful Soquel hills into the turmoil of downtown media wars to found *The Sun* because I felt that Santa Cruz, with its literate citizens and liberal politics and abundant artistic talent, deserved something better to read than was then available. I wanted to evolve from a soloist composing my own improvisations into a conductor who could coordinate the various excellent players I had worked with over the years, and any new ones who might turn up, into a tight journalistic ensemble, an orchestra that could both echo the sometimes cacophonous music of the community and help refine it into a more harmonious sound, setting a tone of rational discourse and creative thinking.

What I couldn't have known at the time was that the end of *The Sun*—or more precisely the Loma Prieta earthquake itself—was a watershed moment in local history after which nothing would be the same. The Pacific Garden Mall—an elegantly landscaped meandering one-lane one-way street where pedestrians and trees far outnumbered cars, and little locally owned shops dominated the commercial ecology—would not return to its funky, intimate, village-like form. And when, in time, the dust cleared and the new buildings were up and the street was straightened back into just plain Pacific Avenue, and the big-mall chains moved in with their Gaps and Borders and Starbucks and multiplex mega-cinemas—and meanwhile the high-tech gold rush boomed and Santa Cruz real estate became unaffordable for anyone who didn't drive a BMW—the town would evolve into another stage of maturity.

For better and worse, downtown changed into a distinctively Santa Cruzian but more conventional if slightly offbeat small-town urban model. It feels like a much bigger town now, and though one still runs into familiar faces, it's easier to be anonymous, as in a city. Even if *The Sun* had survived the seismic shakedown, the city it served was so transformed that I don't know whether we could have sustained the kind of intimacy we shared with our readers. The civic atmosphere was altered, and there's no telling what kind of paper we would have become.

There are those old-timers who complain that Santa Cruz isn't the way it used to be before the quake. But quake or no quake, nothing is ever the way it used to be—ask what's left of the retirees who, in the 1960s and 70s, saw their peaceful little town overrun with students and transplanted professors and blissed-out hippies—so that's the kind of loss people just have to learn to get over. As journalists during a twenty-year period of major creative agitation, we certainly didn't think our job was to preserve the status quo, even if the status quo, such as it was, seemed pretty cool at the time. What we were trying to do—at papers like the *Sundaze* and the *Independent* and the *Express* and *The Sun*—was to give back to Santa Cruz the best of itself and be a bonding force for its anarchic spirit, keeping the community on its toes while opening people's minds to unimagined possibilities. Those papers were fun to read, and as an editor (and publisher) I felt it my duty to make our pages indispensable sources of "news" you wouldn't find anywhere else.

We caught hell from the left almost as often as from the right because our angle of vision was truly independent. (Our marketing slogan was "Independent. Locally Owned.") Would-be but never-were advertisers constantly complained that we were too serious, too political, too irreverent, too intellectual, too literary, not business-friendly enough, too demanding of readers' time and attention—never mind that some fifty thousand people kept our pages open long enough to *read* them and thus give the ads more exposure than if skimmers were just flipping through to check the show times. We didn't have the material ambition to fully realize that a newspaper is more than a public service or vehicle for spirited debate, but is also a commercial enterprise that ultimately lives or dies by how it makes its way in the marketplace. Though my father had been a successful salesman and eventually CEO of his own company (so presumably I had some entrepreneurial genes), I never did fit that model, and clearly I wasn't fooling anyone, least of all my fellow business owners. I was a writer—worse, a poet—with all the defects of those sorry species.

So as I watched from my office window the swarms of tourists and voyeurs observing, from behind chain link, the ruined buildings being razed by gigantic machines and carted away on the backs of enormous trucks, I had to admit I was lucky to have lived through this cataclysm. It was exciting to be part of such a historic ordeal and to have something useful to offer as a record of an unforgettable moment: an account in print that, twenty years later, surely at least a few locals still have stored in their private archives.

The necessity to tell stories was never more evident, as everywhere I went I heard people yakking nonstop about what they had personally been through and witnessed, and what they had heard from others, revealing most vividly the primal need we have to share narratives, even if we don't write them down. The urgency of the tales I heard, the intensity of people's engagement in their own dramas, the endlessness of the anecdotes exchanged, all proved the enduring value of my original desire to start *The Sun* as a medium for such messages. Information is not enough; people need interesting, well-told, compelling stories.

As I put my house back together over the next months, and

closed down the business, and prepared to resume a more purely literary agenda, I felt grateful for the privilege of having ridden out the epic rise and fall of the most ambitious and costly project I'd ever embarked on, and for the honor of putting out our final issue as a testament to our purpose. Though we failed commercially, and thus failed in our long-term effort to serve the community as we'd hoped to, for those three years we reflected and affected the life of our town in all its complex character.

And out of our ruins rose what you're reading now.

No Success Like Failure

[1989]

When I got home from the earthquake my house was junk. The chimney had imploded, littering the living room with bricks and granite and a thick layer of mortar dust pulverized by the shock. Amid the rubble lay much of my library. Artworks and furniture were mangled, shivers of glass strewn over the floor, the kitchen covered with flood and utensils flung around the room. Ancient cobwebs had been shaken loose, drooping like tired ghosts. A large chunk of masonry, still stuck in the ceiling where the chimney once stood, hung over a hole that used to be the hearth, now a pile of debris in the basement. "Take a deep breath, feel like you're chokin'," I thought I heard Bob Dylan wheeze from a track on his new album—"Everything is broken."

Having come from the fresh destruction downtown, roaming astounded among the new ruins in the dazed curiosity and awe of the first hours, I felt oddly calm surveying the evidence of my personal disaster. Perhaps I'd attained the objectivity I never had as a journalist. The scene was so different from what my home had been, I could barely claim a connection. The structure was leaning slightly on its foundation. An atmosphere of pure wreckage lingered in the air, a light sense of detachment and acceptance—humility. It was pointless to be upset; powers far larger than fear had spoken. Such a warm evening, peaceful in its way. Night fell gently. The twilight zone.

All the ordeals at the office suddenly were small. The paper's chronic problems—lack of capital, anemic ad line, staff psychodramas—shrank as survival became the issue. Three friends dining under the stars on crackers, apples and avocado proved the finest banquet imaginable. I relished the taste of my last Pacifico as we listened to the transistor. A camping adventure like this was a vacation from the commercial terrors I'd been suffering for the last three years—advertisers who weasel out on their contracts, unaffordable health insurance, irate readers incensed over our failure to conform to their viewpoint, business owners hot under the collar over an editorial, libel suits, rampaging political power clowns, ruthless competitors, insecure employees working for meager wages, agitated landladies, temperamental typesetting equipment, accounts payable, accounts receivable, meetings, working Sundays, all the nightmares of being your own boss and everyone else's too—it was refreshing to finesse the elements with a cool head and a bag of basic supplies.

Maybe you're familiar with the Fay Wray syndrome. In the movie *King Kong*, female lead Fay Wray finds herself in a sequence of perilous adventures, each more horrifying than the one before, culminating in the climactic scene at the top of the Empire State Building. For Wray all through the movie, it seems like things couldn't possibly get worse—but they keep getting worse. That's how it's been for me in recent months, one calamity after another, mostly to do with business. The disaster and its economic impact have been a breakthrough: now that Nature has stated its case on top of everything else conspiring to sink *The Sun*, I feel like a free man surrendering to Destiny. At last I'm able to lay my burden down.

Actually it's a privilege to witness such earthshaking events and to be a part of this awesome experience. The cosmic dimensions of the general catastrophe put individual afflictions in perspective. Everybody's in more or less the same rocky boat. It's inconvenient but exciting, dredging up lots of creative muck from the unconscious. Living above Soquel near the epicenter, I feel my psychic batteries being charged almost beyond capacity. Everyone I know is completely freaked in one way or another, as if we're all sharing in the same psychosis, having to talk nonstop, tell stories, console each other, promise to see one another soon in anxious phone calls across the state or across town, an affectionate babble of voices expressing love and comfort.

In my case friends have been calling to send condolences for *The Sun*, a loss for us all but for me a relief as well, an opportunity to start again, go back to being a writer, read some books, take a break. Over the years I've often declared I wasn't going to crucify myself on this business, would only sacrifice so much for its survival. I did it because I wanted something interesting to read and nobody else around here was about to provide it. Again and again I heard from would-be but never-was advertisers that our publication was too heavy, too intellectual, too political, not fun enough, not responsive enough to their commercial needs. So what if thirty thousand people picked us up each week—they couldn't read and shop at the same time, could they? Such is the dictatorship of the marketplace.

But as Mikhail Gorbachev might say, there's no success like failure. An honest effort to overcome an impossible situation is better than none at all. If I lacked the wisdom to know when to quit—constantly raising money to keep us going despite all odds—larger forces than the need to publish have made the decision for me. I can look more clearly at the daily miracles—waves of vapor rising off damp grass blades in the morning, the autumnal slant of light in the afternoon, my lover's face by candlelight in our temporary shelter—without the overriding administrative angst of one who is responsible for coordinating a complex collective enterprise like putting out a weekly newspaper.

From our tower at the corner of Cedar and Union streets, across from the great black walnut in the city parking lot, we could observe the drama of people going about their business. A cast of downtown characters ranging from raving homeless evangelists to cultural and political dignitaries made for an entertaining spectacle, a voyeur's orgy of gossip and speculation amid the token facts demanded by our profession. Now we look out on a ghostly scene of cyclone fences and security guards and gawkers in search of historic snapshots, and I'm more convinced than ever that reality is more surreal than any poet imagines. The attempt to represent it otherwise, as journalists often do, is one of the greatest fictions of all.

As I patch my house back together over the next few weeks and months, I'll have the leisure to review the mess of evidence proving I existed and to sort out the salvageable treasures from the trash. I say existed because whoever I thought I was before Quake Tuesday is history, and if I make it through the aftershocks, the storms and the depression, the future is wide open. This morning as I write the air is clear. Life is more beautiful than ever.

Culture & Politics

So Long, Mr. Chips: Democracy, Elitism and the Arts

[2014]

One of the best things to happen to me when I was in graduate school, way back at the dark end of the 1960s, was meeting Norman Harms. I had been exiled by the literature faculty at UC Santa Cruz, due to bad behavior in seminars on critical theory, to a TA-ship in the core course of College Five (now Porter College), whose emphasis was the arts. I was to assist the newly hired Harms, an artist from Berkeley, in his woodscrap sculpture workshop both by participating in "the activity," as he called it, and by assigning arts-related readings to the undergraduates enrolled. I would help the students with their reading and writing, and Norman would guide them in the art of woodscrap sculpture.

The only problem with the class, apart from Norman's utter unsuitability to an academic environment—even one as relatively freewheeling as UCSC in 1969—was that woodscrap sculpture, by design, was not a "fine" art and did not require instruction. The whole point of the activity, which Norman may not have invented (Louise Nevelson was a master of this medium) but did attempt to popularize, was to prove to people, or give them permission to prove to themselves, that they did not need to consider themselves artists in order to discover the artist within. By taking variously shaped scraps of wood that had been reclaimed from furniture factories and pattern shops in deepest industrial Los Angeles, and gluing them together with Elmer's glue, anyone could create their own piece of improvisational sculpture. Art, for the evangelical Mr. Chips (Norman's *nom de guerre*), was not those paintings on the wall but the creativity in everyone. Because everyone, as far as Chips was concerned, was an artist.

Norman had come of age in the heyday of Abstract Expressionism, had trained as a fresco painter with Hans Hoffmann, and was a very accomplished abstract painter himself. A big silvery-blond man with a well-waxed handlebar mustache, of Nordic ancestry from Wisconsin, Norman was large in gesture, loud in voice, vehement in his convictions, on fire with ideas and practically exploding with revolutionary enthusiasm. He told me that the Abstract Expressionists had thought of themselves as revolutionaries, radical overthrowers of the status quo, but had been turned by the art establishment into commodities. Wild geniuses like Jackson Pollock and Mark Rothko had painted themselves into a commercial corner, and their only escape was self-destruction—which only increased the market value of their art.

For less gifted and visionary artists, the great masters like Leonardo and Michelangelo and Rembrandt were tyrannical overlords, hanging judges, elitist icons, overbearing role models, totalitarian taskmasters brutal enough to intimidate anyone.

Mr. Chips's project was to turn people on to their own creative potential and encourage them to do their thing in their own way with the most elementary materials: wood and white glue. He staged "glue-ins"—where anyone and everyone was invited to participate—at Ghirardelli Square in San Francisco, in public parks around the Bay Area, and in front of Bookshop Santa Cruz on what was then the Pacific Garden Mall. It was there, I believe, that some adventurous UCSC faculty recruiter discovered him and offered him a job. Chips's inability to adapt to the culture of even such a seemingly progressive ivory tower (or "City on a Hill," as the campus was called) was only a foreshadowing of the university's gradual eradication of the experimental humanistic vision on which it had been founded. Universities are corporations, corporations run on money, and the big money is in the sciences, not the arts.

Chips lasted but a single quarter because his insurgent fervor was not confined to art. When the rolling meadow to the west of College Five was to be carved into lots for student family housing, Norman was one of the leaders of the protests against such land-mutilating construction. He wrote inflammatory pamphlets and printed and distributed them (a great American tradition dating back to the Founders). He angered black students by distributing a screed called "The Student as Nigger," which encouraged undergraduates to revolt against the oppressive corporate regime that was reducing them to powerless slaves.

Needless to say, his contract was not renewed.

But our one quarter together, before the gates of academe

were slammed shut behind both of us on our way out, was the start of a twenty-year friendship that had a tremendous impact on me and my ideas about art. Norman was then the closest thing I had ever had to a mentor, and he was eager to impart his wisdom. His ideal work of art was the Watts Towers, Sam Rodia's sculptural-architectural creation in South LA, composed of bits and pieces of discarded, abandoned and found materials: scrap iron, glass fragments, broken tiles, wire, pottery shards, rusty tools, auto parts, junkyard crap of no useful purpose, constructed by Rodia, a tile setter by trade, into a monumental work of urban "folk" art. Chips took me there for the first time and gave me a major lecture on its importance. Rodia had demonstrated that people who make no claim to be artists, who don't turn their talent into inevitably corrupt careers, can be the greatest artists of all.

I believed it, having escaped a very Yale-centric literature program where hierarchy of accomplishment, whether in poetry, criticism or the academic pecking order, was paramount. The professors I hated most were the authoritarian know-it-alls who attempted to impose their intellectual vision on uppity hippie poets like me; I felt a stronger connection with the redwood groves than with their whiteman's curriculum. So I was ready to hear Norman's eloquent rants about the art police and the need to reclaim authority for the creative spirit of free imagination. Though I had been initiated into poetry the old-school way, by reading rhymed and metered English poems, and writing my own pale imitations of them, I had finally come around to "free verse" in the effort to expunge my inner conservative.

Forty-five years later, having survived the sixties and managed to spend my adult life doing what I like, which is writing and engaging in cultural intercourse with my community, I confess to being a bit nostalgic for the discredited notion of "elitism," which to me implies not an artistic priesthood or privileged class of tastemakers but an aspiration toward excellence: the effort to create, in whatever medium, not necessarily a "masterpiece" but as strong a manifestation of your talent and your vision as you can achieve, using the old masters not as slavemasters but as examples. W. H. Auden, the English-turned-American poet, as an undergraduate at Oxford, was reportedly queried by a snooty don, "So I understand you want to be a poet." "No," Auden replied, "I want to be a great poet."

I guess it is greatness that I miss in the leveling of the playing field where everybody's a poet or artist of some kind, all people are creatively equal, art is reduced to therapy and mediocrity prevails. Mediocrity is mathematical—the law of averageness demands it—but that doesn't mean that excellence should be ignored, or worse, scorned. Some of the most inspiring work may be what we do as amateurs to show ourselves we can do it—for me, domestic pleasures like cooking or gardening—but I am most inspired by things I know I could never do so well, like Vivian Maier's street photography (the work of an amateur), or Paul Cézanne's oil painting (definitely professional), or the poetry of Rainer Maria Rilke (an elitist for sure). Witnessing greatness makes me want to improve my own game, even if I can never hope to play in the same league as Emerson, Yeats or Kafka.

One of those bossy professors I had in grad school told me that he had wanted to be a writer but when he read Dostoyevsky he realized he could never be that great so he quit his own literary ambitions. What an idiot, I thought at the time; he should have taken Dosty as a role model and written novels of his own instead of promulgating the latest French metaliterary-critical-theoretical fashion.

Another legendary UCSC professor, the art historian and painter Mary Holmes (whom I met only long after I had dropped out), once told me that she taught art history instead of painting because she didn't want to have to look at students' work all day; she wanted to keep her eye on the highest standard, so that she would absorb those values into her own work. "Bad images drive out good," she said. Mary was the warmest person imaginable, and was supportive of anyone who felt called to become an artist, but when it came to "art appreciation" she wanted to look at, and talk about, only the best—not just the latest but the best of all time.

Whose work that is determined to be, and who decides, are political questions, but also personal ones. If we can't discriminate enough to establish our own personal canon or pantheon, how will we ever accomplish anything? How will we know who we want to hang with in eternity? How will we know who to imitate in order to learn the tricks of the trade, develop our chops, sharpen our artistic wits? While I still appreciate Mr. Chips and his populist creativity crusade, as I age I crave more and more to invest my time and attention in the enjoyment and appreciation of excellence, because being around works I most admire makes me want to join them with something of mine, and this desire stimulates my imagination.

Access to such models of accomplishment is not exclusive. Everyone these days has access to pretty much everything, at least in virtual form, and that is paradoxically part of the problem. Like one of those twelve-page deli menus that turns ordering lunch into an existential crisis, the proliferation of cultural artifacts (and arty fictions) at our fingertips is surely more than anyone needs or can consume. But if in the cacophony we can find what has proved enduring, we can tap into some of that staying power and use it to fuel our own creative enterprise. This has nothing to do with self-expression or self-esteem—though both may be side effects of plugging into such energy and doing something with it—and everything to do with serving your muse as truly and devotedly as you can.

No App for Humanities

[2014]

In case you've been so absorbed in the pages of *The Redwood Coast Review* for the past fifteen years (we start our sixteenth with this issue) that you haven't paid much attention to the world outside—nor to the world of academe—the study of the humanities at the college level has fallen off precipitously. Literature, philosophy and history programs are suffering from an absence of student interest, and thus of students. Economic anxiety, job insecurity, the escalating cost of tuition, the digital revolution and its rapidly multiplying repercussions have combined to redefine, in the public mind, the purpose of education. Like the vocational schools of old, our current universities have become training camps for employment rather than safety zones where young people can begin to learn how to think and to develop as well-rounded individuals. The liberal arts are just too, well, liberal to be of any use in our culture of relentless material competition.

I've been thinking about what this means, not just for literature majors like me, but for the world my granddaughter will grow up in, and for a society where the study of what it means to be human is seen as too impractical to be worthwhile. American pragmatism taken to this extreme becomes pathological, and while it may be too late to arrest this techno-functional paradigm of education as we hurtle toward our own post-human future, the "uselessness" of the liberal arts needs not only to be acknowledged but celebrated. It is precisely in the non-utilitarian aspect of the humanities that their value resides.

This truth should be self-evident to anyone who has ever read a great work of fiction, poetry, philosophy or history. Such works serve as both an escape from and a deeper immersion in everyday reality. They provide a timeout where extraordinary things can happen in the imagination or the reason of the reader. We discover common patterns of human behavior, ethical dilemmas and how people have dealt with them, ideas that have driven civilization and, most gratuitous of all, the sheer beauty of language raised to its highest power. If such an interruption of the grindingly mundane appears to have no practical purpose, it is only because people's imaginations have become so impoverished as to render them slaves to their devices—constantly on-call, plugged-in, interconnected, multitasked, attention-deficit-hyperactivity-disordered victims of the progress that has made contemplation a luxury.

Most religious traditions honor some version of the Sabbath, an interruption of the routine of survival for a more meditative, spirit-restoring interlude. A liberal arts education is such an interlude between adolescence and adulthood, a period in which the student may explore traditions that record humanity's investigation of itself and at best reveal what a human being is and how such a being navigates existence in an indifferent universe.

The ordeals of Odysseus, of Adam and Eve—literary characters of mythic significance, as both the Bible and Milton prove—of Alonso Quijano (Don Quixote) and Anna Karenina, of Emma Bovary and Huckleberry Finn and Kafka's Joseph K. are journeys in which we all participate, at one time or another, in one form or another, and so we recognize in their stories something of our own.

This doesn't mean that literary works are guides to self-realization, self-improvement or happiness, but that at best they tell us tales with lasting resonance, tales that explore and illustrate and offer inspiration or consolation for what T. S. Eliot called "the boredom, the horror and the glory" of being alive. Some philosophers do try to tell us how to live, but mostly they try to teach us how to think, whether in the form of abstract arguments and elaborate syllogisms that go on for hundreds of pages, or of pungent epigrams that cut through everything to reveal some revelatory truth. Historians try to figure out what happened, and sometimes why, and thereby show us how things have come to be the way they are. My late friend Mary Holmes, a painter and professor of art history at UC Santa Cruz, once told me that knowing what has happened in the past reveals patterns and cycles in human conduct that put current crises in perspective, and such knowledge has a calming effect on the mind.

The student given the chance to explore these stories will be better equipped to live, no matter what professional path he takes. Doctors and lawyers and factory workers and entrepreneurs and engineers and grocery cashiers can all be enriched by exposure to the humanities. If only for the value of reading good sentences, which is a prerequisite to writing them, studying the best of what has been written may be helpful to whoever wishes to make their way in a morally mixed-up world. The manufacture of increasingly "smart" gadgets that do our thinking for us may or may not be a good thing, but if the people who make and use such gadgets have no grounding in a humanistic tradition, the content and function of their devices will be more and more dehumanized until their users can be programmed like robots. This appears to be where we're headed and, despite those techno-utopians convinced that it's all for the best, this future world does not suggest to me any happy endings.

But it's not all technology's fault that the humanities are on the defensive. I know that in the study of literature, at least, the rise of critical theory as a domineering force has surely driven lots of people out of the English departments and into other disciplines. "The death of the author," the ethnic and gender identity wars, political and pseudo-political agendas, all the various mumbo-jumbos of postmodernism have combined to make reading poetry and fiction subordinate to arguments about how to read them, so that what is read is of interest only insofar as it can be construed to bolster the power of one or another theoretical camp. These turf wars over academic predominance do tons of collateral damage not only to the minds of scholars but to the books they're supposedly studying. As long ago as 1969, when I was in graduate school, I could see this coming and bailed out of there to try to become a writer.

Surely the proliferation of creative writing programs is partly a result of the dehumanization of the English departments, so that people interested in reading, and in exploring their own humanity, have embraced the option of becoming writers themselves, and possibly making a career of teaching writing.

And while this may not be entirely a bad thing, considering the alternatives in the current economy, it is not a good thing for literature as it generates an ethos of writing as mere "craft" and gluts the marketplace with competent mediocrity while the classics and the irregular standards they set fade further and further into the mists of lost time. Now there are more and more hundreds of thousands of writers and fewer and fewer readers. No wonder the English professors are nervous for their own futures.

Some of my best friends are literature professors and teachers of creative writing, and I know how devoted they are to books and to their students, and that current trends and turns of academic events are not their fault. Like me editing this skinny magazine, they are doing their best in what is probably a doomed last stand to defend the things they love, as well as to earn a living that in many cases supports their lives as writers. With journalism drying up as a viable profession, I hope my friends in academia are able to adapt to this rapidly changing landscape as teachers and champions of literature. But I am not especially optimistic.

For students who are drawn to neither math nor the sciences, and who have an affinity for the written word, hard as it may be to find a job with a humanities degree (especially in an environment with diminished opportunities for teaching, at least at the college level), I would encourage them to indulge whatever passion they may have for literature or history or philosophy, and to learn how to read closely and write with clarity, because regardless of their ultimate career path these skills will certainly prove useful. Being able to understand what you read, and to communicate your thoughts, are vital attributes no matter what you end up doing. And the human experiences and mysteries of these "soft" disciplines may help you to make sense of, and make your way along, whatever hard road you choose.

My wife, a recovering academic who is fluent in four languages and reads more fiction (in all of them) than anyone else I know, reminds me that anyone interested in reading literature rather than studying critical theory would do well to study a foreign language because after the fundamentals are in place you advance your understanding of an idiom by reading its literary texts. And despite the dominance of English in so many spheres of commerce, knowledge of foreign languages not only exposes one to other cultures, but provides a very practical skill in dealing with an increasingly multicultural world.

While the humanities may continue to shrink as a share of the university curriculum, and while knowledge of literary and philosophical traditions may not contribute to one's immediate prospects for employment, I would argue that their intangible benefits—in terms of personal enrichment and appreciation of life's less material pleasures—will prove in time to have value beyond measure. Allegedly dead white males like Homer and Cervantes, Dante and Dostoyevsky, Whitman and Joyce and Rilke are more fully alive on paper than the most technically amazing video game or dazzling digital device because their writings, however marginalized, will never be obsolete. They not only need no batteries, they will charge yours.

The Hill and the City According to Page Smith

[1985]

Around this time in 1965, the University of California Santa Cruz campus opened its doors—or, perhaps more accurately, circled its wagons—on the hill overlooking this little city. With Cowell College still under construction, a small but adventurous band of students and teachers gathered in trailers and rustic meadows to discover one another and chase the elusive grail known as a liberal education. A mile away, the downtown community was beginning to change from a sleepy seaside resort and retirement center to an outpost of what would soon come to be known as the counterculture.

In the intervening decades, both the university and the city of Santa Cruz have gone through some radical transformations. The campus has evidently striven to become a center of science and high-tech enterprise. While the town's attraction as a tourist magnet has increased dramatically, its cultural life has flourished with almost cosmopolitan vigor, and the political climate has shifted from a fairly reserved conservatism to an atmosphere of progressive experimentation.

What relationships can be traced between the university's arrival twenty years ago and the new shapes life in Santa Cruz has taken? In search of informed, opinionated perspective on this subject, I asked Page Smith—one of the founders of UCSC, teacher, historian and community activist—for his views on the debatable dynamics between the campus and the changing town.

Currently at work on the closing chapters of the eighth and final volume of his monumental *People's History of the United States* (Volume VII, *America Enters the World*, is recently out from McGraw-Hill), Smith was at first reluctant to venture any observations on this local theme, but once we got started talking a number of unexpected insights began to emerge.

"Santa Cruz is full of people that fifty years ago wouldn't have been caught dead in a small town," said Smith. "But I think the university had relatively little to do with this. Cabrillo College is really much more important in terms of sowing the seeds of a cultural and intellectual renaissance in Santa Cruz.

"When I got here, in 1964, the Hip Pocket Bookstore was flourishing. Norm Lezin, who had been head of the NAACP, was mayor of Santa Cruz. There was already that strange conjunction of the underground and the intelligentsia. The Hip Pocket Bookstore was where the counterculture hung out, and there were also 'criminal' types hanging out there.

"As soon as the first groups of students began to graduate, a little residue of them stayed here, but that was not until 69 or 70. And the character of the community as a countercultural center was pretty well established by then. Furthermore," he added, "the faculty remained very aloof from the community—the university faculty, as opposed (to some extent) to the Cabrillo faculty—they were not immediately and actively involved in the intellectual and cultural life of the community, and by and large still aren't."

Asked what the ideal relationship might be between the university and the community, Smith replied, "I think universities are vulnerable to the charge that they are a world apart. Marvelous as the setting of the campus is, if it were my doing, it seems to me that the university should have been in the *town* of Santa Cruz, or Watsonville; just that physical separation has very considerable psychological implications or consequences.

"If anybody had decided to have the university in the town—if the faculty felt it was an important part of their own conception of their function to be actively involved in the life of the community—it would already be an indication that they didn't need to be in the town. If they thought of themselves as part of the town, then it wouldn't matter particularly where they were."

So, culturally and intellectually, in Smith's view, the presence of UCSC has been merely incidental to the evolution of Santa Cruz over the last two decades. Economically, however, it's another story. "I mean it's provided an important stimulus economically to the community," Smith said. "Students obviously spend a good deal of money here," and the campus provides jobs for local workers in various clerical and service capacities.

But outside the campus, according to Smith, "It's kind of a funny situation because it is a community that you can't stay in unless you're willing to make substantial financial sacrifices.

There's just not enough employment here to make it worthwhile for certain talented people. I know dozens of people in New York City who'd much rather live in Santa Cruz—some of whom tried for five or ten years to do it—and it's not just the money that keeps them in New York, it's the opportunity to have an interesting job. I think people care about having a sense that their capacities are being utilized."

But what about the many individuals—a significant portion of the *Express* staff, for example—who initially came to Santa Cruz as university students and stayed to start small businesses or become involved in local cultural institutions. "It's relatively inconsequential in terms of the overall economy of the county," says Smith. "It would be interesting to have a sociologist take some groups of several hundred people and look at their role in the community's cultural and intellectual life and then calculate how many of them were here because of the university connection initially.

"I'm sure there are quite a few and that it's more evident in certain areas than in others—certainly in the arts community I would think that probably as high a percentage as a third or a half were graduates of the university.

"But then again, the arts community is such a special case because the people in it have no reason to believe they'd do better in New York or Los Angeles or anywhere else—it's just a hand-to-mouth existence at best."

Smith feels that the most important impact UCSC students have had on the community has been in the political realm. That they tend to vote liberal on political issues, and that the university's presence tends to attract politically liberal kinds of people to the area, are more significant factors in the life of

Santa Cruz than any contribution the campus makes in the area of culture.

"When you look at the Cultural Council," Smith observes, "there are very few university people on it. And if you take somebody like [County Supervisor] Gary Patton, who's a staunch liberal on most political issues, Gary isn't really very interested or knowledgeable in the arts. The person who's been most helpful in the realm of the arts over the years, I think, has been [conservative supervisor] Dan Forbus. And Marilyn Liddicoat, when she was a supervisor, was much more sympathetic and responsive to the arts than some of the more liberal members of the board."

Looking ahead, we asked Smith what, if any, changes he foresees in the evolution of the university or its relation to Santa Cruz. "I think there are some hopeful signs or possibilities," he said. "There is a strong group of older faculty and emeriti faculty and ex-chancellors who are anxious to do everything in their power to move the campus back more toward some of the ideals that were held in its early years. So I think there's a possibility of that happening. I don't know how good the odds are.

"But at the same time, I think that for there to be any real change in the relationship between the academic community and the town—the county, the natives—there'd have to be a very profound change in the academic world's notion of what its role in the world is, or what scholarship and learning and teaching and so on are all about.

"When I was at Dartmouth, my great teacher, Rosenstock-Huessy, got faculty and students together to talk about the relationship between the inside and the outside, between the academic community and the world—or the setting, the particular community. And I didn't know any better, it didn't seem to me a novel or revolutionary idea, but just getting faculty and students together to talk about an issue like this, I realize now, in retrospect, was extraordinary.

"And yet, in all that time I haven't seen anything to indicate that that idea, which he was so committed to, has come any closer. It couldn't get much further away, but I certainly haven't seen any substantial change. You see, the academic world is not really an intellectual world, it's a professional world."

Like other professional worlds, the academic community has become specialized and isolated from the surrounding reality, or so Smith sees it. But this doesn't necessarily mean that all educational institutions have to fit this pattern. "The junior colleges," he notes, "have appeared in almost every community of any size with any intellectual get-up-and-go, and are much more interesting, much more vigorous, or contain much more potential than the universities because they're not locked into all these crazy academic pieties.

"I think there's an inherent snobbishness that we all partake of, whether we are conscious of it or not, that the university is the big stuff and Cabrillo is the small stuff. But if you consider the issue of Cabrillo and UCSC and the community, as you think about it and talk about it with various people, you may come to the conclusion that Cabrillo has been the more interesting and that it remains the more promising institution in regard to this matter of change."

During the nineteenth century, Smith said, when the American character was flowering and some of our greatest thinkers were spreading their ideas, there wasn't the same separation we now experience between scholarly or intellectual and popular consciousness. Philosophers such as Emerson took their thoughts to the people. But in the 1920s, in Smith's reading of history, "a new kind of intellectual class formed, and that class felt very much against the mass of Americans," and that split has never entirely healed.

"To me," says Smith, "the real issue is, what is the character of American life? How do intellectuals relate to it? What is the role that they play?"

Waiting for JFK

[1999]

November is the cruelest month. In election years it's the time when we must choose among lesser and lesser evils. In off years we are inevitably reminded, just before Thanksgiving, of that sickening afternoon in Dallas thirty-six years ago when history took an irrevocable turn for the worse. The assassination of John F. Kennedy was the watershed event after which everything went to hell. Somewhere in our uncollected unconsciousness many Americans of a certain age have held the hope for a second coming of JFK, as if the idealism of The New Frontier, of the torch being passed to a new generation, might somehow be resurrected. For a minute, before he too was murdered, Robert Kennedy appeared to be that person. While John Kennedy Jr. was never a serious candidate for this role, his very existence, even as a nonpolitical celebrity, embodied a certain imaginary sense of the possible. His beauty, his cool, his amused response to the accident of his own renown, gave the illusion that his father's premature death might not have been so fatally tragic after all, that if John-John could take life lightly, so might we. Then, last July, he went and crashed his plane, reminding us all that the nightmare continues.

John Kennedy's death is nothing if not absurd. It may have a rational explanation—carelessness, bad judgment, inexperience, inattention—but the randomness of its happening and the shared distress of its reality are more than his family and the rest of us should have to bear. How many assassination flashbacks can we take? Yet that's to regard things from a merely human perspective. Looked at in mythic terms, Kennedy flying his airplane into the ocean is an elegant finish to a perfect story that illustrates, like the Greek tale of Daedalus and Icarus, the tragic limits of even the most ingenious men. Like many others, I was surprised at how shaken I was by news of this event. What little I knew of JFK Jr. had not especially impressed me. His disappearance reveals how well he served as a living symbolic antidote to everything that has gone wrong since his father's murder.

Now he will always be our golden boy, perpetually promising, vigorous, happily married, embodying good clean liberal values, a citizen without cynicism or tacky sentimentality, easygoing under the burden of unearned fame. That handsome philanthropic grin has been emblazoned in our collective imagination like the faces of James Dean and Marilyn Monroe. Little kitsch statues of his three-year-old funereal salute will be marketed on the shopping channels and on the shelves of tchotchke shops coast to coast. Leonardo DiCaprio will have several JFK Jr. screenplays to choose from. The celebrity Kennedy suffered in his lifetime will expand exponentially in death, but luckily for him he won't be around to experience it. It's clear now that we needed him a lot more than he did us.

I see no reason to doubt the wealth of anecdotal evidence suggesting that John Kennedy was a great guy. More interesting to me is what his magazine reveals about his view of the world and his place in it. Kennedy himself had a skeptical, ironic response to all the attention he attracted; he recognized the ridiculousness of his own celebrity and its relation to his cultural and political identity. *George*, the magazine he founded, played with the concept of politics as glamorous yet farcical entertainment; it made a mockery of media-obsession while at the same time exploiting its most frivolous tendencies. Mildly amusing in a sophisticated frat-boy kind of way, it lacked the substance to transcend its own flashy fluffiness.

At best, *George* under Kennedy's direction faintly evoked a 1960s-Esquiresque insouciance, only without the literary daring of original *Esquire* political writing—like Norman Mailer's "Superman Comes to the Supermarket," his classic report on JFK's ascension to power as the Democratic presidential nominee at the 1960 Los Angeles convention. *George* had no such radical journalistic ambition, partly no doubt for marketing reasons and partly because its editor lacked the imagination to make it anything more than a reflection of what it was trying to satirize. I was disappointed in *George*, not because I expected anything exceptional, but because it seemed an inane waste of money and talent to publish a slick magazine with such lightweight aspirations—another glib, smirking offspring of *People* and *GQ* and *Cosmo* and *Vanity Fair*.

Now that *George* is headed for the recycling bin of history, I see its late editor in a new light, or more precisely, as Kennedy Lite: the comic face of historic tragedy, harmlessly clownish, not taking the world too seriously, having a little fun with the superficiality and silliness of public life, living the imposed role of Prince Charming and laughing it off at the same time. I think the lightness of his style is what we miss, the sense that history is not, as Page Smith called it, tragic drama but more like comic opera or commedia dell'arte, and its mediated distortion nothing more than a glorified photo shoot. Young John-John's Secret Service code name, Lark, could hardly have been more poetically just. Flying, for him, both figuratively and literally, was a natural mode of transport. You can hardly blame him for the desire to soar on his own wings beyond the theater of public scrutiny. But as Heraclitus told us, the way up is the way down. Gravity beats buoyancy over the long haul. Tragic drama outlasts comedy.

The Kennedys as First Family had class, which is not to be confused with royalty. The style and brains of JFK and Jackie were all the more appealing for the fact that they weren't entitled to the White House. As it turns out, they got there fair and square through a close election whose result was fixed, according to some historians, by JFK's father. This is the American way, as in a Mario Puzo novel. Surely John Jr. felt both the obligation of *noblesse* and the desire to escape the bizarre scenario into which he was accidentally born. His last flight turns out to have been the ultimate career move, taking him from mild renown as the editor of a mediocre magazine to immortality as a hypothetically heroic figure whose best work may or may not have been ahead of him.

Historian Douglas Brinkley, a friend of Kennedy and collaborator on *George*, reported that JFK Jr. had been a fan of Bob Dylan and that his favorite Dylan song was "Chimes of Freedom." That's the civil-rights/JFK-era ballad (circa 1963) in which the singer sees, in an electrical storm, a vision of liberation for all the oppressed. Brinkley says the song represented for his friend an identification with the downtrodden and the righteous struggle for social justice, but for me Dylan's invocation in the same song of "the warrior whose strength is not to fight" more fittingly epitomizes Kennedy's courageous refusal to be his father's avatar. There was an integrity to his conscientious objection. Maybe later he would have changed his mind, but who knows?

Crashing, he joins the ranks of Amelia Earhart, Buddy Holly, Patsy Cline, Roberto Clemente, Ritchie Valens, Ricky Nelson and so many other All-Americans who prematurely met their fate in airplanes. After the tears have been shed and the piles of bouquets composted, the Cultural Icon Formerly Known as John-John, along with his star-crossed passengers, will remain eternally gorgeous, rich, always about to arrive. Our grief is greater for Kennedy than for other eclipsed icons not because of his accomplishments, nor even his presumed promise, but for his representation of those early-Dylan—and early-JFK—visionary values of a world that would inevitably get better, a world of which John-John's sexy and witty and high-powered father would turn out to be both false messiah and martyr.

There's cosmic synchronism in the fact that John Jr. died on the thirtieth anniversary of the moon landing, another mythic-historic event inspired by the ambition of his father. The fearful symmetry of JFK's space program, his abbreviated presidency, jet-pilot astronauts walking on the moon, and his amateur-pilot only son's plunge in the Atlantic precisely thirty years later is worthy of the ironic plot twists of some futuristic Victorian novel—Dickens meets H. G. Wells meets Henry James. A contemporary fiction writer who penned such a narrative would be laughed out of the office of most editors. But history isn't restricted by plausibility. As we have witnessed again and again, what passes for the real life of our time is more incredible than anything we could imagine. How could this happen? we ask. But it keeps happening.

Ecclesiastes' dictum that a living dog is better than a dead lion is little comfort to those of us still alive yet strangely grief-stricken by the unexpected loss of someone we never paid much attention to. At the same time, the spectacle of this mediated death—or three deaths, ghoulishly magnified via electronic replication and acres of magazine covers and printed pages, including these—was an absorbing distraction from our own more doggish disasters, our mundane mistakes and routine screw-ups that go unnoticed in the world at large because we're not that important. The small plane flying over dark water, its pilot losing control and spiraling down, is a terrifying image of human error, of helplessness and solitude amid forces stronger and more obscure than we know. But dying anywhere at any time, as each of us will, young or old, famous or anonymous, at home or in some twilight zone, must feel just as mysterious as losing it all in a few fateful moments of vertigo. In some way it must have been ourselves we were mourning.

At his mother's request, John Kennedy gave up his youthful notion of a life in the theater—or worse, as an actor in Hollywood—for the more serious and potentially political business of law, then abandoned law for a half-baked hybrid of showbiz and journalism. Now it's clear that his true calling was to be a star on the biggest stage of all, more worthy of pity and terror in sudden death than he ever was alive. As an accidental public figure he finally found his most commanding role: a Sophoclean character as rewritten by Samuel Beckett, caught in the spotlight through no fault of his own and for no comprehensible reason, amused and bemused by his predicament, conscious enough to know he was no hero, and destined, like his dad, to vanish into the netherworld of legend.

Summer of 68: What I Learned from Robert Kennedy

[2008]

Ted Kennedy's brain tumor is the same kind that killed my father, and the doctor who did the surgery on my dad was one of the team of neurosurgeons called in to try to save Robert Kennedy's life the night he was shot by Sirhan Sirhan in the kitchen of the Ambassador Hotel. That hotel had other primal associations for me—taking a date to see the Kingston Trio at the Cocoanut Grove in my junior year of high school, or being introduced to Willie Mays in one of its cottages where a friend and I were taken by someone who knew someone who knew the immortal Mays and had arranged a brief meeting when the Giants were in town to play the Dodgers. This means, according to a certain paranoid narcissistic logic, that I'm related by five degrees of separation to all of the above.

Ted Kennedy, my father (whose name was Jack), Bobby Kennedy, Sirhan Sirhan, the Kingston Trio, Willie Mays—these are just a few of the more emblematic dramatis personae of my 1960s-addled imagination, whose forty-year flashbacks have been set off by this year's many historic commemorations, further stirring up an already twisted memory field like so many psychic tornadoes. My father left this world on July 19, 1983. Willie Mays is still with us at the age of seventy-seven, but his greatest plays—the clutch home runs, the amazing catches, the stolen bases, the dead-on throws from center field, the completely poetic grace of his moves, the ebullience of his style—are long gone, like the boy I was who witnessed them in awe. Most difficult to accept, still, four decades later, Robert Kennedy was taken in his prime at a time when the United States, and I personally, needed him most.

In mid-July of 1968 I had just graduated from college, and had returned to California from the East Coast to go to graduate school in the fall. Friends and I had arranged to rent a Berkeley house together for the summer, and got there in time for the tear-gas police riots and sexual chaos of that city in the vanguard of antiwar and countercultural agitation. The sense of dread, excitement and depression was an incoherent mix of emotions that I don't believe was mine exclusively. Amid the festive protests and the militant fucking, the rock music and the revolutionary rhetoric, the burning cities and the burning joints—self-medication for those unable or unwilling to deal with the darkest realities descending on the nation, most gravely the unending nightmare of the Vietnam War, an unimaginable horror in the distance which invaded the culture pervasively spreading its poisons—amid all this, it was hell to be young that summer.

Staying as stoned as possible in a Berkeley at its most berserk, at a time when I might have been looking ahead to a budding adulthood and a fellowship welcoming me into the parentally approved respectability of an academic career, it's hard to remember ever being more distressed than I was that July. Just a couple of months earlier, for those of us young and liberal enough to be hopeful that Lyndon Johnson's decision not to run for reelection meant that Robert Kennedy would win the presidency, it was possible to envision the realization of our ideals in the body politic. A Kennedy restoration meant that what Lincoln called "the better angels of our nature" might be mobilized to end the war, bring the races together in mutual respect and understanding, defeat poverty and invigorate the collective imagination. Despite another Bob's admonition not to follow leaders, Bobby Kennedy was one leader who still might inspire multitudes with a fresh sense of the possible.

From his early days as an attack-dog anticommunist assistant to Joe McCarthy, Kennedy had evolved through his brother's assassination and subsequent cultural upheavals of the mid-1960s into a more humble, more moral, more visionary politician—a man imbued with a certain tragic wisdom—but a politician nonetheless, and that was part of his strength. He was tough-minded about the workings of Washington power and he seemed to think the machinery could be put to the service of higher purposes. The movie *Bobby* a couple of years ago (not a great film but admirably ambitious) made me cry because the news clips of Kennedy's speeches—especially after the murder of Martin Luther King—were a heart-crushing reminder of the optimism he engendered and the utter devastation of his death.

It was too late to lose our innocence—that had been lost less than five years before in Dallas—but Bobby Kennedy's murder triggered, in me at least, a total hopelessness. It meant that there would be no political figurehead, no president with the intelligence and passion and compassion and strategic shrewdness to lead us out of the war and through the exciting yet also deeply troubling confusion of a culture in turmoil. Kennedy embodied an engaged pragmatism, not exactly countercultural but experimental enough to dare to do the right thing and do it creatively. He and many less-establishment figures, activists who challenged the system itself, set an example and inspired many of those currently trying to hold the line against the most destructive forces of Bushism. These idealistic pragmatists in nongovernmental organizations, human rights groups, environmental movements, law firms still defending the Constitution, among other causes, prove that some people, sparked early on with the fire of ideas of justice, fairness and creative evolution, are still in the game and refuse to be defeated even when things look bleakest.

When I think of public figures at the heart of the beast who've tried to make a positive difference, no one comes to mind more readily than Robert Kennedy. I cried in the movie about his assassination—and afterward sat in my car in the parking lot sobbing until I could regain composure enough to drive—because of the sense of tragic waste that came with his loss, and the memory of the misery I felt that summer when prospects for any improvement in the public realm looked utterly grim, and the increasing feeling in subsequent months that there was nothing to be done to redeem this country so we might as well just blow our minds and kiss our asses goodbye.

Forty years on, in the hopeful heat of another electoral season, many survivors of 1968 are very cautious in their optimism, knowing how suddenly the tectonic plates of history can shift. Barack Obama's candidacy, as many have noted, is reminiscent of Robert Kennedy's in its combination of political skill, instinct, intelligence, eloquence, idealism, charisma and evident sincerity. Obama has inspired millions of citizens who weren't even born in 1968 and are perhaps more realistic than the I-have-a-dreamy students and earnest hippies of my generation. My twenty-seven-year-old daughter and her boyfriend have told me that they are for Obama but they don't have illusions about him—as some of us probably did about Bobby Kennedy—as any kind of political messiah. Still, his realistic engagement with the monumental problems of the moment, his poise, his cool and can-do attitude, suggest that the status quo may be improvable.

Oddly enough, Ted Kennedy's illness is also a reminder of what can be done within and despite the system. His possible disappearance from the Senate invokes his near-half-century record of defending progressive principles, which makes him in some ways a far more consequential political actor—in terms of actual accomplishment—than either of his older brothers. Kennedy, at first the least impressive of the three, has proved himself a major mensch in taking the best of his brothers' legacies and making a significant material contribution. Whatever his character flaws, he emerges in the end as a figure of near-heroic stature.

Robert Kennedy never had that chance. His martyrdom makes him a noble historic personage and someone who touched people personally as the last, lost hope we had of a moral recovery from a war at least as horrific as the one now destroying Iraq and ruining the lives of so many sent there to fight. It is unfair to Barack Obama, even should he be elected, to burden him with the expectation that even an enlightened administration can effectively turn things around. The government, the nation and the planet are too far gone at this point to expect much good news even in a best-case scenario. And anyone who's not an idiot fears the worst—the most mentionable manifestations of which might be, say, the invasion of Iran or the lengthy tenure of a McCain Supreme Court.

Maybe I'm getting soft in my old age, bitterly clinging to a sentimental secular humanism in the naïve belief that humanity is not a total loss, but what better time than the summer of a national election to be audaciously crazy enough to hope for the best, and work to make it happen, if only by voting. I may have lost my illusions with Bobby Kennedy, and lost the rest of my mind in the months that followed, but what else do I have to lose? Things are likely to get much worse than they are before they get better—if ever—and optimism may be the opiate of "elitists," but from the heights of despair you can sometimes see in the distance something that moves you to keep on. It's never too late, as Kennedy suggested (quoting Tennyson), to seek a newer world.

Anarchism and Responsibility

[1984]

A couple of weeks ago, when Rock Against Reagan rolled through town, stopping at the Vets Hall for an eight-hour orgy of music and dance and discourse, I was asked to speak as a resident philosopher on the subject of "anarchy." With only a smattering of historical background and readings in anarchist literature, I felt I might not be qualified to discuss such a volatile political idea. But when I considered how many rebellious spirits disgusted with government in all its forms and shunning elections on principle might think of themselves as anarchists, and how the rest of the political spectrum—from Communists to Republicans—regard the notion of anarchism with a nervous horror bordering on hysteria, I decided it would be worth debunking some anarchist stereotypes that might be plaguing the Yippies, hippies, punks and post-traumatic musicians gathered to blast the president.

Rock Against Reagan, first of all, was a remarkable event, one of the liveliest and most dynamic cultural/political conventions I've attended. A caravan of cars and buses originating in New York City and gathering strength en route west arrived in San Francisco in time for the Democratic Convention at Moscone Center, staging a counter-concert elsewhere in the city, leading to a spontaneous demonstration and the subsequent arrest and abuse of numerous youthful citizens in attendance. When the tour arrived in Santa Cruz the following week and set up at the Vets Hall on a Thursday afternoon, the place was charged with that electric energy which comes from being part of current events.

A row of tables in the entry hall displayed a range of anti-authoritarian literature ranging from posters and bumper stickers to pamphlets and magazines, the most visible of which was the Youth International Party organ, *Overthrow*. Admission was free, with donations requested to help finance the tour's expenses on the road to Los Angeles and Dallas, where soon these neo-wave mutants and lunatic-fringe visionaries intend to enact a theatrical alternative to whatever the Republicans are doing. No alcohol was for sale, so the Santa Cruz crowd ranged from teenagers on skateboards to gray-haired grandmas with petitions, from Mohawk-headed slam-dancers to mellowed-out middle-aged bohemians still recovering from the sixties. The vibes were positive, the bands were loud and the speakers who gave their spiels between musical sets showered the crowd with a rich diversity of perspectives.

Predominantly word-of-mouth publicity brought hundreds of people to the Vets Hall long before dark, with attendance building throughout the evening as people clustered outside the doors in earnest and festive interplay. Despite the noise of the more aggressive music and the post-denatured appearance of some of the dancers, there was a wholesome feeling in the air, suggesting that the dreaded punks were really clean-cut kids with a critical point to make by dressing up in apocalyptic costumes. On top of this sense of good clean fun, the mixture of generations present gave the gathering a festive atmosphere—not exactly the family the Democrats had invoked from the podium at Moscone, but an antinuclear extended family whose parents and children look out for each other beyond the property lines and walls of what used to be called home.

It was to this friendly, unruly group—primed by a punk band and a moronic comedian—that I was to offer my rap on anarchism. Without attempting to reproduce that extemporaneous discourse, I may be able to outline the basic argument, which ought to begin with a distinction between the political philosophy of anarchism and the condition of formless chaos commonly associated with "anarchy." Anarchism is based on the principle of voluntary cooperation rather than state coercion; it implies a trust in the capacity of humans to conduct themselves sensibly in both their individual and collective interest. Like communism and democracy in their ideal forms, it is a utopian philosophy whose difficulty of realization increases with the size of the community. Thus there can be anarchist households and even anarchist organizations but no anarchist nations.

The cooperative principle implies a sense of social responsibility. Each individual must be responsible for his or her actions and their consequences, instead of referring to some bureaucratic authority where the buck supposedly stops. This includes the presumed authority of anarchist ideologues, who believe that anarchism too is bound by dogmatic rules, like the spoken and unspoken prohibitions against voting. I would argue that even anarchists can use any means necessary, including elections, as a tool toward abolishing the state. In the current circumstances, a conscientious anarchist might vote against Reagan for the sake of having a chance to create some other society in the future—a future gravely threatened by the continuation of present imperial trends.

Rock Against Reagan itself was an excellent example of anarchistic people getting organized and creating a social microcosm that worked. It took planning and a great deal of cooperative effort, with specific persons taking responsibility for various aspects of the project but with no apparent hierarchical pecking order. Such horizontal organization and distribution of power toward a common goal, a functional goal involving many individuals, is a structural paradigm for many of today's most progressive political movements. People are gradually becoming aware that the limited dialectics of partisan politics and ideological rigidity must give way to a more holistic community/planetary vision if civilization is to stand a chance.

Collaborations and alliances among people and groups who share the desire for a non-repressive society, a peaceful and just society of egalitarian relations, are tactical necessities in a long ongoing effort, regardless of our respective political models. The sectarianism and doctrine-mongering that have traditionally divided the progressive sector can no longer be afforded. The concept of anarchism could serve as a catalytic element in frontline politics by promoting creative flexibility capable of embracing diverse perspectives and methods of change, a critical appreciation of our *compañeros'* paths of action without necessarily endorsing their imagined systems.

Since the ideal society is a long way off and the threat of

obliteration so imminent, the notion of "no government like no government" is wishful thinking at best and at worst a forecast of post-holocaustic polity, where leftover humanoids might start from scratch with no state in sight. What's left of our powers of self-preservation might best be employed in devising ways of cooperating consciously to dismantle the state—rather than letting it destroy itself and everything else with it—and create in its place a livable, plural, nourishing social organism.

Beyond Faith and Family

[2000]

The rhetoric of this political season reveals some dubious assumptions that currently seem to prevail in American culture. The emphasis on "family and faith," especially by the alpha Democrats, as the bedrock of all virtue and morality, implies that secular and/or single persons are somehow morally inferior and socially suspect. Even married couples without children or religious affiliation—let alone unmarried couples—are likely, in the present climate, to be regarded as vaguely unsavory or at least far enough outside the imagined mainstream to deserve little or no acknowledgment as valued contributors to the commonwealth. And if you happen to be gay, forget it—by declining to breed you are obviously out of bounds; you may be tolerated in the big tent of happy-face cosmetic diversity that even the Republicans have fabricated, but when it comes to "family values," yours are at best questionable.

Now, I don't mind if Al Gore wants to ask himself what Jesus would do about the budget surplus or the strategic oil reserve, or whether he'd run for president. And if Joe Lieberman would like to declare every Saturday a national day of rest, I don't consider that such a bad idea. And even if that big-league Bible-hugger George W. Bush believes he's exercising Christ's compassion as he signs off on one more Texas execution, that's a moral riddle I leave to scholars of deeper Talmudic wisdom than mine. But when these guys suggest that rational faithlessness and deliberate or circumstantial singleness are less than moral, or maybe un-American, that gets my goat. How many scamming evangelists and pedophilic priests and adulterous rabbis have to be publicly busted before the virtue-mongers are forced to acknowledge that there's no correlation between proclamations of righteousness and actual ethical or moral conduct? Didn't Jesus himself expose the Pharisees as a bunch of pious hypocrites? And wasn't Jesus single?

One likely source of this new moralism is a backlash against the perceived excesses of the 1960s—the pot-smoking, draft-dodging, sexually promiscuous self-indulgences personified by our lame-duck scapegoat president. Never mind that the greatest obscenity of that era was an insane war that some people had the good sense to resist. "The sixties" are still being bashed by those too old or young to have been tormented by that decade's terrible contradictions, and by those who used the turmoil of the times as a smokescreen for their own irresponsible experiments and now, unable to govern their own children, are desperately reaching for some controlling moral authority. Religious institutions, with their "thou shalt nots," are an appealing refuge from the dizzying changes currently wracking the planet. Some folks who sought spirituality in drugs or exotic cults or Eastern religions or the Internet are returning with relief to their Judeo-Christian roots.

But one philosophical movement that gained currency in the 1960s and remains, for me, a wellspring of ethical and moral inspiration—with or without God—is existentialism. Without reducing this various and complex body of thought to some simple formula for living, I would say that one of its core principles is that of personal choice and responsibility. If God's existence is in question and, as Dostoyevsky noted with anguish, "everything is permitted," the burden of moral conduct is on the individual rather than the rules of some higher authority. It is up to each of us to live in accord with our conscience and in conscious consideration of those around us. This assumption of the power to shape our lives without the benefit of institutional guidelines is, in my experience, both humbling and exhilarating. The freedom to become what we are and do as we will, without the comforting fiction of a supreme being, affords us, as humans, a certain modest dignity. It is this existential dignity that I invoke against those who claim that morals are impossible without religion. Any thinking adult should be able to respect the integrity of those who consciously choose to live without false faith. Better to remain honestly apart from hollow ritual than mindlessly go through the motions.

As for the family and its apotheosis as the model of wholesome citizenship, sure, it's hard to raise kids and to support, both materially and emotionally, such a volatile and complicated bio-social unit. But it's also hard to live alone in a culture that promotes marriage and children as the natural goal of anyone who wants to be considered normal. If contemporary memoirs are to be believed, the average family is steeped in destructive psychodrama and hardly the paradigm for a harmonious social order. The joys of family life, like the joys of independence, are mixed with its agonies. The Democratic presidential ticket appears to take for granted the support of a majority of single voters, so it's strategically understandable for Gore and Lieberman to court the "family" vote; but a lot of single people are struggling too, and in a time when half of all marriages end badly it seems a bit myopic to ignore the legions of the unmarried. Certainly being a husband or wife or parent, while imposing an array of serious obligations, has historically failed to force people into virtuousness. And there are enough adulterers and lousy parents out there to raise the troubling question of whether some couples are morally fit to procreate.

Maybe once the election is over we'll be spared the bully-pulpiteering of the self-righteous. One redeeming aspect of Bill Clinton's moral lapses has been to disqualify him from copping a holier-than-thou attitude. He's a flawed person, like the rest of us, and everyone knows it, so instead of pretending to have a hotline to heaven he has proceeded, for better or worse, to attend to business in the earthly realm. His public humiliation in the Lewinsky fiasco—not to mention his continuing legal problems—have had the ironic effect of making him far more likable than the sanctimonious obsessives who tried in vain to evict him from the presidency. One lesson, or "moral," of the impeachment spectacle was that most of this country's citizens don't look to the nation's chief executive as a role model. Even Martin Luther King Jr., that icon of righteousness, was famously unfaithful to his wife. Does this diminish him as a heroic figure, a man of honor and a fighter for justice? Not as far as history is concerned.

In the secular Jewish tradition that I come from, doubt is

no obstacle to goodness. One's deeds in working for a better world, one's contribution to the community, one's ethical conduct in dealing with other people, are infinitely more valuable than self-serving declarations of faith. In matters of religion, as of politics, I choose to cultivate a scrupulous skepticism.

Language and Politics: How Cheap Is Talk?

[2008]

Much has been made, this political season, of Barack Obama's skills as a public speaker and of whether or not his eloquence has any substance. It's a legitimate question to ask about any lawyer or politician—from Abraham Lincoln to Hillary Clinton—or poet or philosopher, for that mater. Socrates, by way of his ghost writer, Plato, complained of his contemporaries the Sophists who, through fancy rhetorical footwork, made superficially persuasive yet spurious arguments about the true nature of things. And we're all familiar with contemporary examples of artists whose works are all style and no content—the films of Quentin Tarantino, for example, or the Coen brothers.

Obama's use of his adviser Deval Patrick's riff on the theme of "Just words?"—citing Thomas Jefferson, Franklin Roosevelt and Martin Luther King at their most lucidly acute—provoked charges of "plagiarism" from his opponents. But any politician in 2008 who claims to write her own speeches is being ridiculously dishonest. What's refreshing about Obama is that most of the time he sounds as if he's thinking on his feet, and the natural ease of his spoken language gives an impression of authenticity. Scripted as much of campaigning is, by numbingly repetitive necessity through endless months of nonstop blather to the masses, a candidate's ability to improvise in coherent sentences, with wit and candor, makes an impression on a public sick of the same old political clichés. That's one thing some people like about John McCain, and it was one of the most appealing qualities of John F. Kennedy.

Lincoln spoke extemporaneously for hours in debates, and also wrote his own prose; many of his phrases have entered the lexicon as permanently as Shakespeare's. I can almost still recite the Gettysburg Address, which I learned in the fifth grade, not because I understood what it meant at the time but because the rhythm and beauty of its rhetoric—like those of the equally incomprehensible Jewish prayer book—were both seductive and memorable. Language, for anyone with an ear for its sound and a sense of its meaning, reaches deep into the psyche and touches both emotion and intellect.

The late historian Page Smith, one of the founders of UC Santa Cruz, whom I had the pleasure of interviewing several times as a journalist, used to speak of history as "tragic drama"—an epic narrative whose endings are seldom happy—and of the founding of the United States as, essentially, a debate, a battle of ideas among a gathering of brilliant Enlightenment minds who literally talked the nation into existence through what Smith called "passionate, rational speech."

Newspapers, pamphlets, broadsides and speeches were the means by which such founding American revolutionaries as Jefferson, Adams, Madison, Franklin, Hamilton, Tom Paine and Patrick Henry persuaded each other and the public of the need for independence from England, and of the form that independence should take. Language counted because it embodied thought and delineated both ideas and the forms in which those ideas might be realized politically. Talk, then as now, was plentiful but not cheap—words had weight, and consequences.

In our current multimedia cacophony, contaminated by advertising and every kind of bad-faith salesmanship, not to mention rampant know-nothingness and pandemic half-baked opinion-mongering, the sound of anything real or true is hard to discern in the din. Even poetry, once a refuge from the marketplace and a zone of intimate truths, has been industrialized by the institutionalization of "creative writing" and the manufacture of countless careerists in a landscape where once roamed various lone artists possessed by individual vision absent of any professional utility. The career poet, like the career politician, typically traffics in formulas and therefore must be regarded with similar skepticism.

When someone like Obama comes along who speaks and writes (he's authored two books by his own hand) as if he actually means what he's saying, and inspires the otherwise unengaged to suddenly pay attention and to participate in what's left of a democratic process, even those with no faith in any messianic salvation from the political catastrophe of the last eight years can't be blamed for feeling encouraged by the prospect of a more intelligent, more creative, more humane and more representative government.

While the institutions of the system, capitalist to the core, may show little promise of deep reform, the only hope for correction of the country's disastrous course is a change in leadership that might begin to steer the battleship of state in a different direction. One thing proved by Kennedy's brief and in some ways illusory reign was that when you have a smart, attractive, tough-minded, quick-witted liberal in the White House, someone unafraid of artists and intellectuals, who actually invites them to join in the effort to recreate a national identity, a lot of people can be moved in positive ways.

Whether or not such inspiration may translate into meaningful "change" remains to be seen. Bill Clinton—also a great speaker, of keen intelligence and decent instincts but fatal character flaws—was ultimately a disappointing president for those who, perhaps naïvely, had hoped for a transformation after a dozen years of reactionary rule. The two-term nightmare of his successor makes Clinton look like a saint in retrospect, but his performance this year on the campaign trail has only proved his egomaniacal arrogance and unquenched lust for the heady pleasures of the West Wing. It's not Hillary's fault that she happens to be his wife, but it hasn't helped her candidacy—except for the fact that she wouldn't be running if she hadn't been married to the president—and if by some historic reversal or desperate deployment of dirty tricks she turns out to be her party's nominee, her brittle style and wonkish command of issues aren't likely to inspire enough confidence among voters to get her elected president.

Obama's cool self-assurance, like Jack Kennedy's, and his ability to put in words the aspirations of the young especially, but also those with any belief left in the experimental potential of the United States and what survives of its ideals, his basketball player's grace and winning attitude, are what excite his half-hysterical mobs of admirers. Surely they're putting too much faith in the power of one man to rescue us from our world-historical mess, but if the sound of his passionate rational speech, with its optimistic air, can change the mood of a nation, that may be a prerequisite for policy decisions that might begin to mitigate the damage done by his predecessor.

Adlai Stevenson and Eugene McCarthy were smart and eloquent, but square. Jack and Bobby Kennedy were smart and articulate and charismatic and sexy and sufficiently Machiavellian to succeed, but never got the chance to really show what they could do. Barack Obama may be a collective hallucination conjured by the desperation of the electorate, but when he speaks he commands not just attention and respect but a sense of possibility—a sense that both his hopeful audacity and his nimble intelligence may be contagious.

Sympathy for the Devil

[2012]

The cover of Walter Isaacson's best-selling biography of Steve Jobs makes the book look like an Apple product. If not in fact designed by the control freak Jobs himself, as it appears to be, it faithfully adopts his signature esthetic: The simple black-and-white image, the elegant minimalism, the clean sans serif type at the top all reflect the subject's fine eye for functional design and sensory seductiveness. The tiny bookstore code on the back, beneath a portrait of the younger Jobs with the original Macintosh computer in his lap as he sits cross-legged on the floor, reads "BIOGRAPHY & AUTOBIOGRAPHY," suggesting this is a collaboration between author and subject. Indeed the forty interviews Jobs did with Isaacson over the last two years of his life form the core of the narrative. Jobs recruited the author for the project out of respect for his previous biographies of Benjamin Franklin and Albert Einstein—clearly considering himself in the same league, creatively and historically—and did not ask to read the result before publication, trusting Isaacson the ace reporter to tell the honest, truthful, unfiltered story of Jobs's highly unusual life.

And the cover image itself: a head-on portrait, the man gazing directly into the camera through the round lenses of his wire-rimmed glasses with the faintest trace of a smirk at the corner of his mouth, wedding-ringed left hand held lightly to his chin, close-cropped grayish hair combed forward over his balding dome, and precisely trimmed beard above his uniform black mock-turtleneck. The subject shows supreme self-confidence, directness, intense engagement with the viewer, and a certain magnetic wickedness in those eyes. This guy has charisma to burn, and part of that power derives from his dark, I dare say demonic, side.

Even for someone scarcely enamored of bestsellers, mogul biographies, business histories, animated movies or digital gadgets—not to mention six-hundred-page books, very few of which I find I can read anymore—I found this tome compulsively engrossing. Isaacson's research is thorough, his style limpid, his sympathy for his subject almost contagious despite the many unsavory aspects of his personality and character. I was reminded of William Blake's famous note, in *The Marriage of Heaven and Hell*, on Milton's style in *Paradise Lost*: "The reason Milton wrote in fetters when he wrote of Angels & God, and at liberty when of Devils and Hell, is because he was a true Poet and of the Devils party without knowing it." Isaacson may not be a poet, but he was inspired as he wrote this story.

One of the most fascinating aspects of *Steve Jobs* is the way it reveals in the early chapters its subject's intellectual and cultural formation as a child of the Bay Area coming of age in the 1960s and 70s. The Santa Clara Valley, until then a pastoral landscape of apricot orchards, was then becoming a rapidly developing habitat of the cold-war aerospace industry, its engineers taking up residence in the spreading suburbs. Parallel to this high-skilled high-tech industrial culture was the counterculture of psychedelic drugs and rock and roll, with its mystical-visionary overtones, its openness to the East, its alternative ethos of experimentation and utopianism. Jobs—whose adoptive father was a machinist (he never knew his biological father, though according to family lore he may have met him accidentally without knowing it) who had a shop in his garage where the young Steve picked up his first taste for crafty precision and elegant design—also took acid and smoked pot and experimented with extreme diets (which plausibly may have contributed to his fatal pancreatic cancer) and studied Zen Buddhism, and thus embodied a merging of these cultural streams, as did so many of the engineering wizards who created the computer industry and the Internet. Jobs was part scientist, part artist, part entrepreneur, part seer and part magician. Another of Blake's Proverbs of Hell comes to mind: "What is now proved was once, only imagin'd."

Jobs's imagination was so persuasive, his co-workers testify, that he generated what came to be known as his "reality distortion field," whereby he would ask his engineers or designers to do something hitherto impossible, they would explain that it couldn't be done, he would insist that it could and they could do it, and then they would do it, often on a timeline they considered totally unrealistic. Not an especially accomplished engineer himself, part of his gift as a business executive was his instinct for and skill at recruiting first-rate talent and putting it to work in the service of his ideas. There are some who say it was the people Jobs hired who should be credited with Apple's many innovations, and that may be so, but it was Jobs who assembled the team. He was the orchestra conductor—ruthless, tyrannical, almost maniacal at times, a whacked-out maestro—who was also charming enough to win the confidence and loyalty of his players, many of whom were able to perform at the level of his extremely high expectations and thus create a corporate music previously unheard in the halls of American business.

Like some sociopathic character out of Dostoyevsky—Ivan Karamazov, say, or Verkhovensky, the possessed revolutionary of *The Devils*—Jobs, according to Isaacson and various Apple alumni, was more than merely *driven* in pursuit of the "insanely great" products with which he meant to "change the world." His impatience with lesser intelligences, his tantrums, his verbal brutality, his intuitive brilliance, his indifference to other people, his lack of empathy, his uncompromising esthetic, his aggressive bargaining tactics, his shrewd dealmaking, his instinct for creative marketing, all combine to set him apart from many more-sympathetic successful people, even in the cutthroat world of capitalism. And for better or worse, he did indeed change the world. Apple did not exactly invent the personal computer but they made it cool and sexy and easy enough to operate that even the technically challenged could make it their instrument. The portable devices they pioneered are now ubiquitous and certainly are rearranging human neurons by the hour, changing brains that now depend on these nifty extensions that do your thinking for you. The borderline madman Jobs has implanted himself in our collective psyche, whether or not we personally use his fiendishly ingenious machines.

In recent months a lot more has been revealed about the inhuman working conditions in Chinese factories where Apple products are made (in part because, the company says, they can't find the trained workers and manufacturing plants in the States that could set up and produce at the pace required to fill the orders for iPhones): twelve-hour shifts, dormitory housing, locked shop floors where workers can't take breaks, suicides on the premises. Apple has agreed to an independent investigation of what industrious reporters have already documented, as the company tries to control the public-relations damage and respond to protests at its retail outlets. The result may well be improvements in such conditions and a general humanization of labor practices in the industry as a whole. But Isaacson, an otherwise deep-digging reporter, doesn't touch on this subject—not a single sentence, much less a paragraph or chapter in his account of Apple's remarkable saga—which is perhaps his book's most egregious omission and defect as corporate history. What it reveals about Jobs's character is far from the image of glorious creativity otherwise promulgated by his biographer.

Another shadow of Apple's techno-consumerist achievements is that the company's remarkable innovations (a word Isaacson uses almost exclusively in a tone of gee-whiz wonderment) carry as a byproduct an accelerated obsolescence. And what happens to all those cool little units—old desktops and laptops, iMacs, iPods, iPhones, iPads—that have outlived their groovy newness? A lot of them wind up in third-world landfills where children attempt to salvage their components and in the process are exposed to all sorts of toxic chemicals and metals. The swift advances in Apple engineering and user-friendly design leave a nasty trail of debris in their wake and look far less appealing against this background of collateral damage to people and the environment.

Which is not to say that Jobs was not an extraordinary character of historic stature. He is surely the most notable exception to F. Scott Fitzgerald's famous declaration that there are no second acts in American lives. Forced out of the company he'd founded and led to its first heights of success in 1985, he returned a decade later not only to rescue its sagging fortunes but to take it to vastly greater command of the market. By narrowing its focus to a few superior products (rather than expand its offerings as its post-Jobs management had, with increasingly poor results), Jobs used his Zen-minimalist intensity of attention to revolutionize the way people use and think of their portable e-tools, and thereby turned Apple into the most valuable corporation on the planet. Fitzgerald, for all his poetic insight, could never have imagined such a commercial, cultural and creative comeback.

Jobs told Isaacson that among his formative experiences were his youthful experiments with LSD. Without getting too explicit about its specific influence on his thinking, he clearly found its mind-expanding powers revelatory, and (unlike less-brilliant and less-lucky acidheads who were launched over the edge by the drug) was able to harness his psychedelic awareness to his vision of a synthesis of science and the humanities—except that Jobs's notion of the humanities appears to have been grounded not in literature or philosophy or ethics but in pure esthetics. He was stuck in what Kierkegaard called esthetic arrest, the first stage of moral development; and, in Nietzchean terms, felt himself a superman who operated in a creative zone beyond good and evil. His contempt for PowerPoint presentations and the people who give them ("If you know what you're talking about, you don't need PowerPoint") is emblematic of his valuing deep understanding and extemporaneous intelligence, a jazz musician's mastery of technique in the service of improvisation. Only stupid people, in Jobs's mind, needed such pointless technical assistance. And only soft-headed idiots were less than ruthless in their decision-making.

The "i" in iMac, iPod, iPhone and iPad stands most explicitly for Internet and the ability of those devices' design to connect with the Web as organically as possible. It also suggests individual identity, one's use of those devices as a means of designing and defining one's own person. I would also argue that it implies isolation—typified by the user's deep, Narcissus-like absorption in the magical powers of the technology, the sight of the small screen or the head full of self-selected sounds coming through earbuds so captivating a representation of reality that one loses contact with one's actual surroundings. Internet addiction, which has been documented as a syndrome of our hyperconnected times, is facilitated by the Wow appeal of its delivery devices. Apple products, thanks to Jobs and his team, are irresistibly transporting, not unlike LSD itself. As with any such consciousness-changing substance, the dangers of its abuse are abundant.

So Jobs's legacy is double- or triple- or quadruple-edged, a mix of blessings and curses for the contemporary techno-connected soul. *Connected to what?* is the key question. Instant access to virtually everything, combined with the hazard of narcosis, can mean being so entranced by one's devices that they take on a life of their own—like Siri the talking info-girl inside the iPhone 4S, who is probably more intelligent than many of her users. The robotic consciousness of such software should give pause to those still rational enough to wonder who or what is running whom.

Steve Jobs's brilliance, his visionary genius, his uncompromising standards, his artistic sensibility and his transformational entrepreneurial skills are beyond dispute. His interpersonal insensitivity, his narcissism, his emotional cruelty, his sense of his own exceptionalism—that other people's laws and customs and manners and courtesies did not apply to him, and that in the search for innovation and market share the people who do the physical work are expendable—are also worth considering, along with the counter-corollary that not every genius needs to be a jerk.

Art Abuse

[1987]

According to a report last week on National Public Radio, tourists in Florence, Italy, have been suffering severe esthetic stress in the face of that city's many museums. In what sounded like a near-epidemic outbreak of "Stendhal's Syndrome"—named for the French novelist who complained in his journal of a similar malaise while visiting Florence—foreign museum-goers have been getting literally sick from exposure to an overabundance of Renaissance masterworks, their vacations ruined by a curious form of cultural poisoning. It was suggested that art gluttons guard their health by cutting back on consumption.

When I was in Paris with my friend Dave Mann in the summer of 1966, he came back to our hotel one day complaining of an overdose of Monet; he'd gotten dizzy and nauseous at the Impressionist museum faced with the sickening richness of all that paint. Like French haute cuisine with its goopy sauces, French impressionism is best relished in small amounts. Mann (who last I heard was a public defender in Santa Clara County) probably couldn't have guessed that he had Stendhal's Syndrome, but

I was feeling the same way from looking at the August clouds floating by whitely in the cerulean sky, so what disease did I have? The NPR report didn't say, but it did imply that a person can stand only so much beauty.

Santa Cruz is in no danger of outdoing Florence as a repository of immortal art, so Stendhal could no doubt hang out here with little to worry about in the way of art sickness. But of course he doesn't have to; we do. And as I contemplate the transformation of this town from backwater resort to cultural smorgasbord, I can't help wondering what we're in for as the local art scene becomes increasingly institutionalized. Festivals, museums, concert halls and patrons are indispensible to the infrastructure of Big Art. As in Big Business, the entire community may benefit, with artists enjoying jobs or grants, the public feasting its eyes and ears on exhibits and performances galore, and the promoters basking in the prestige of the money that makes it all possible. I know from experience that even when you lose your shirt putting on an event or building an institution, great satisfaction can be had from the act of making it happen.

But the establishment of cultural institutions and the onset of artistic self-consciousness bring with them hazards of an attitude that kills real art. Andy Warhol made an ironic fortune by exposing Fine Art as a consumer item, his parodies of pop icons reflecting perfectly the supermarket mentality of the art economy. Art is a great investment: you can decorate your house with it as it appreciates in value. But when art becomes merely a decoration—or worse, a vanity mirror for the collecting class—it has lost its life.

In feudal Europe many great artists survived by serving power, delivering portraits of the royal family for a piece of the royal pie. In the late eighteenth century, Spanish painter Francisco Goya brilliantly subverted this genre of portraiture by depicting Spain's nobility of the moment as a bunch of buffoons. Without blowing his own cover, Goya subtly recorded for posterity the pomposity of his patrons; his penetrating insight and technical skill revealed his subjects stripped of their mystique.

The artist as social critic is not exactly a radical concept. As the raw nerves of society, creative types are as likely as anyone to feel and communicate pain. But if they scream too loud or in the wrong direction, they could lose their funding—and then what? Perhaps the turn to a more conventional career with a little time for art "on the side"? If a painter or writer or dancer or actor or musician can pay enough dues to begin to make a living at their profession, good for them, but watch out for the symptoms of success: receptions, for example, where the artist is swamped in a bog of big spenders eager to objectify his or her talent by grabbing a piece of the action. It's the tradeoff that sometimes has to be made for the privilege of carrying on the work.

Official persecution of the graffiti writers of San José and elsewhere stems not only from the defense of property, but from the absolute independence of the artists. Rebellious youths who leave their signatures on public walls are contesting the notion of art as a precious item to be stashed in galleries and museums; theirs is a rough-edged statement that runs against the grain of the status quo. Once these artists are "discovered" and adopted by the art world, controlled and sold to the highest bidder, no problem—but let them spray their obstreperous identity on some freeway underpass and the cultural police will be on their case. Such artists on the far side of respectability, who show and tell what the connoisseurs don't get, are often the ones who are opening the way for the creative advances of their successors.

Clearly, we're not in Florence anymore. If our museums and cultural centers are to be more than tombs for embalmed artifacts, and our artists more than the domestic pets of those who can afford to support them, we need to cultivate imaginations daring enough to make the authorities uneasy. Guerrilla artists operating independently of any formal approval are the spice in the soup being brewed collectively beyond consumers' control. The vitality of Santa Cruz or anyplace else as a "center for the arts" depends as much on this undercurrent of obscure ferment as it does on the more visible triumphs of sanctioned spectacle. In a healthy climate, each would fertilize the other in a nonstop dialogue blurring the boundaries between them.

This is how I like to imagine this community: a cauldron of creative energy where "high" and "low" culture, popular and fine art, artists and audience are constantly changing places in a dynamic neoprimitive dance. While I personally can resist such revelry in its more theatrical manifestations—for example, the tribal hoedown of the typical rock-and-roll ritual—I like to know that it's going on, just as I value the poetic efforts of thousands of unsung bards without ever having to read or hear their stuff.

Luckily, I suppose, I'm bombarded anyway by tons of cultural fallout both institutional and intimate. Like the Paris sky to my nineteen-year-old senses tasting the world for the first time, such intense drenching of everyday beauty can be burdensome to one who is moved to respond to the accidental gifts of experience. You don't have to be a tourist at the Uffizi Palace to feel overwhelmed by the richness of your surroundings— faces and forms endure in memory as surely as they do in marble.

It is in the effort to record this understanding that revelations occur, whether or not the finished product ends up in some museum. Neither the canvases nor the catalogs quite capture what Botticelli was up to, any more than van Gogh's actual misery can be seen by looking at his pictures. But inspiration is contagious, and if the artist succeeds in bringing it across, it gives you something to work with.

Miss America Unbound

[1983]

When they repossessed my tiara as punishment for my posing as a lesbian in *Playhouse*, at first I felt raped, ripped-off of the woman I imagined myself, but as days went by I began to realize that like the Statue of Liberty's torch, my identity as Miss America is unsnuffable—sort of like having let the immigrants in, you can't put the omelet back in the broken eggs. I saw myself walking around a parking lot in front of some political convention wearing an egg-carton crown, gray-faced, carrying a Bible. My very existence makes evangelists' blood boil because they want what I've got and can't get it to save their souls. Nobody fucks with Miss America.

Let's get this straight. I do what I want, with whom I want, and it's nobody's business. When you elected me Miss America you elected everything I am—a strumpet, a virgin or a presidential candidate, depending on the lay of the law that day, on who got sent back at the border and what color the light was on Old Faithful—and now you're stuck with me for eternity, stark raving naked, delivering news you never had the nerve to hear. Look closely, my race is *other*, my skin transparent.

So we were married, you and me, that first night we met on TV, you in your apartment eating a frozen dinner or down at your favorite dive remarking over beers the size of my breasts, me on the runway like something the Air Force dreamed up; it was a scholarship I'll never forget, like having sex with a senator in an elevator on Capitol Hill. I read in *The Washington Post* that the hostages who tried to free me were intercepted by the CIA and interrogated in a basement in Tegucigalpa, their genitalia investigated for communist connections. While you and I were on our honeymoon air raids were spreading obscenities more awesome than magazines across the countryside.

Remember that time we were flying home from Hollywood, dropping the images off everywhere, and the pilot informed us we were heading for San Salvador instead? Remember the Buddhist stewardess, how she tongue-lashed those nuns because they claimed to have done it with Jesus? She was sending a message to you, man. It meant you don't marry a god or goddess, she does with you whatever myth demands, and my myth is to possess you with visions of independence, a state traditionally ascribed to guerrilla fighters.

I saw some spraying a mural in a tunnel, it was a long sentence in unintelligible script, a calligraphy that worked on your mind like the sound of a beeswarm, musical but scary, they moved over that surface like a wedding dance, loving that wall with their whole souls, hugging it with paint. They're the ones I'm bonded to, big boy, not you.

But our affair has had its tender moments—all those nights

in hotels where the entrepreneurs had slept, all those afternoons in limousines en route to meet the press, all those mornings over croissants and coffee reading *USA Today* and weeping. It wasn't that we were doomed but that we weren't prepared to perish: we were expecting to last forever, packed with preservatives, but even dictators die. I entered the pageant because it was my best way out of the ghetto next to basketball. You showered me with credit, with cosmopolitan cosmetics. It's been a plastic romance, and unforgettable.

Somehow all those automobiles just don't shine for me anymore; I want a rifle and a speculum, an office with a view and a few kids to leave at home with my husband. Forget you ever met me, if you can, though I'm everywhere, like Patty Hearst when she was on the lam only much more numerous. Most of the girls on your stage have made much funkier scenes than me, and tell me you haven't whored around yourself. Forgive my language, I don't mean to be unladylike, and I'm not angry at all, just a little disgusted at the double standard.

Last night I dreamed I was a dolphin and was swimming in the Black Sea with Isadora Duncan and being serenaded on the shoreline by Lebanese mariachis who were on a world-tour-for-peace mission. Isadora was like a sister to me and as we hugged and gossiped underwater we discovered ourselves in love, not with each other exactly but with everything, and our gratitude overflowed, wave upon wave.

The personal is political, remember? Or as I learned from you, everything is political. That's why you could send your goons around to take my title away. But money's only skin deep, and beauty's thicker than water, and any man who comes near me does so at his own risk. I have intimate friends. We understand each other. When one of us is in danger a kind of radar goes out and somebody comes to the rescue. There was a movie I saw once something like that but the friends were all boys. The political is personal, right? Our time has come.

When you think of me, daddy, look across your lawn and see the rainbow hanging in the sprinklers. I am the glint on the windshield of the oncoming car as you drive home from work to your cocktail. Flick on the radio and hear my voice selling you the come-ons you'll never use. Everyone I trust touches me, leaves me filled with inexpressible affection, a wireless eros binding us beyond sex, lovingly. It is a connection that can't be explained, least of all on television.

But in the street, yes, our ceremonies are happening all the time, those brief embraces shared on the sidewalk with different destinations in mind but entwining paths, and the conversations that digress endlessly and end in kisses. Your Sunday religion means less to me than a swimsuit; I and mine are devout in our unholy alliance with the living, celebrating our sexiness with the glamour of athletes and actresses, only more real, committed to drama which is history.

If they censor this tape, imagine your own: you are the most beautiful and talented young thing in the country, men will masturbate to your picture while you and yours have gone on to greater embraces, every day the world is revealed to you as a gift you pass on gladly because it keeps coming. The juice of summer makes you feel like a free country, in love with the future, humming a tune the beautiful can hear.

Oscar Night

[2013]

Watching the Academy Awards this year was even more painful than usual—not because of who won or did not win Oscars but that the show looked like amateur night at the fall of Rome. From the exceptionally obnoxious and unfunny master of ceremonies to the embarrassingly self-parodic (though perhaps postmodernly ironic) song-and-dance production numbers to poor best-actress winner Jennifer Lawrence tripping on her ridiculous dress as she ran up the steps to fetch her trophy, the whole spectacle reeked of Hollywood self-love/hate, vanity, bewilderment and panic at the fate of movies under the onslaught of private digital entertainment.

The same technology that enables filmmakers to stage ultraviolent apocalyptic visual orgies of mayhem without physically destroying too much property has also made movies, in the old-fashioned sense of something one goes out to see on a big screen with other people in the audience, all but obsolete. So Hollywood, like a publishing industry increasingly driven by ebooks and their instruments (if new multimedia book products can still be called books at all), is freaking out in the effort to adapt. Presumably in an appeal to smartphone-mesmerized youth by way of their great-grandparents' type of music-hall entertainment, The Oscars (don't call them the Academy Awards, as that sounds, well, academic) rolled out the singing and dancing movie stars to make fools of themselves in front of a billion or so voyeurs around the planet.

It's not that it was such a bad year for movies. A few of the nominated films actually had more to do with human beings (by way of the writing and acting) than with gee-whiz digital effects. *Lincoln*, *The Master*, *Silver Linings Playbook*, *Amour*, *Argo*, even *Zero Dark Thirty* examined humanity with some compassion. But the dominant trend in big-budget Hollywood spectacles (think *James Bond Diehard Zombie Killer Goes Ballistic*) remains a steroid-pumped testosterone-addled gun-worshiping explosion-happy bloodthirsty animated facelifted breast-inflated spectacle that translates easily into any language (since language is beside the point) for the international mass market. Smaller, more intimate, independent movies do get made, and sometimes even distributed but, like small-press literature, seldom reach big numbers of people.

I confess to having roots in both indy culture—having started a number of quixotic little publishing ventures—and, reaching deeper into my privileged past, the world of movie stars and media moguls. I used to feel ashamed at having grown up in Beverly Hills, but eventually I came to understand that it was not my fault that my father made a fortune in the garment business and moved the family there in 1950 to take advantage of that city's excellent schools. It was in those schools that I met, and selectively made friends with, many kids born with a silver screen in their mouth.

My big brother Bruce was a semi-famous racing driver in his twenties, which first led him to friendships with the likes of James Dean and Steve McQueen, and later to directing jobs in Hollywood where he enjoyed a long and lucrative career in television. My own schoolmates (but not friends) included such current eminences as Rob Reiner, Albert Brooks, Richard Dreyfuss and Academy president Howard "Hawk" Koch, most of whom went into the family business and have done as well as or better than their parents.

So I grew up in a Hollywood-centric universe and, though drawn as a clueless teenager to the "fast cars, fast girls" ethos of my brother and his friends, by the time I was a freshman at UCLA and discovering the inexplicable allure of poetry, I was already growing increasingly disillusioned with the emptiness and desperation I perceived behind the stylish façades of the LA movie illuminati. I fled that scene at nineteen, about the same time I stopped watching television, and took a left turn into literature, from which I've never found my way back.

But I love the cinema, and go to the movies whenever something worth seeing is playing, because at its best it is an amazing synthesis of the visual and dramatic and novelistic arts—storytelling of the highest order. A great movie can be as esthetically, intellectually and emotionally engrossing and moving and revelatory as practically any other experience, in or outside the arts. Screen gods and goddesses were born of this mythic storytelling power—since then abetted by ever-advancing technologies—to captivate the receptive imagination.

Our current movie culture, with its stars reduced to mere celebrities (even if they happen also to be first-rate artists) about whom we know more than we ever wished to, and with its shrinking share of the media landscape and therefore mythscape, is a rather pathetic shadow of its former glory. That glory may have been built on grand illusions, but somehow it was glorious and bigger than life and full of romance and adventure. I don't think it's only my own advancing years that make today's stars and their shrunken illusions seem so pitiful.

So to witness something like the Oscar show—probably no more decadent than ever but somehow so much cheesier with its facelifted, Botoxed leading men and surgically altered grand dames and nubile starlets sewn into absurd outfits and stumbling on their sky-high heels—is a sad reminder of how all-too-human the professionally famous are, and, once the layers of glamour armor are removed, how ordinary all but the most transcendently talented seem to be. A glimpse of the great Robert De Niro slumped half-asleep in his aisle seat having flown out from New York only to lose for best supporting actor was somehow emblematic of the whole disaster—as if the sight of the snarling troglodyte Quentin Tarantino clutching his little statue for *writing*, of all things, were not depressing enough. Clearly the industry doesn't know how to regain its dignity much less supremacy in the contemporary cultural landscape. Even forty years ago Marlon Brando had the self-respect not to show up to accept best-actor honors for his classic performance in *The Godfather*. It seemed the stars onstage at the Oscars this year were desperately dancing their socks off to keep from crying over their own irrelevance.

Because technology has always played an instrumental role

in cinema, evolving with the times to add sound, color, scope and special effects of all kinds, there's no reason to expect the magic made possible by computers to return anytime soon to merely human scale in the art of narration. And whatever kinds of movies are made in the years ahead, they are likely to be watched on the very devices—smartpads, dumbphones, wristbands, brainchips—now driving Hollywood nuts. The content provided to such devices will be targeted to individuals whose tastes in entertainment are tailored to suit their well-tracked consumer preferences. The movie theater as a public space, like the bookstore and the record shop, may continue to exist, but for a self-selected minority of retro-hipsters and old fogies who don't get all their kicks from a computer screen, however tiny and portable.

The fragmentation of the marketplace we're currently witnessing in the publishing and music industries will no doubt continue, with self-produced recordings and micro-brewed books proliferating for smaller and smaller markets yet also potentially empowered by the Internet to "go viral" at a moment's notice. My hope is that movies made on smaller budgets and at a human scale, like many of the independent productions currently circulating on DVD or, if they can find distributors, in whatever art-house cinemas are left, will begin to gain audiences tired of being assaulted by the brutality and inanity that now dominate the mass-market box-office blockbuster offerings that most of the public still seems to prefer.

As in other art forms struggling to adjust to changing cultural demands—dance, theater, opera, painting, poetry—perhaps movies can recapture some of their lost mojo by scaling down their more spectacular ambitions and attempting to hold people's attention (or at least the attention of a significant minority) with sensitive intelligence and subtle attunement to more intimate human experiences. Maybe all those mobile devices will enable some artists to reach people where they live and remind them they are not mere extensions of their gadgets and hapless victims of whatever the producers throw at them.

Or maybe I'm dreaming of a golden age that never was and never will be beyond the marginal communities created by out-of-the-way newspapers and low-budget online artifacts like the one you're reading. If you've read this far, you could be a member of this endangered species of new-old media users who don't need the self-debasing antics of overpaid, cosmetically enhanced, manufactured objects of desire and distraction to tell you how to stay brainlessly entertained.

Is California Wine Too Much of a Good Thing?

[2013]

One of the most delicious things about living in Santa Cruz in recent years is the abundance of excellent, more or less affordable restaurants with locally sourced organic foods and a dizzying array of very good wines to choose from. The far Westside, which used to be almost entirely industrial, has gradually been turning epicurean, with cafés and bakeries and brewpubs and pizzerias and wine-tasting rooms replacing little factories and warehouses. The wealth of these new businesses all over town greatly enhances our quality of life.

But as I travel in California outside Santa Cruz—in Monterey and San Luis Obispo and Santa Barbara and Sonoma and Napa and Mendocino counties—I have noticed a troubling transformation of the landscape: Where orchards and meadows and groves of trees used to be there are now grapes and more grapes as far as the eye can see. And I begin to wonder just how much wine we need to keep us happy in our Golden State.

I realize California's wineries are a booming industry and a boon to the economy, exporting much of what they produce and bringing in tons of money and pleasing tourists by giving them lovely places to stop and sip off the fat of the land. And there is nothing like an alcoholic drink or two to loosen up one's shopping inhibitions. Without its wine, the state would yield much less homegrown pleasure and economic activity for natives and visitors alike.

Still, the sprawling monoculture of vineyards deserves a hard look for its esthetic as well as environmental impacts. The amount of herbicides and pesticides used on California's vineyards is staggering—more than 20 million pounds per year—and the soil must be replenished with chemical fertilizers. This can't be healthy for the environment, the workers or the consumers, and is a strong and rational argument in favor of small, organic growers.

And does anyone really prefer the rigid, rectilinear, almost military look of rows and rows and rows of tied-up grapevines to the grace of trees and rolling hills and grasses? Orchards too are planted in rows but at least they cast some shade and absorb some carbon. The current legal battle over a clearcut of redwoods in Sonoma County by a Spanish company that wants to plant more grapes exemplifies the worst and most destructive tendencies of a wine industry run amok. For the sake of the watersheds, and the visual appearance and health of the natural landscape, there should be a limit on how much wine can be grown.

I can imagine a time when there is so much wine grown in California—our signature crop, like Idaho potatoes or Iowa corn or Cuban sugar—that non-viticultural rural real estate becomes nearly nonexistent, whole counties planted from here to hell with wall-to-wall grapes. It would be tragic if such a tasty fruit were to spread with such viral virulence as to become a blight on the state.

I enjoy a glass of good wine as much as anyone—and am glad that some of my friends are in the business—but I know when enough is enough.

Geezers, Relax, It's Okay to Be Old

[2014]

For the past several years I've been taking advantage of my advancing age by enjoying the senior discount here and there, especially at the movies. The previews of coming attractions (at least at the theaters I frequent) often seem to be stories of old people falling in love or acting otherwise a fraction of their age in uplifting, feel-good, childlike antics even if in the setting of some nursing home. I never go see these films because they tend to infantilize the elderly, as if there were something wrong with acting one's age.

In most traditional cultures, elders are accorded a certain respect for their having survived an extended period of time, and for their presumed wisdom. While certainly in the United States there are plenty of clueless older people, there is something to be said for accepting with grace the reality of a certain physical diminishment, which at least in some cases is offset by gains in self-knowledge, an enriched understanding of the world and its workings, and a certain satisfaction in having come through the ordeals and absurdities of existence, and perhaps even accomplished or contributed something. Such older folks enjoy a sense of confidence and self-respect that compensates for the wear and tear of time.

But television commercials and the cosmetically altered visages of aging movie stars (remember a grotesquely facelifted Kirk Douglas at the Oscars a couple of years ago, or the stretched and stitched-up mug of Sylvester Stallone?) would have us think that aging is a disease that must be treated with pharmaceutical interventions—if not cosmetic surgery then at least testosterone gels or "erectile dysfunction" drugs that promise to resurrect our drooping manhood. As if a decline in libido where not in fact the most natural thing in the world for men of a certain vintage, we are urged to believe there is something pathological about being less horny than we were a few decades ago.

Perhaps just as pathetic as the fitness-obsessed, sexually striving, hair-dyed dudes who cannot bear to concede they are past their physical prime and are too hung-up on their fading physiques to notice what they might know, are the codgers who look their age but haven't outgrown their adolescence, so they feel they must assert their lost machismo by wearing a t-shirt that proclaims: OLD GUYS RULE. To these contemporaries of mine, I say: No, we don't rule, and we don't need to; what we need is a little dignity.

The notion that pseudo-youthful looks (which far more often look ridiculous on age-inappropriate bodies) and sexual athleticism are the only things worth living for reveals a failure of imagination. Testosterone causes more problems than it solves, and the pleasures of growing older—if one's health holds out—include not only remembering the romance of earlier days and nights but perceiving with poignant sensitivity the transient delights of the ongoing show, the daily dramas we witness in ordinary human interactions. To observe with a certain compassionate detachment the behavior of our fellow creatures is one of the gifts of being old enough to know better. I would rather harvest and savor such wealth of experience than try to impersonate a self that no longer exists.

As Heraclitus and Ecclesiastes both observed long ago, all things come in seasons.

An Unknown Artist, Even to Herself

[2012]

Vivian Maier (1926–2009) was a career nanny in New York and Chicago who in her free time carried a camera on the streets of those cities and through the years around mid-century took more than one hundred thousand pictures, only a fraction of which were ever developed and even fewer printed. After her death a young historian, John Maloof, purchased Maier's archive when it was auctioned out of its Chicago storage locker and discovered an astonishing trove of images—spontaneous black-and-white shots of people, mostly, of various ages and social standing but mainly invisible types—old men and women, derelicts, children, unknown citizens going and coming from work or shopping or mere survival, the expression on each face or language of each body suggesting a privately epic tale of human existence.

With perfectly timed clicks of her shutter—and a sharp eye for striking composition and implicit drama—Maier caught these moments of city life with great compassion, her cool empathy somehow evincing in her subjects their unconscious cooperation so that deep humanity is revealed in both the photographed and the photographer. The belated discovery of Maier's work has led thus far to several shows in Europe and the States and to a book, *Vivian Maier: Street Photographer* (PowerHouse Books), which have revealed her to be one of the outstanding practitioners of this genre. I would put her pictures up against anyone's—Elliott Erwitt, Lee Friedlander, Diane Arbus, Robert Frank, Ruth Orkin, Garry Winograd, Rebecca Lepkoff, Weegee, Brassai—as consummate examples of the art.

(Another great street photographer, much published but with no artistic pretenses, is Bill Cunningham of *The New York Times*, whose photo-essay on popular fashion trends appears every Sunday in the Style section. Cunningham, now in his eighties, rides his bicycle around Manhattan shooting what he sees as various forms of vernacular flair and elegance in pedestrians' dress. The wonderful documentary *Bill Cunningham New York* is an inspiring portrait of someone with the soul of a true artist. Also a photographer of society affairs, the monklike Cunningham declines a hostess in the film who invites him to dine with the guests, cheerfully replying, "I eat with my eyes.")

Little is known about Vivian Maier, but one thing is clear: she had no ambition for a career as a professional artist. Whatever inspired her to take all those pictures, fame and fortune were not among her motives. It may not even have been art for art's sake, or conceived as art at all, but something moved her to document what she saw, to use her extraordinary eye and sympathetic insight to catch a vast collage of human experience and urban serendipity and then to put most of the pictures on ice indefinitely with little chance of their ever being discovered. I imagine she felt intense infusions of joy from the click of her Rolleiflex with an image passing just so through its viewfinder, an image she was able to *see*, and to sense its transient eternity.

While in New York in January I saw a show of Maier's pictures in a high-end gallery on 57th Street and was happily stunned to discover them. After marveling at their still yet moving beauty, I stepped back outside into midtown Manhattan with my senses sharply refreshed, reminded that the simple act of paying attention—especially in such a swarming human landscape—can reveal endless wealth to the observing eye, the listening ear, the nose alert for reality. Maier's utterly modest yet subtly ambitious art reminded me again that, even though I'd seen it in a fourteenth-floor gallery, a down-to-earth engagement with the world is all the foundation one needs to begin constructing a masterpiece.

Maier's modesty is understandable, given her job of caring for others' children, her never pairing up and her plain looks—revealed in several self-portraits shot in shop windows with other reflections and dimensions interestingly complicating the composition—and her solitary wanderings suggest a soul at home in its aloneness, perhaps akin to Emily Dickinson. But this first taste of her work is a revelation, and I look forward to seeing much more of it as she becomes more visible in the years ahead. And I can't help wondering how many other such unknown artists have been hidden among us, not driven enough to wish to make even the smallest name for themselves, content (or at least willing) to work at the extreme margins, beyond the marketplace, where virtually no one will notice.

We all know people who work diligently, with varying levels of skill, and try without success to be published or discovered in one form or another. And we know too well the ongoing contest for stardom among brand-name artists and writers and musicians—the vast vanity of celebrity—but the absence of such ambition embodied by Vivian Maier combined with her astounding gifts of vision feels to me quite rare. And yet surely there are thousands of obscure masters who have practiced their craft assiduously without it ever seeing the light of day.

So in addition to making me see the world in a fresh way, Maier's pictures succeed in making me think of art and the artist's job in a different light—not of career or reputation or public presentation but the anonymous act of attention, the presence of mind that records and thereby creates something—some moment, some expression, some perception—worth saving. In this acute attentiveness it is the act itself that matters; what follows is of little or no concern.

Last summer I spoke at a panel in San Francisco on the topic of projecting one's work into the world, a theme at odds with the privacy and modesty of Vivian Maier's project—far more in tune with our contemporary culture of exhibitionism, of blogs and YouTube uploads and Facebook mugging and Twitter blather and reality TV. Among writers both amateur and professional, everybody and their cousin wants to publish and can do so with the technology at hand; a few clicks and you're "live," your words or sounds or images flashing around the globe at the speed of light. Indeed all three other people on the panel with me spoke of ways to exploit the Internet as a means of reaching the maximum number of readers. By now even Vivian Maier's pictures are out there for all to see and download, so even she can't escape the currency she managed to elude during her lifetime. But as my fellow-panelists were excitedly explaining how to make one's work go viral in the virtual world, I couldn't help feeling out of place in the conversation.

True, I've published a lot, in various forms and media, and if, in the 1960s and 70s when I was starting out, the Internet had been available, I surely would have jumped into its Web like pretty much everyone else is doing now. But at this stage of life I look back at those early strivings for attention as youthful folly, premature ejaculations, unripe harvests, unready revelations of whatever I had to say. And if I could do it again I would wait a while, because poetry (or any art) that's fresh and true to life stays new whenever (or whether or not) it may go public. It was Horace (65–8 BCE) who famously counseled "nine years in the drawer" before a poem is ready for publication.

For better or worse, a lot of talented, hardworking, committed, creative people are never acknowledged for the work they've done beyond a small circle of friends—if that—while lots of on-the-make, self-promoting, variously talented bullshit artists rise to the heights of "success" on the strength of some combination of salesmanship, connections, gumption, persistence, marketing and luck.

Literature, I've come to understand, is not a popularity contest. The same goes for painting, music, dance, photography, sculpture, theater, cinema—so many of the greatest films I've seen have been commercial flops—and life itself. Many of the most gifted, dedicated, authentic artists I know have minimal or nonexistent public profiles, and their anonymity doesn't in the least diminish their accomplishment. I think of my friend Greg Hall, who died at sixty-two, unknown as a poet outside the few dozen people he shared his work with over the years; who made his living in nursing homes and hospitals, but on his own time created an exceptionally rich body of work. Or the legendary Santa Cruz psychedelic bluegrass band from the early 1970s, Oganookie, whose five virtuoso musicians eventually split up as a group and went on to other professions—law, dentistry, teaching—but have continued to play music at a very high level for their own pleasure ever since. Or others, including some RCR contributors, who toil in obscurity on poems and stories and novels and visual art that may or may not ever see print or a gallery wall. They can self-publish if they wish to, of course, or launch their pixels on the rolling seas of the Web, but being "discovered" is almost out of the question.

As Vivian Maier's strange career arc proves, however, such a discovery may eventually happen. Or maybe not. And if it does not, so what—the loss is ours, that is, the world's—yet that does not negate the mundane miracle of what Maier did with her life, and by extension what anyone of similar devotion to a vision may achieve. The evidence shows she was completely engaged in what she was doing with her instrument, her camera, and through its lens found a deep connection with the world, and with other people, even if she never met them or knew their names, and though neither they nor scarcely anyone else ever knew hers. The click of the shutter that catches life in flight, the hours in the studio immersed in the act of art, the timeless minutes at one's writing table when the words are streaming like sunlight onto the page—such moments of creation are ends in themselves and their own reward.

Stein versus Salomon at the Jewish Museum

[2010]

Was it a subversive stroke of curatorial genius or just a perverse coincidence that San Francisco's Contemporary Jewish Museum mounted concurrently this summer its Charlotte Salomon and Gertrude Stein exhibits? Stein of course is the Mother of All Modernists, the Paris salonkeeper who not only cultivated the budding geniuses of Picasso and Hemingway and Matisse among many others but was herself a formidable literary force, a daring experimenter with language who—for better and for worse—has influenced generations of writers. Salomon was a young German woman who had the bad luck to come of age just as the Nazis were coming to power and, despite fleeing to the south of France in 1938, was arrested there in 1943 and sent to her death at Auschwitz. She was twenty-six.

Salomon was an artist, writer and musician who authored a single sustained work, *Life? or Theatre?*, a series of several hundred gouache paintings with text telling a highly imaginative version of her life story, including a "soundtrack" of German popular and classical music—what today might be called a mixed-media or multimedia piece, or the book for a musical tragicomedy, or a graphic novel. Whatever it is, it was truly experimental for its time, but with none of the intellectual trappings or glamour of Stein's Parisian salons. Stein, much older and making her way assiduously up the cultural hierarchy as an avant-garde tastemaker, reputation-establisher and high priestess of Modernism, was about as far from Salomon's circumstances as can be imagined, but both were in France at the same time and both were Jewish. Yet they experienced very different fates and fortunes.

The Salomon exhibit was a linear tour through a substantial portion—about three hundred painted pages out of more than seven hundred—of *Life? or Theatre?* To follow the tragic story of the artist's family, including the suicides of her mother and grandmother, her own coming of age and falling in love with her music teacher, her exile and ultimate doom under France's Vichy regime, is to be moved both by the urgent energy and beauty of the work and by the terrible sadness of her young death. You wonder what she might have become as an artist, writer and/or musician had she had the chance, but because she happened to be Jewish at a time in Europe when that was a death sentence, all we have of her is this one epic work.

The Stein show, just upstairs, was a completely different kind of exhibition—not of the writer's writings nor of the art patron's collection, but a tour of her personage at home in Paris of the 1920s and 30s—many photos and portraits of Stein by her pet artists (and portraits of her white French poodle), her home décor, her clothes, her jewelry, swatches of wallpaper, restaurant menus, napkins, newspaper clippings, magazine pages, editions of her books—an artifactual record of her cultural persona, the *things* in her domestic and public life that defined her. I could feel as I strolled through this elaborate collection of artifacts the storied force of Stein's formidable personality, her tireless promotion of her favored artists and of herself, her mastery of the art of self-mythmaking. A genius in her own mind, she aggressively championed that idea in the minds of others, and through a shrewd combination of true accomplishment and skillful public relations established a permanent place for herself in twentieth-century cultural history.

Ezra Pound, her chief American expatriate rival for the throne of modernist pope, referred to Stein as "that old tub of guts," according to poet and publisher James Laughlin, who worked for both of them one summer as a Harvard student in Europe. Stein in turn dismissed Pound as "a village explainer." These two monumental egos, like King Kong and Godzilla, fought it out between the wars to determine who could be the bigger blowhard, know-it-all and scoutmaster of up-and-coming literary talent. One thing they had in common was a fondness for fascists: Stein publicly endorsed Franco during the Spanish Civil War and translated for American readers the speeches of Vichy leader Maréchal Pétain (whom she compared to George Washington) during the Nazi occupation of France, while Pound in Italy affiliated himself with Mussolini and famously ranted on the radio during World War II about the sinister conspiracies of Jewish bankers.

Despite her Jewish background, Stein breezed through the war unscathed, protected by her alliance with Bernard Fay, director of France's Bibliothèque Nationale. (This relationship is explored by Stein scholar Barbara Will in her book *Unlikely Collaboration.*) In other words, Stein was a collaborator with the Vichy government and, by association, with the Nazis. She told *The New York Times Magazine* in 1934, perhaps sarcastically, that Hitler deserved the Nobel Peace Prize "because he is removing all the elements of contest and struggle from Germany. By driving out the Jews and the democratic left element, he is driving out everything that conduces to activity. That means peace." Even if, as seems plausible, she was being sarcastic, in light of history this is a rather lame idea of a joke.

None of this is mentioned in the Jewish Museum exhibition, certainly an odd omission in this context, and doubly disturbing when considered alongside the story of Charlotte Salomon, who, lacking Stein's connections and not sharing her political sympathies, was left to a less distinguished destiny. How the museum could have mounted both shows without acknowledging this grim irony is something I'm still trying to figure out. Was it, as noted above, a subtle and profound curatorial comment on the terrible contradictions of these parallel exhibitions? Or was it simply a sign of cluelessness to celebrate Stein the shameless self-promoter and collaborator directly upstairs from the desperate creation of a victim of those she was collaborating with?

Crisis, experience teaches, tends to bring out people's true character. Knowing her days were likely numbered, from 1941 to 1943 Charlotte Salomon threw herself feverishly into painting and writing an artistic record of her life. As a Jewish woman she understood her prospects were bleak, yet rather than despair and follow her mother and grandmother into self-destruction, she embarked on the path of creation and managed to leave an extraordinary testimony of her difficult existence. Under such depressing circumstances this strikes me as a remarkably courageous course of action. It does not, as the cliché has it, reveal "the triumph of the human spirit"—quite the contrary, her spirit was brutally exterminated—but it does show that a human being can summon the gumption to go down fighting for life in the form of a deathless work of art. In such disheartening conditions I wonder whether I could have risen to the occasion with such creative aplomb.

Stein, in her way, also revealed her character during the war. Her choice was to preserve her privilege (unlike such non-Jewish intellectuals as Beckett and Camus who worked in support of the Resistance) in order not only to live in comfort but to promote her esthetic program. A lifelong conservative Republican, she apparently had no serious problem accommodating herself to a fascist French government in the interest of staying alive and furthering her cause of literary and artistic experimentation. Her commitment to her own genius and creative agenda overrode whatever moral qualms she may or may not have had about the Holocaust in progress all around her. Perhaps she was oblivious or willfully ignorant of the ambient atrocities—and who knows to what lengths people will be driven in their instinct for self-preservation—but there is something exceedingly creepy about her cultivation of her own importance in a such a horrendous historical setting.

That the Contemporary Jewish Museum, of all places, should avoid these questions completely strikes me as nothing less than obscene.

But such are the politics of cultural celebrity—and of marketing. To raise such questions in public (if indeed they were privately discussed or debated among the curators) would have utterly changed the tone and poisoned the atmosphere of self-congratulation permeating the Stein exhibition, all the more so in light of Charlotte Salomon's fate.

Equally revealing of the compound ironies embodied by these simultaneous shows was the fact that, on the Friday afternoon when I saw them both, the galleries of the Salomon exhibit were all but empty—affording me the chance to contemplate the art with virtually no distraction, pausing before the artist's pages long enough to absorb their unspeakably sad beauty—while upstairs the Stein show was swarming with voyeurs, just as Gertrude would have wished. She self-fulfillingly prophesied her own immortality, and indeed in this exhibition her particular brand of highbrow exhibitionism reached its apotheosis. She herself, or her enduring afterimage, had become the indestructible artifact. Her writings, patronage and collecting, it seems, were merely means to an end: the creation of her own towering legend.

Stein died at age seventy-two in 1946, and so did not live to witness our current culture of competitive celebrity, but I expect she would have felt fully at home in our multimedia spectacle of personality and taken advantage of every chance to advance her personal fame. Charlotte Salomon, like some geeky graphic novelist or librettist or mixed-media artist, would likely also have made some modest mark in our cultural landscape. But the contrast between these artists' destinies, the triumph of one's indomitable will in the afterlife and the relative obscurity of the other—even though her snuffed-out gifts showed enormous accomplishment and promise—is something I find very hard to accept.

Forbidden Island

[1984]

It's hot in Havana in the middle of June. Sitting in the back seat of a Soviet sedan parked in the loading zone at José Martí International Airport, sweat running down me like a waterfall, I could think of nothing better than a cool swim in the Caribbean. With a North American eye for cars as icons, I couldn't help noticing the 1950s-vintage Chevys, Fords and Buicks scattered among the Ladas in the parking lot. People waiting for friends and family to come through customs were crowded around the airport doors; unlike most such terminals I've passed through, technology didn't dominate the scene.

I'd come to Cuba as a delegate of the San Francisco committee of the Intellectuals' Meeting for the Sovereignty of the Peoples of Our America, a project launched in 1981 some months after the election of Ronald Reagan. A gathering was held in Havana in September of that year, under the auspices of Casa de las Américas, which brought together more than three hundred writers, artists and other cultural workers from all over Latin America and the Caribbean to discuss the problems of human rights, freedom of expression, political tyranny and military intervention faced by the peoples of the hemisphere, and to propose cooperative actions intellectuals might take in dealing with these cultural and political issues.

Three years later, after subsequent meetings in Mexico City and Managua, Casa de las Américas invited representatives from the various national committees to report on the work of their respective groups, and I was sent to give an account of our efforts (thus far unsuccessful) to organize a meeting in the States on the model of the Dialogue of the Americas held in 1982 in Mexico. Perhaps as important, the conference this June in Havana was an opportunity to interact informally and exchange ideas with a number of *compañeros* from other countries.

Casa de las Américas is a cultural institution founded in the spring of 1959, shortly after the triumph of the Cuban Revolution. Its festivals, art exhibits and publications have drawn the participation of most of Latin America's outstanding creative workers; the annual literary awards, judged each year by a different panel of eminent writers, are among the most prestigious in the Spanish-speaking world. In the 1960s, when Cuba was ostracized by the Latin American political community (Mexico being the only country that didn't interrupt diplomatic relations), Casa de las Américas kept the country culturally in touch with its neighbors. As I was to discover during my weeklong stay, the Casa remains, after twenty-five years, an actively dynamic organization.

My wish for a dip in the Caribbean came true soon enough. After being met at the airport by the suave Conrado Bulgado, one of the Casa's social directors and foreign-relations functionaries, I was driven to the Havana Riviera, where the rest of our party—an assortment of writers, cultural activists, artists and one priest, from Costa Rica, Panama, the Dominican Republic, Puerto Rico, Chile, Uruguay, Brazil, Grenada, Jamaica, Trinidad, Barbados, Spain and Sweden (where there are large Latin American exile communities)—was preparing for an outing to the beach. It was Sunday, no meetings were scheduled, and our Cuban hosts seemed more than eager to show us a good time and demonstrate their tropical hospitality.

We were bused to a lovely beach house east of Havana, where a team of bartenders was breaking out the rum and mixing a variety of indigenous drinks to cool us out for the afternoon. After a couple of mojitos (a refreshing and powerful combination of rum, lime, mint, sugar, sparkling water and ice) and some snappy chatter with the comrades, I retreated for a plunge in the green Caribbean, relieved and delighted to be in this water so soon after getting off the plane.

It was a beautiful afternoon, with continuous servings of drinks and hors d'oeuvres, followed by the arrival of Cuba's minister of culture, Armando Hart, and intense discussions of politics and the role of religion in popular movements in the region. While novelist George Lamming of Barbados complained that the evangelical Christian crusade in the Caribbean and Central America is "a political virus," and Fray Beito, the Brazilian priest, replied that the only way to combat this virus is to not let people forget that "Jesus was a political prisoner," Hart pointed out that the moral and ethical element in the church is its revolutionary force—Nicaragua being an example of a Catholic country whose church has been instrumental in mobilizing the population.

The themes of politics and religion were to recur and intertwine throughout the several days of meetings, alongside the realities of food and drink, which our hosts lavished on us with an almost excessive extravagance. Sunday's beach party culminated in a huge buffet whose variety and quantity of dishes could have fed a group far larger than the thirty or so people in attendance. I assumed that the cooks and bartenders and their families would finish what the guests couldn't. We returned to the hotel sated (I hadn't drunk so much rum since the cocktail party two years ago in Mexico City at the home of the Cuban ambassador), our brains primed for the next few days of serious work and tourism.

The Havana Riviera is an air-conditioned nightmare more than twenty stories tall built in the 1950s by legendary Mafioso Meyer Lansky and expropriated after the Revolution for use by the National Tourism Institute. Situated around the corner from Casa de las Américas, it's a convenient and well-appointed place to lodge official visitors. The front of the building faces north, toward Florida, and through the lobby's enormous windows one notices lots of freighters and tankers on the horizon—no less than four or five at a time—steaming in or out of the port of Havana. International languages abound: I heard voices from Latin America, Eastern and Western Europe, the Soviet Union and Scandinavia, among others. Since a significant portion of the Caribbean population is black, the racial heterogeneity of the guests was also far more visible than in most North American luxury hotels. Asians, however, were noticeably absent.

There's an acute shortage of consumer goods in Cuba—due in part to the US trade embargo—but the hotel gift shops are pretty well stocked with items desired by the average tourist: most notably clothing, tennis shoes, records and tapes. Ironically, the Yankee dollar is the preferred currency in these shops, which places the dollar in great demand among natives unable to purchase things in other stores. Walking the streets of Havana, I was approached by numerous young people eager to trade their pesos for bucks, with which they might buy the jeans or sneakers or cassette recorders they crave. It seemed a little strange to me that most Cubans should be deprived of these things so easily obtained by tourists.

Outside the hotels there is a general feeling of austerity. Due to the shortage of paint, many of the buildings have a run-down appearance, the combination of salty sea wind and humidity imposing a constant wear-and-tear that leaves its mark on the Spanish colonial architecture. And perhaps the most obvious civic problem is public transportation: the buses tend to be old and overcrowded, often leaving potential passengers stranded on the corner waiting for the next one and hoping it will stop to let them on.

Cuba's poverty gives it the look and feeling of a third-world country, which it is, but the poorest of Cuba's poor don't seem half as bad off as their counterparts in Central America or Mexico. There are health clinics in virtually every neighborhood, open night and day, into which anyone can walk and receive free medical treatment. Education is also free and universal, no doubt loaded with political biases, as is ours in the States, but breeding a certain alertness that encourages critical thinking: the young Cubans I met were earnest and articulate—sharp-minded—whatever their politics.

Latinos love to talk, the Spanish language is a feast of delicious phrasing, so discussing politics is an almost sensuous proposition. Our meetings and off-the-record conversations were laced with political themes, which are inescapable in any country as politically sensitized as Cuba. While Cuba's social reality appeared to me to be as riddled with contradictions as anyplace else, what distinguishes Cuba from the rest of Latin America and makes it a beacon and an inspiration to people fighting for independence is Cuba's ability, at whatever cost (and with Soviet support), to tell the Yankees to bug off.

North American domination of the Caribbean and Latin America has a been a daily reality for generations, so when a Central American or West Indian militant uses words like "imperialism," he's not just mouthing rhetoric like some textbook radical. The recurrent urgent theme of our talks at the Casa was the fear abroad in the hemisphere that Ronald Reagan may be reelected and embark on some cowboy-style conflagration. Each national committee reported on its efforts to mobilize artists and intellectuals in the contest of ideas and imagination that must play a key role in any political struggle.

Although there were various political philosophies represented at the conference table, there was total solidarity in opposition to further armed intervention in the region following the invasion of Grenada. Reagan is seen as a gravely dangerous individual whose policies and propaganda must be fought by all available means. Culture is considered a unifying force, a creative instrument for demonstrating morality, an instiller of revolutionary values. By forming friendships and sharing information and encouraging one another to carry on, the Intellectuals' Meeting is attempting to multiply and strengthen the connections of that force for unity.

That's why Casa de las Américas is such a vital institution: it has invited the liveliest minds and most gifted creative spirits of Latin America to enjoy the shelter of its sponsorship. As Armando Hart kept reminding us, culture can be the spearhead of political transformation. Book fairs, festivals and exhibitions have an important educational value. The mass media—print and electronic—are major factors in shaping as well as reflecting current events. In Latin America, according to Hart, the intellectual is more integrated into popular and political culture than in Europe or the US, and naturally is more disposed to reach for means of mass communication.

The common ground between Marxism and Christianity, said Hart, is in the moral realm. While a revolutionary government should keep its nose out of artists' formal experiments and encourage imaginative explorations of diverse media, "we are not going to allow counterrevolutionary content in our art." Precisely what such content might consist of I was never able to determine but there is in Cuba some line of criticism or dissent beyond which one isn't permitted to cross without repercussions. When I questioned Roberto Fernández Retamar, editor of *Casa de las Américas* magazine, one of the world's outstanding literary journals, about freedom of the press, he assured me that "there is no censorship in Cuba." Of course, he added, we don't publish everything. "There is a very famous publication—I believe it is not a communist publication—which has as its motto 'All the news that's fit to print.' We also publish all the news that's fit to print."

Granma, the official organ of the Central Committee of the Cuban Communist Party and the most widely available daily paper, is about as reliable a source of news as the *San Francisco*

Chronicle. In the upper left-hand corner of the front page of every issue the reader finds an excerpt from the wisdom of Fidel Castro, usually a paragraph or two from a speech in which he exhorts the people to work hard for the Revolution and against the imperialist menace. The rest of the paper is a kind of scoreboard detailing, with a maximum of righteousness and a minimum of analysis, all the great things the socialists did today and all the terrible exploits of the capitalists. Ideally, for ideological balance, one should read *Granma* alongside *The Washington Times* or *The Wall Street Journal*.

Cubans can sometimes pick up mainland radio from Miami and get the Voice of America on the shortwave, so there's no shortage of right-wing propaganda. My impression was that those who believe in the Revolution are willing to make sacrifices for what they hope will be a better life in the future. It is a constant effort, but the dignity gained by the population with the overthrow of the dictator Batista (and his Yankee backers) makes Castro's regime seem heroic, even benevolent, to many.

Among the writers and activists I was with there was a universal admiration for Fidel, even though individuals took issue with his policies. I found a willingness among my fellow visitors to question frankly and critique some aspects of Cuba's political rigidity, but always with respect for its achievement of independence. The US embargo has obviously hurt Cuba economically, but now there is an element of national pride in Castro's defensive posture toward the States. (Jesse Jackson's accomplishment on his pending diplomatic mission could be a breakthrough toward dissolving this stance of reaction.)

The "fever of ideas" which Armando Hart invoked in his closing remarks to our meeting represents the essence of "our moral force" as artists and writers, he said; creative work is the most human expression of politics. Diplomacy, the art of being able to speak with one another, is the political arm of this cultural campaign. "Art," he said, quoting Antonio Gramsci, "is politically useful always, as long as it is *art*" (not propaganda). "Dogmatism, sectarianism and division," Hart admitted, "are the biggest problems the Revolution has."

Hart's speech went on for nearly an hour, official video cameras and tape recorders blazing away in the conference room at Casa de las Américas; I noted that my Puerto Rican colleague was denied permission to tape the talk herself. Highly developed countries, Hart said, have in many cases lost touch with the popular roots of their culture. Folk art and music are more vigorous in the Caribbean and Latin America than they are in Europe because in developing nations these arts are connected to their popular roots. And, he added, most of the leading artists in these forms tend to be politically on the left.

"Commitment," said Hart, "is part of our cultural tradition; the artistic vanguard is linked to revolutionary change." He also stressed the importance of positive relations with Christian movements because the broad popular base of the church must always be respected. "We must study the religious element not from a theoretical or philosophical point of view but from an ethical and political perspective."

After this lofty discourse, the Cuba libres and mojitos and hors d'oeuvres were passed around, and the assembled delegates and media people milled excitedly about, taking the conversation in more personal directions. I had a funny conversation with eighty-year-old Panamanian novelist Rogelio Sinán, who compared the mint in his mojito to the marijuana plants some South American diplomat used to grow in his courtyard in Panama. Sinán, a longtime leftist, was much amused when I told him of the legendary herb known in California as Panama Red.

After a few drinks our group was rounded up and bused back to the Riviera with instructions to appear in the lobby at ten o'clock for a field trip to the Tropicana, Havana's answer to Las Vegas, a nightclub under the stars with a (presumably socialist) floor show. We were escorted down front, of course, where we could get a closeup view of the wiggling torsos of the dancing girls and boys all shaking their stuff to the accompaniment of an orchestra and chorus of salsa technicians. I smoked a cigar and ogled the spectacle along with the rest of the tourists in attendance, sipping rum and Tropi-Cola and gobbling little morsels of baked ham.

The connection between religion and politics became clearer to me every day in Cuba, although probably not in the way the minister of culture meant it. I saw how faith in the Revolution is reinforced by iconographic images: José Martí, Fidel and Che Guevara are the father, the son and the holy ghost of the Cuban Revolution, and their pictures—especially Che's—are visible in public and private places as iconic reminders of the movement's ideals. Martí and Che, being dead, are more easily idolized than Castro, and those who don't see Fidel as a savior may view him as a demagogue, a tyrant wielding power as absolute as, say, Haile Selassie's in Ethiopia during his lengthy reign.

Wandering around Havana on my own on my last day there, I was approached by a young black man who initiated a friendly conversation. I joined him and some of his buddies, cats in their mid-twenties, sitting on a park bench and we raved for a while about sports and pop music and politics in the US, of which they had only fragmentary news. They were excited about Jesse Jackson's impending visit and wanted to know how Jackson was regarded in the States, and whether Reagan might pick him as a running mate. I told them there wasn't much chance of that, nor did I have any inside information as to whether Brooke Shields was really going to marry Michael Jackson.

These guys were warm and animated people hungry for contact with US popular culture, which they feel is closely linked with their own as part of their living heritage: Stevie Wonder is as American as José Martí. To be deprived of access to such resources makes them angry. They want interaction with North Americans, so to them a person from California with any degree of hipness is like a messenger from an exotic realm they can only imagine through their TV sets.

Our conversation soon turned political. It was a hot day, and I asked if we could find a place to have a beer and continue the discussion. Three of them—Raúl, José and Luis—joined me in the search for cerveza, which proved fruitless because there is a beer shortage in Cuba and you can't find a bottle in the bars between certain hours. We settled for Tropi-Cola in a little café by the port. Everyone was eager to talk, asking each other questions and answering with opinionated enthusiasm. When my queries became too directly political, my companions lowered their voices so as not to be heard by nearby customers; but the urgency with which these guys expressed themselves testified to the fact that they didn't often have the chance to speak this way, honestly sharing their thoughts with a stranger.

Raúl proposed that I record their comments, which seemed fair enough to me since I'd been taping conversations with writers all week and had been interviewed twice myself for Cuban radio. We made plans to meet that night where we'd first run into each other, in the park in front of the Museum of the Revolution, which was closed for repairs. I returned with my Sony around 9 pm and we walked to the stone wall across from the lighthouse at the mouth of the port, ships going in and out tooting their horns and a fire blazing in some oil tank up in the harbor spewing its black smoke and burning a gorgeous orange.

There were only four of us but in the course of our stroll my companions would signal by whistling to their partners out of sight, communicating locations and who knows what else. They were assuming acoustic command of this turf, monitoring the terrain as subtly as possible. Born around the time of the Revolution, growing up as their president was consolidating his power—the charismatic Fidel assuming personal and absolute control—these dudes were ready to flex their muscles and exercise some authority of their own. They were physically in good shape, working ordinary jobs—teaching physical education, working on a fishing boat, studying to be an engineer—and as cynical about their government as most of us are about ours.

"For Cuban youth life is pretty monotonous," said Raúl. "Sure, we have free health care and education. But we don't have freedom. We have no freedom of speech, we cannot have a demonstration. We are not allowed to travel. We want to be able to know the world like the youth of other countries. We want democracy here in Cuba."

When a passerby would approach we'd change the subject or flip on the Sony's radio and pretend to be grooving to the music. They were amazed by this machine, wanted to know how much it cost and could I bring them one when I came back. The same for my t-shirt and Levis, they wanted to get their hands on some of this stuff we in the US take for granted. Raúl, the most talkative of the three, said the reason they wanted to talk to me was to let people outside know that there are many problems in Cuba that the government doesn't publicize. He assured me that in the port of Havana—the old colonial neighborhood slowly being restored—there are families living five and six people to a room in virtually ruined buildings, and that there is much more crime and delinquency than reported.

Asked what he'd do if Cuba were invaded by the United States, José replied that he'd "take advantage of the confusion to escape the country." Raúl said he didn't think the US would "stain its dignity" by attacking Cuba and that anyway the Soviets are too well established on the island for the US to risk a confrontation. All three expressed a desire to be friends with the people of the United States and engage in full social and cultural interaction. They blamed communism, not the American embargo, for the denial of these rights.

It struck me that these guys might represent a new generation of rebels. Their politics were less ideological than experiential, even though they had their own ideas about communism and democracy. They wanted access to ways of life more interesting and varied than what was offered them, and I imagined that some of today's Cuban adolescents may be the next wave of cultural revolutionaries, kids born since the revolution who've never known anything else and are more and more curious about the outside world, including the material pleasures of capitalism. As things are, you can't leave the country except with government approval, and to leave without it means a one-way trip.

I thought of my hosts' generosity at Casa de las Américas, the way the arts are actively promoted and the encouragement given cultural workers, and I wondered if this intellectual vanguard isn't the new social elite in revolutionary Cuba. Cuba's artists are among its greatest political resources, according to what Armando Hart was saying, so they would naturally enjoy a certain prestige. But workers, like anywhere else—and poor black workers especially—appear to be missing many of the benefits of Cuba's cultural renaissance, even though they can attend exhibits and concerts and movies at little cost. The fact remains that while visiting intellectuals are feasting at the state's expense in their hotels, there are people on the streets who are equally hungry for those little extras in life that lure the tourists.

Standing in the midnight bus en route back to the Riviera, I noticed a Nicaraguan passport sticking up out of the shirt pocket of the young man next to me and asked him what he was doing in Havana. He was very shy, but his compañera said that they were studying "electricity and medicine" so they could go back to Nicaragua and help their people build the country. When I told the young woman I was North American and that there are many people here working for peace in Central America, she said it was a good thing because if the US invades Nicaragua "it will cost your mothers many sons."

By the time I boarded the plane the next morning at Martí, I felt like my brain had been through a blender. One week in any country is scarcely enough to gain a comprehensive picture of the culture; a place as cloaked in radical mystique and reactionary prejudice as Cuba presents more complex puzzles than most. One has to spend more time with people, discovering their perspectives and getting to know the texture of daily life. The irrational taboo on travel to the island makes it all the more inviting for freelance diplomats and investigative poets to explore this forbidden zone and record their impressions.

Managua Made Easy

[1987]

It's Thursday night at the Ministry of Culture and four pigs are roasting over an open pit. A giant ceiba tree dominates the walled garden, where hundreds of guests in Managua this week for the First International Book Festival are milling around, chattering in several languages, seemingly enjoying the evening drizzle and getting increasingly looped on Nica libres. Nicaragua's famous rum, Flor de Caña, is flowing generously and the Atlantic Coast dance band—one part Dixieland, one part Zydeco, one part reggae and two parts calypso—is warming into a groove. It's hot, as usual in July, but the light rain following the daily downpour is refreshing, the company's interesting and the food, when it's finally served, is a delicious feast. Minister of Culture Ernesto Cardenal, Interior Minister Tomás Borge and Vice President Sergio Ramírez are among the distinguished hosts, and the guests include a number of cooks and maids and maintenance workers having a fine and uninhibited time.

Nicaragua is not the most likely place to take a vacation these days, but newspaper business being what it is I seized the chance to take a week off and check out the book festival. The National Library of Nicaragua, devastated in the earthquake of 1972 (and a little smaller than the downtown branch of the Santa Cruz Public Library), desperately needs books, the Sandinistas need friends, and some of us need a glimpse of reality virtually ignored in the North American press. I wanted to see firsthand this much-maligned country where the Soviet Union is rumored to be planning a takeover of Texas. What I found were far more gringos than Russkies, and a sense of fellowship that rendered borders irrelevant.

As the night darkened and the dancing escalated, the libido level increased and I was accosted by one of the women in the US delegation asking if I would protect her from a lascivious Soviet-bloc poet: "I'm drunk," she said, "and the Bulgarians are on the make."

In fact it was a Russian publisher who soon sidled up to us with a leer in his eye, asking my friend why she'd disappeared and giving me a big diplomatic grin. "What country are you from?" he asked in Spanish.

"The United States," I said.

A flicker of dismay crossed his face. "There are so many of you!"

"We're everywhere," I reminded him.

"Yankee go home," he said jovially.

"This is America," I said.

Nicaragua is indeed as American as corn and baseball, a country where the kids listen to US pop music and watch Hollywood movies on the Sandinista Television System. The second night I was there, laid low with a cold I'd brought with me from California, I watched *The Graduate*, a film made more surreal by its regular interruption for noncommercial public service messages about picking up litter, driving safely, doing one's homework and taking care of the school grounds. A couple of days later the front page of *El Nuevo Diario*, the independent paper, announced with exclamation points that Dustin Hoffman had been signed to star in the forthcoming film biography of Augusto César Sandino. Kris Kristofferson had just performed at the eighth anniversary victory celebration in Matagalpa. While the US Congress debated the most effective way to unseat the Sandinistas, hundreds—maybe thousands—of North Americans were in the country working and playing with the people. I'm sure Dustin Hoffman will make a great Sandino.

"The Book: A Window on the World" was the slogan of the festival, its logo an opening book in the shape of a V with its pages doubling as dove's wings. Forty-five countries and five hundred presses were represented, most of whose books—ranging from political economy to technical manuals to poetry to volumes on sexuality—would be donated to the National Library. The US delegation was large and typically diverse, with people from all parts of the country representing such independent small enterprises as Kitchen Table Women of Color Press, New Society Publishers, Orbis Books, South End Press, Children's Book Press, Curbstone Press, The Feminist Press of the City University of New York, Thunder's Mouth Press, Open Hand Publishing, West End Press and other obscure but feisty representatives of progressive publishing in the States. This motley group shared a large booth with the US Embassy, which was freely distributing *New York Times* reporter Shirley Christian's anti-Sandinista account of the revolution along with other propaganda hostile to any form of socialism. At first the tension was rather thick between the embassy officials and the literary lefties, but as the week went on a cold peace settled between them even as their ideological warfare continued.

Nicaraguans, enduring six years of a "low-intensity" war that has wrecked their country's economy and has affected practically every family in a land of some three million people, are hungry for books and came swarming into the festival grounds as into an intellectual oasis. Culture has been a high priority since the revolution's triumph in 1979, but with fifty percent of production directed toward defense, every other sector of development has suffered. Books, said Cardenal in his opening speech, are a means of democratizing a culture; education is liberation.

On the plane from Mexico City I'd sat next to a man who turned out to be Cardenal's first cousin, an entrepreneur and philosopher who said that despite an initial "revolutionary arrogance" and "immaturity" among the Sandinistas, he felt good about their respect for intellectuals. This man, Carlos Cardenal, was doing well in the revolution because as a businessman his skills are in great demand—sixty percent of the economy remains in the hands of private enterprise, and much of the wealthier business class has fled to Miami. The book festival was typical not only of the Sandinistas' genius in the field of public relations but of their emphasis on the arts as an integral part of revolutionary change, the combination of exhibits, readings, panel discussions, concerts and performances creating a richly stimulating setting for individual expression.

Uruguayan writer Eduardo Galeano—along with South African poet Dennis Brutus and US novelist Alice Walker among the international guests of honor—spoke in a tribute to Julio Cortázar of the supernatural dimension of everyday life that Cortázar consistently captured in his stories. "Reality," said Galeano, "is richer than its interpreters," and life is magical in its capacity to surprise. Cortázar, an avid champion of the Nicaraguan Revolution, saw in the people's daily life "the magic of childlike possibility." Despite the many difficulties of the moment, that sense of hopefulness and possibility, an enthusiasm for learning and communication, pervaded the atmosphere of the festival.

Tropical heat is hard on paperback books. Many covers were curling in the humidity. It rained nearly every afternoon, sometimes in torrents, but a warm rain that only seemed to enhance the general steaminess. One of my traveling companions commented when we first arrived that Nicaragua always smells like a kitchen, because the country itself is cooking. After my first trip here two years ago—when I stayed with some twenty other gringos in a large open-air dormitory—it felt funny to be lodged in the relative luxury of the Hotel las Mercedes with its air-conditioned bungalows. Three Korean microbuses were assigned to the US delegation, and the tour guides and drivers were young men eager to please their guests and give them a good time.

This hospitality, a warmly genuine friendliness, is common among the Nicaraguans I've encountered there. Under the surface of appalling poverty and a certain weariness born of the war and the hard times, the people carry themselves with the physical assurance and self-respect of those who've fought for their dignity. National pride is high, in part perhaps because the endurance of so much suffering—the earthquake, the insurrection and now the contra war—has given people a sense of the depth of their own strength. The country's happiness and hope can be seen most vividly in the children's faces; walk around with a camera and they ham it up with great energy. When they ask you for something, it's usually a pen. Take a stroll through Managua with a pocketful of Bics and you can make a lot of little Nicas jump for joy.

Managua is a very peculiar city, though. Its downtown demolished in the 1972 quake, the landscape is a spooky mixture of empty lots and half-collapsed buildings. Cattle wander among the buildings, and lots of kids, but you don't see many dogs because there's not that much to eat. Hardly any of the streets are marked with signs, so you need to know where you're going if you want to find your way around. That's why a tour is often the best introduction. Since I was there for only a week and there was so much going on in the capital, I was able to take just one day-trip out of town—a rainy excursion to nearby Masaya, the arts and crafts capital, and the colonial city of Granada, which appeared to be the wicker rocking chair capital of the world. As night fell, many families could be seen rocking in front of their TV sets in simple rooms with doors and windows open on the street.

This sense of relaxed openness is almost everywhere, even among the gun-toting security guards patrolling the hotel grounds. Seeing armed soldiers on the street, rather than provoking paranoia as it would in the typical military state, has a way of making a tourist feel secure. You know these guys are there to protect you. A huge percentage of the population is armed, but they don't go around shooting at each other in a frenzy of urban aggravation, as Los Angeles commuters have been doing lately. The country may be at war, but the people are at peace, trying to keep themselves and each other alive.

Mauricio, for instance, one of our guides—wounded while serving in the special forces, released from military duty to work in the ministry of tourism and soon to resume his formal education—had the gentlest personality imaginable, a humorous tenderness perhaps derived as much from his combat experience as from his inherent character. One understood the strength behind his easygoing humility. Or Jorge, one of the drivers, who informed me matter-of-factly over lunch one day that, like so many other Nicaraguans, he writes poetry—"just romantic poetry, nothing political." Little encounters with individuals like these—people casually carrying on in the midst of a major crisis—make even a brief visit to their country a time of rich and resonant impressions. You understand you're witnessing a moment pregnant with potential, and you can't help wondering what might happen if these people were not besieged.

How I Became Hispanic

[2013]

More than thirty years ago I attended a conference in Mexico City called Dialogue of the Americas, a gathering of leftist activists and intellectuals from the United States, Mexico, the Caribbean, and Central and South America occasioned by the presidency of Ronald Reagan and his aggressive anticommunist policies toward the region. Reagan had yet to invade Grenada, but was funding the contras against the Sandinista government in Nicaragua and propping up the right-wing dictatorships in the civil wars of El Salvador and Guatemala. The meeting was held on the weekend of the ninth anniversary of the September 11, 1973, coup in Chile that had overthrown the democratically elected government of Salvador Allende, a coup assisted by the support of President Richard Nixon, his right-hand man, Henry Kissinger, and the Central Intelligence Agency. A group of Latin American writers had organized this event in the quixotic hope of arresting further American intervention in the hemisphere by way of engagement with their US counterparts who might somehow influence the national discourse regarding the supposed communist threat south of our border.

I had come to the conference with Fernando Alegría, the Chilean writer and Allende's cultural attaché in Washington before the coup, who during most of the 1970s and 80s also headed Stanford's department of Spanish and Portuguese. Fernando had come to the States originally to study English literature, had gotten his PhD at Berkeley, met his wife, Carmen, and started a family there in the 1940s. Carmen was from El Salvador, and the four Alegría children, born and raised in California more or less contemporary with me, were completely bilingual, tri-national Californian Americans.

Recruited as a translator by Fernando in the mid-1970s and gradually invited into his family, I felt more at home with him and Carmen than I did at that point in my parents' house. As a Los Angeles native who had grown up surrounded by the Spanish language, had become a poet and had a knack for turning poems from Spanish into English, I fit right in with *los Alegría* (Spanish for joy). It was at their home near Stanford where I first met, among other interesting people, Nicaraguan poet and minister of culture Ernesto Cardenal; the great Argentine writer Julio Cortázar; and Fernando's former graduate students the now-acclaimed Chicano poets Francisco X. Alarcón and Juan Felipe Herrera. Alarcón now lives part-time in his native Mexico and teaches at UC Davis. Herrera, the child of migrant workers, is now a professor at UC Riverside and poet laureate of California. Thanks in part to Fernando's introductions I have since had the pleasure and privilege of working with each of these writers on one or another project and, in the case of Juan Felipe and Francisco, formed friendships that endure to this day.

Fernando had asked me to join him in Mexico City as part of a Bay Area delegation that included the Reverend Cecil Williams of Glide Church in San Francisco, his wife the poet Janice Mirikitani, SF State professor and editor Robert Chrisman of *The Black Scholar*, and Oakland writer and all-around cultural agitator Ishmael Reed. In a program of sessions and panels where almost every speaker, in Spanish or English, took the opportunity to condemn Yankee imperialism and by association almost everything else American, Reed addressed the highly ideological audience with a defense of US culture as one that had welcomed the Latino elements that have enriched it, reminding them that in music, in cuisine, in language, in architecture, Anglo and Latino cultures in California are inextricably intertwined. The insults to the United States that he had heard were personally offensive to him as an American, and if this were to be truly a dialogue of the Americas, more respect should be paid to their gringo guests and to the things we had in common.

Reed's reminder of our cultural connectedness was one of the most controversial speeches of the conference and had the effect, in its pushback against Marxist and anti-imperialist rhetoric, of helping to make the meeting more like a true dialogue than simply an anti-Reagan rally. Standing in the lobby of Mexico City's magnificent Museum of Anthropology, where the sessions were held, I was discussing what Ishmael had said with some of the others in attendance when someone, identifying me as a translator, called me over to act as an interpreter for a live television interview with Cecil Williams. While it may not be obvious to the uninitiated, a literary translator's job is nothing like that of an interpreter, even though both require proficiency in at least two languages. A translator like me typically works in one direction, from Spanish to English, in writing, whereas an interpreter must be orally fluent enough in both idioms to switch effortlessly from one to the other in both directions. I managed to fake my way through the interview as an ersatz interpreter, grateful that my vocabulary in Spanish had not been stressed beyond its limits.

Later it occurred to me that virtually any first- or second-generation Latino-American high school student, the kind of kid who has routinely spoken mostly Spanish at home with her parents and mostly English at school with her peers, could have served at least as effectively as I had as an extemporaneous interpreter. You can see such students anytime, in any town from San Diego to Eureka, and I am in awe of their facility in two spoken languages, a facility I'll never have despite my skills as a translator of poetry. Because I never studied Spanish until high school and have spoken it mostly in my travels—and only felt half-way fluent when I was drunk enough to abandon my grammatical inhibitions—I still can't claim to be completely bilingual, certainly not as much so as those children of immigrants.

After graduating from an elementary school called El Rodeo, I started taking Spanish as a high school freshman with the great *maestro* Juan Padilla, a Mexican immigrant who had mastered English and was the most excellent language instructor imaginable. Señor Padilla's teaching techniques were so lucid and effective that I continued in his classes through my senior year, and Spanish proved the only subject I aced consistently. My mastery of the fundamentals, achieved under his guidance, served as the foundation for whatever competence I had, leading some twenty years later to that conference in Mexico City.

As if all this weren't enough to make me feel half Mexican (because of my brown complexion my big brother Bruce has called me Pancho since I was little), it was in the lobby of that same museum the following afternoon, September 11, 1982, that I happened to meet a woman—a *chilanga*, as Mexico City natives call themselves—with whom for the next three years I was to carry on a border-hopping romance, a turbulent affair including bumpy flights and Montezuma's revenge among other discomforts (climaxing in the Mexico City earthquake of 1985), which we were ultimately unable to sustain. During one of my trips to see Citlali we visited the Frida Kahlo Museum in Coyoacán. This was long before Frida became a popular icon mass-marketed on t-shirts and coffee mugs, so we had the place, her former home shared with the monstrous muralist Diego Rivera, virtually to ourselves.

I didn't know it at the time, but Coyoacán was also the neighborhood where the Spanish exile poet Luis Cernuda had lived (and where he died in 1963 after teaching briefly in California at both UCLA and San Francisco State), a writer who, thanks to the Spanish Civil War and subsequent forty-year dictatorship of Francisco Franco, necessarily took up residence outside Spain in England, Scotland, the US and finally Mexico. Cernuda is someone whose work I continue to translate, having over the last ten years or so done versions of two of his books. Apart from his importance as one of Spain's leading twentieth-century poets, it is the beauty of his poems in Spanish that has inspired me—as did the beauty of my Mexican sweetheart—to embrace his work for love more than anything else. I find that when I am translating his poems I enter a zone of psychic pleasure that feels to be outside time, as if his spirit, by way of his language, were somehow streaming through me.

What I am trying to convey by way of all these associations unfolding out of that one weekend in Mexico at the *Diálogo de las Américas*—backward in time though the Hispanic LA of my boyhood and forward though my maturity and continuing practice as a translator—is that Spanish, though I am not a native speaker, is "in my blood like holy wine" (in Joni Mitchell's phrase) that keeps on infusing my life with hybrid flavors I would otherwise never have tasted. A translation is in many ways a piece of original writing, and all my original writing (including this essay) is permeated with what I've absorbed from the sounds and rhythms of the Spanish writers I've had the good luck and madness and passion to try to bring into English.

So when I hear some xenophobic politician invoking the specter of immigration as some sort of threat to American values or identity (Latino immigrants' economic contributions are well documented and their demographic majority is inevitable) I have to wonder what country they think they're living in. The California I know has always been part of Mexico and its language has been part of me for as long as I can remember. The constant cultural intercourse among the Americas—the US Marines brought baseball to the Caribbean, for example, an unintended side effect of empire, and many Latin American writers acknowledge their debts to Whitman, Faulkner, even Ezra Pound—has vastly enriched and seasoned our respective sauces. Though I can't claim to be representative of anything beyond my own experience, I wouldn't trade my native Californian multilingual multicultural border-defying formation for all the tortillas in Texas. And I can't help wondering what my Russian-Jewish immigrant grandparents (who came to the States by way of China, where my mother was born) would make of the kind of Judeo-Hispanic American I've become.

Writers & Writing

On Writing

[2013]

Writing is a gift that can ruin your life.

Writing is a vocation and an affliction.

Writing is a game of skill, like poker.

Writing is a curse that can save your life.

Writing books, like diet books, are a waste of time.

Writing can be a good form of revenge.

Writing can be a substitute for seduction.

Writing is small consolation.

Reading literature is the only workshop.

Promiscuous imitation is the road to originality.

Make it old!

Show *and* tell.

Who says?

My philosophy of writing on a bumper sticker: NO WAY.

Critics: Exterminating Angels or Johnny Revelators?

[2012]

One of the first editorials I published in *The Redwood Coast Review,* back in the summer of 1999, was headlined "In Praise of Criticism." In its three short paragraphs I invoked the idea of the critic as enthusiast, an *amateur* in the original sense (one who loves) eager to share his appreciation and understanding of the arts. I invited writers who shared this concept of criticism to send their essays to the RCR so as to enliven and illuminate the cultural landscape of our readers. In the years since, such clear-thinking, straight-talking and creative critics as Daniel Barth, Rebecca Taksel, Jonah Raskin, Roberta Werdinger, Zara Raab, Alta Ifland, Hilda Johnston, Jane Merryman, Marc Hofstadter and others have risen to the occasion, writing with passionate and informed intelligence on books and arts that have excited them. Sometimes this kind of excitement can take the form of skepticism, of questioning received assumptions and interrogating trends or inflated reputations, the critic serving the public as what could be called a fiction-checker. Facts, as Ronald Reagan famously said, may be stupid things—but imagination aspires to a higher truth.

This idea of criticism as enthusiasm and illumination runs counter to the common misconception that the critic is a frustrated artist who takes some sort of perverse pleasure in demeaning the work of others. Fault-finding is a terribly impoverished concept of criticism. The best criticism, like the best art, helps us to see and experience the world in a new way by freshening our perception of whatever it engages. And the greatest criticism is great writing, or should be if it wants to hold the reader's undivided attention—especially now, amid the cacophony of distractions assaulting us constantly via the magical devices that exert ever more pull and power over our consciousness. A good critic, like a good poet, can stop time long enough for us to notice what's going on around us.

I've learned a lot from critics, both about the subjects they were addressing and the styles in which they made their arguments. John Ruskin's prose on Gothic architecture captivated me both for what it showed me about medieval cathedrals and their gargoyles and for the sensuous pleasure of his sentences. Kenneth Rexroth, in his highly literate, no-nonsense newspaper columns, demonstrated that the classics can be as fully alive in the present as popular culture. Pauline Kael proved that a good movie review can be almost as much fun to experience as a good movie. Robert Hughes pugnaciously questioned, in a most entertaining way, a lot of dubious common wisdom about the arts. Alfred Kazin showed that a literary critic can be both a historian and a creative participant in the moment, elucidating the works of his contemporaries and contributing to the cultural conversation with his own powerfully personal and original writings. Such models as these prove that first-rate criticism beats second-rate "creative writing" any day of the week.

So I noticed with interest an essay by Dwight Garner, a book critic for *The New York Times*, in that paper's Sunday magazine a couple of months ago, titled "Not Everyone Gets, or Deserves, a Gold Star," a defense of criticism against the complaints of those who consider the creative act sacrosanct, and not to be violated by judgmental commentary, even after it's published. Despite its unfortunate title, which plays into the notion of the critic as schoolmarm, Garner makes a good case for the value of criticism as a defense against "mass intellectual suicide." He uses this memorable phrase to describe what Dave Eggers calls for in an astonishing quote from an interview he gave to *The Harvard Advocate* in 2000: "Do not be critics, you people, I beg you. I was a critic, and I wish I could take it all back, because it came from a smelly and ignorant place in me and spoke with a voice that was all rage and envy. Do not dismiss a book until you have written one, and do not dismiss a movie until you have made one, and do not dismiss a person until you have met them.... What matters is saying yes."

This is one of the stupidest things I've ever heard or read from the mouth of an otherwise intelligent person. Eggers is confusing his own meanness and immaturity and psychological problems with criticism just because he was a jerk at the time he was writing it. He has since gone on to prove his generosity and creativity in many big-hearted books and constructive community projects, and I salute him for his hard work and imagination and activism. But I will continue to write criticism (in addition to other things) because it helps me understand the world and what I'm thinking about it, and I hope it helps others think for themselves as well.

The poet, translator and editor Jerome Rothenberg once called Harold Bloom "the Exterminating Angel of poetry," presumably because of Bloom's authoritative pronouncements about the Western canon, something Rothenberg has spent a distinguished career proposing alternatives to by arguing for a global counter-canon that includes the works of far-flung "primitive" cultures. Rothenberg's landmark anthologies, starting with *Technicians of the Sacred* and *Shaking the Pumpkin*, have had a significant impact in widening the scope of American poetics. Bloom is one of those know-it-alls who really has read and thought about practically everything, and from his perch at Yale has declared himself the Big Kahuna of criticism. He's the kind of professor who inspired me to flee graduate school, so sure of himself and full of himself that he brooks no difference of opinion because nobody else could possibly know as much as he does about anything.

That may be true, but it doesn't mean there are no further arguments to be made. I'm not for a dictatorship of the intelligentsia, or any member of it, any more than for any other kind of dictatorship. People who are sure they're right are among the most dangerous of all, especially if they have guns or other instruments of institutional firepower. But this doesn't mean that Bloom should be dismissed; he's a really smart guy who has a lot to teach. His love of Shakespeare and the Bible and the Romantics and the classics can be felt in the heat of his writings. Still, he is not some Godlike figure entitled to tell the rest of us what to think. This is what I believe Rothenberg was getting at when he called him an exterminating angel (a reference to the amazing film by Luis Buñuel in which the guests at a bourgeois dinner party find themselves strangely unable to leave the room).

At the opposite pole of "critical" commentary these days is the unmediated blather on millions of blogs and book review sites and Twitter and Facebook, ad nauseam. It's not that you can't find great writing and thinking online—there's lots of it—but that the Babel in which it is embedded can make for a kind of white noise that renders almost everything unintelligible because it affords no chance to contemplate what you've just read before you click away to something else. As the *Times* reporter David Streitfeld wrote in a recent story in the Business section, "Reviews by ordinary people have become an essential mechanism for selling almost anything online," and this democratization of reviewing, at least in the case of books, has debased the public discourse. The millions of reviews of millions of books on Amazon, for example, have not only leveled the playing field but have killed the referees; there are no rules or standards, and all opinions are created equal.

Of course, critics can be obnoxious when they have a prestigious platform from which to incidentally advance their own careers. Some are reluctant to say anything negative for fear of the repercussions. Others make a point of being nasty—like bad-boy critic and novelist Dale Peck, or the poet and critic William Logan, both of whom specialize in the snarky takedown. It doesn't necessarily mean they're wrong, only that their smart-ass personas often obscure the value of whatever they have to say. Nevertheless, they can be entertaining—at the expense of the victim of their review—and that contradiction can make the reader squirm, which is generally a healthy antidote to complacency.

I question authority every chance I get, but it doesn't mean I don't want to hear what smart, knowledgeable people have to say about things that interest me—or who can arouse my interest in a subject with the force of their impassioned point of view. Polemical critics like Christopher Hitchens, philosopher-critics like Susan Sontag, critical comedians like Leslie Fiedler, contrarian critics like Cynthia Ozick, all-around writer-critics like Mark Twain and John Updike—yes, they can be a little excessive, a little annoying with their overbearing personalities, but most of them are usually interesting to read, and show me something I didn't know before.

As the editor of this slim but wiry paper, I guess I qualify as a gatekeeper, some combination of talent booker, stage manager and bouncer who gets to decide who performs in my little club. This issue marks the end of our fourteenth year in print, and we're still looking for the smartest, wittiest, most imaginative writers we can find and asking them to show us what they've got. Criticism is an art like any other and can be manifest in countless variations. It can be writing of the highest order. It can be original scholarship. It can be as "self-indulgent" (as a former professor of mine once called my early efforts in poetry) as any other form of self-expression, but isn't that what art is all about, indulging one's inner angels and demons so as to discover something? The critic can serve as a bridge between the specialists and the amateurs, or as a pointed stick in the flabby flanks of the overrated, or a finger pointing at the passing show, pointing out things we might otherwise not have noticed.

Lost & Found: My Life in Translation

[1985]

It makes sense that translation should be the most invisible and least understood of the literary arts. A translator's job, after all, is to be transparent, creating a window of words so clean as to give the reader an illusion of the original text undistorted by the inevitable changes a work undergoes in transit between one language and another. The translating process is riddled with paradoxes, contradictions, multiple choices, acts of creative faith and lucky accidents.

It was Robert Frost who reportedly said that what gets lost in the translation of a poem is the poetry. Indeed, anyone who's ever written one knows that if it can be said some other way it's not a poem. The composition of a literary text—poetry especially, but prose too—is so integrally rooted in the language of its conception that the sounds and rhythms and cultural assumptions of the idiom play an instrumental role in determining content, and creating meaning. Once the genetic code of those primary associations is broken, the reader is faced with a different creation.

So what's a translator to do, and how is it that so many basic sources—the Bible, Confucius, Homer, Chaucer, Dante, Cervantes, Dostoyevsky—are known to most of us, if at all, only in translation? And what about all the modern works, in verse and fiction and other fields, without whose translated presence our knowledge of the world would be impoverished? Existing translations answer these questions, but let me explore some aspects of the mystery whereby these "secondary" works come into being.

Speaking some years ago in New Orleans at the annual conference of the American Literary Translators Association, W. S. Merwin began his address to his colleagues by saying, "Some people think that translating poetry is difficult, but we all know that's not true—it's impossible." Acknowledging the impossibility of the task is the first leap a translator has to take in order to proceed with the act. Translating *is* an act, not only in the sense of action taken but of a theatrical performance. The original text is a script the translator has to interpret with sympathetic attunement to its emotional tone, its music and its mood. Or the original can be seen as a musical score the translator plays on his own instrument. Just as an actor or musician can say all the words or hit all the notes correctly and still deliver a terrible performance, a translator can make a perfectly adequate, seemingly "accurate" or "literal" version of a poem or story and fail to bring across its animating spirit, thereby missing its meaning. (On the other hand, as sometimes happens, he can obliterate any sense of the original with the quirks of his personal style.)

Translating demands that its practitioner be a writer with the nerve and imagination to impersonate the author whose work is being rendered. It involves what Keats called "negative capability," the capacity to live in uncertainty and to abandon one's own identity in order to speak in another's voice. It means taking creative chances based on intuition, on listening to the subtle nuances of the original and letting them direct one's inner ear to verbal analogies in the new language. As with other forms of art and intercourse, translation requires a synthesis of understanding, feeling, technique and inspiration.

Examples of inspired translation abound: Robert Fitzgerald's Homer, Kenneth Rexroth's and Arthur Waley's versions of the Chinese sages, Dudley Fitts's Greek Anthology poems, Mary Barnard's Sappho, Walter Kaufmann's Nietzsche (which captures among other things the manic humor of the mad philosopher), William Arrowsmith's Cesare Pavese, Gregory Rabassa's remarkable renditions of Cortázar and Vargas Llosa and García Márquez (who reportedly has said that Rabassa's version of *One Hundred Years of Solitude* is an improvement on the original), and Constance Garnett's Victorian Tolstoy, to name a few, all convey the feeling of what reading these great writers must be "like."

And yet every translation, however brilliant, is provisional, never definitive. The last few years alone have seen a half dozen new attempts at getting Rilke in English. The greatest works, which in a sense are the least translatable, are also those whose essential genius somehow manages to come across even in a poor translation. And it's these same works that continuously ask for fresh interpretations. Changing times, idiomatic and cultural evolutions demand new versions of everything worth preserving. So in addition to strictly literary transformations we have cases like that of Pasolini (a poet and polemicist as well as a filmmaker) translating Boccaccio and Chaucer and

Sophocles and Sade and St. Matthew into movies, and new-wave Shakespeare directors translating Renaissance plays into neo-postmodernist theater, and revisionist Christians trying to improve on the King James Bible—all in the effort, for better or worse, to keep the classics current.

As if it weren't discouraging enough to know that one's work will sooner or later be superseded, every translator lives in fear of the critic Rabassa calls Professor Horrendo, who reviews your translation in *The New York Times* with one eye on the dictionary and the other on the original, meticulously picking at every "mistake" he detects and sniveling over every interpretive liberty you've taken.

But these occupational hazards of the translator's trade, and the mechanical and mental pains of the actual labor involved—the strained eyes, the stiff back, the brain-twisting puns that keep you up all night in search of equivalents—fade in the light of the revelations delivered to the writer who puts himself at the service of a masterpiece he would otherwise never come to know so intimately. The care and respect and sensitivity ideally brought to bear in the act of translation—and the depth of relation one develops with the original author, dead or alive—can return a soulful satisfaction closely akin to love.

My adventures as a translator began in earnest in the early 1970s, when the versions of Pablo Neruda I was reading didn't seem adequate to the originals and so much of the Chilean poet's voluminous output was not yet available in English. I'd studied Spanish in high school, traveled some in Spain, and read a moderate sampling of Spanish literature in college. More important, I was writing poems and intensively involved in explorations of the American idiom, experimenting with the sinewy changes this language lent itself to, its expressive possibilities, its texture.

In June of 73, while traveling in Spain, through a fortuitous sequence of events I was introduced to the Spanish maestro Vicente Aleixandre at his home in Madrid. Aleixandre, then seventy-five, was one of the few survivors from the extraordinary Generation of 1927 who, due to poor health, had remained in Spain during the civil war of 1936–39 and come to be known not only as one of the greatest living poets in the language but as a point of reference and source of encouragement for younger writers coming of age in the oppressive years of the Franco dictatorship. Without knowing it at the time, I was participating in a ritual that countless young Spanish and Latin American poets had been enacting for nearly five decades: the visit to Aleixandre's house to sit in his salon—where García Lorca used to play the piano in the twenties and early thirties—and converse in the spirit of poetry and friendship.

Aleixandre was a beautiful Old World gentleman, frail and bald with pale translucent skin and sparkling sky-blue eyes. He spoke of his art with passionate enthusiasm, invoking both its esthetic pleasures and the spirit of fellowship it engendered. In the course of our conversation, during which he exhibited a surprising amount of interest in me and what I was doing, he encouraged me to translate one of his books, a collection of poems called *La destrucción o el amor* (*Destruction or Love*) originally written in 1933. As it happened, I had purchased a copy of that very book a few days before while browsing in a Madrid bookstore, not even knowing whether the author was still alive, much less expecting to meet him. These surreally erotic love lyrics, composed in a rhetorically elegant English-defying style, had not been translated into this language in all the intervening years, and here the author was entrusting them to me, a young American he scarcely knew.

After extensive study and several false starts and months of correspondence, I agreed to take on the project. Some three years and thirty poems later (from which we selected just twenty-two for inclusion) a small edition was published in 1976 by the Green Horse Press collective in Santa Cruz. The following year, much to our astonishment, Aleixandre received the Nobel Prize for literature. Since our little book was one of just two volumes of his work available at the time in the United States, the edition soon sold out. It was happily received in the literary community and, presto, I was certified as a translator.

One of the people who liked my work was the Chilean writer Fernando Alegría—novelist, poet, critic, diplomat, and professor of Latin American literature at Stanford—who recruited me into the world of his own writing. As with Aleixandre, to whom I'd become a kind of apprentice in the course of working with his words, the relationship with Alegría became a major learning experience for me. As he introduced me further to contemporary currents of Latin American writing (and often enough to the writers themselves when they came through the Bay Area) I began to discover the inevitable connections between literature and politics in this hemisphere.

As a Chilean who had worked in the Allende government and had barely escaped with his life at the time of the 1973 coup which brought General Pinochet's dictatorship to power—a spooky echo of the fate of Aleixandre's generation in Spain—Alegría and his fellow exiles from various political tyrannies in Latin America were engaged in an act of cultural resistance every time they sat down to write or stood up to speak. The humanist tradition embodied in books was being systematically exterminated by military regimes afraid of the subversive power of words. Neruda's books had been burned by the junta's troops in the streets of Santiago, and many other progressive writers were (and are) unable to publish in their own countries, unable to reach the readers to whom their works had the most to communicate.

The more I became acquainted with these realities—almost incomprehensible here, where writers are either totally ignored or turned into talk-show celebrities between commercials that trivialize whatever they have to say—the more I realized the responsibilities inherent in being a translator. Not only did one have to maintain a high level of stylistic agility in order to do justice to the inventiveness exercised by so many authors in the Spanish-American language and its regional variations, one had to make an ethical commitment to speak for the silenced, to tell the censored stories, to make available living texts that might otherwise be lost.

Ideological blackouts, I've since discovered, are not confined to formally totalitarian regimes. To get an essay, for example, by any important writer deemed "leftist" by the standards of the Reagan-era political climate, published in a widely circulated US magazine or newspaper is next to impossible. It's true that the poems and prose of such writers can be published, but usually in the more marginal journals unseen by readers bombarded daily with official propaganda issued by Washington and obediently repeated by the mainstream press. My version of a speech by Sergio Ramírez, novelist and vice president of Nicaragua, unsuccessfully made the rounds of several respectable magazines before being printed by a smaller-circulation progressive journal—only to have its literary style, which I had taken pains to translate faithfully, reproducing its rhetorical elegance, chopped into more readily comprehensible newspaper-like sentences by an editor with his own political agenda. So the formal beauty of the medium—in this case Ramírez's eloquent language—was ironically sacrificed to the urgency of the message and the editor's inability to see beyond its ideological thrust.

Under the current critical circumstances in Central America, this is just one example of the fine line a translator may have to walk in the course of trying to be true to art while at the same time providing a socially useful service. Those of us working with writers from that region feel a special urgency in helping their voices be heard in styles that approximate the original character and feeling. Translators of both literary texts and personal testimonies give broader access to what's going on elsewhere in forms that are often far more informative than mere news. Working as I do with poets and essayists and storytellers under fire or forcibly exiled from their tortured lands, I feel connected to their creative struggles in ways that strictly political work or purely literary endeavors would never allow.

This integration of literature and history, attributable in part to the experience of translation, has proved a tremendous resource in the growth of my original writing. Whether in poetry, fiction, journalism, essays or criticism, the dynamic give-and-take of translating—the exchange of energy and understanding with distant persons of another tongue and culture—informs and expands my reading of the world and puts me in touch with voices I might not otherwise have found.

Translator Tricksters Take Kansas City with Sauce

[2011]

On the drive into Kansas City from the airport, an anomalous building appears on your left in the shape of a monstrous yet elegantly sculpted seashell that rises up out of the landscape like a hallucination. It is the Kauffman Center for the Performing Arts, KC's new opera house and symphony hall, designed by architect Moshe Safdie. Coming toward the building from the other direction you see its soaring glass façade and can't help marveling at this extraordinary example of urban design and engineering. This could replace those "crazy little women" of the Leiber and Stoller song as the signature attraction of this heartland metropolis.

I'm in town for the annual conference of the American Literary Translators Association, a meeting of several hundred translators held each year in a different part of the country. ALTA is a very congenial organization, and most unusual for a congregation of writers in that virtually every member, even those with their own careers of original writing, is devoted more to serving literature than to serving his or her personal ambition. Other writers' conferences I've attended tend to be crawling with people either trying to hustle a book project or attempting to get close to some renowned author or, in the case of such famed literati, basking in the adulation of their admirers. The collegial fellow-feeling and mutual respect of ALTA members are a refreshing antidote to such power-strivings and social-climbings.

Margaret Sayers Peden, Willis Barnstone, Bill Johnston, Marian Schwartz, Alexis Levitin, Geoffrey Brock, Katherine Silver, Esther Allen, Jonathan Cohen and Roger Greenwald may not be household names, but they and others like them are instrumental in bringing foreign literature into English for the benefit of readers who would otherwise have no access. Spanish, Greek, Latvian, Estonian, Chinese, Persian, Danish, Norwegian, Arabic, Portuguese, Polish, Serbian, Turkish, French and Russian writers, among others, can be read in versions so artfully wrought you scarcely realize they are not originals, thanks to the tireless efforts of these obscure workers who toil on the margins of literary celebrity but play a central role in bringing novels and stories and poems and plays from other languages into the lives of those of us who still read books.

Also, and very encouragingly for a grizzled veteran like me, there are two or three generations of younger translators coming up the line behind us, so that however dubious the future of literature in these increasingly digitized times, interesting writings from other cultures will continue to be turned into works in English, in one medium or another, and cross-fertilization will go on among the world's writers and readers.

It's a curious subculture, this world of literary translators, and surely its eccentric position in the larger culture is part of what makes for such camaraderie among its members. In Kansas City there was plenty of shop talk—about certain technical and stylistic issues, questions of publishing and politics, theory and practice—but for me the most interesting part of the conference is always the social connections, the extracurricular conversations and friendships formed or refreshed at night in the hotel bar, or during coffee breaks between sessions, or at lunch or dinner in neighborhood restaurants.

I met a young Iranian-American poet who drove up from Arkansas for the occasion and whose intense *passion* for poetry reminded me why I got into this game in the first place—for love of the words and the music and the inspiration and consolation of dynamic language dancing on the page. There was a young Israeli fiction writer attending the conference for the first time who told me what a great experience it was for her to meet all these other dedicated people and hear what they had to say. I encountered people I see just once a year, if that, whose projects—translating huge novels, editing anthologies, writing original books—somehow spur me on in my own endeavors in a spirit of encouragement and friendly rivalry.

Yelling over the loudness of the live music in the hotel lounge on a weekend night when other conventions are also in town and the conventioneers and other guests are determined to have a good time and making no secret of it, your annoyance with the cacophony of competing noises is somehow overcome by a sense of being alive to the chaotic drama and absurdity all around, even the hotel staff confused by the swirling intensity of interactions, the clusters of friends gabbing and drinking, the strangers getting acquainted over cocktails, the scholars getting loose under the influence of booze and shmoozing, the traveling salesmen on the make.

You get a wonderful feeling of anonymity staying in a big hotel, yet paradoxically at a conference like this you're constantly bumping into people you know, and this contradiction makes you feel oddly at home and in an exotic realm at the same time. Like the low-ceilinged rooms where most of the sessions and readings are held, this whole scene seems an unlikely place for any kind of esthetic experience—it is much too unnatural and commercial, claustrophobic, with bad acoustics—how could one begin to appreciate a poem or consider an idea or engage in a private dialogue in such a setting? And yet, again and again, something said in a panel discussion or read in one of the bilingual readings or confessed by a friend over a drink or a meal touches me in unanticipated ways, so that by the time I return home several days later I feel recharged and ready to proceed with work that often seems gratuitous, a pointless exercise in creating something beautiful or revelatory that hardly anyone will notice.

The art of translation, like any other art created in the solitude of one's study or studio, or even in the collective setting of a stage or bandstand, is an act of faith, a leap in the dark, a long-shot bet that what you are doing serves something beyond your own amusement—or, more likely, obsessive compulsions—something that others somewhere, sometime, eventually will recognize and be grateful for, something that speaks to and possibly for their own experience or spirit. Those strangers, even if as yet unborn, may be no more strange than the locals you see at Fiorella's Jack Stack Barbecue chomping on their spareribs slathered in the restaurant's signature sauce, or the gangs of school kids running through the Nelson-Atkins Museum past the imposing Henry Moore sculptures, or the blond-haired black-clad cocktail waitresses dodging the drunks in the hotel lounge while carrying trays of iced beverages over their heads without spilling a drop. These might as well be the people we are writing for, oblivious as they are, because we madly trust that somehow one day someone may open one of our books and be astonished by what they discover.

How strange that in the middle of a country whose religion is football a performing arts center can spring up like a lovely mushroom and be sustainable, and that an otherwise ordinary hotel can host a gathering of oddball intellectuals who temporarily turn it into a hotbed of highbrow culture, as if they were really an association of magicians dedicated to the creation of completely convincing illusions. For translators are tricksters, shape-shifting smoke-and-mirrorists, sleight-of-hand card-shufflers playing with unmarked decks that nevertheless turn up full houses in the form of stacked pages that read as if they'd been dealt that way by luck of the draw, when in fact those unfolded hands are mirages fashioned from alien tongues whose mysterious messages are patiently transformed by multilingual literary gamblers who often feel more like monks.

These usually invisible illusionists are an unusual breed indeed, working more for the sake of some obscure honor than for any sort of worldly glory, and for the pleasures and satisfactions of making something out of something else. More than the blues and the barbecue sauce, more than the sexy curves of the opera house, more than the bends in the Missouri River reflecting the heartland light, a renewed belief in the art of translation and the half-crazy people who do it is what I brought home from Kansas City just in time for Thanksgiving.

Lorca Rorschachs

[2010]

With the possible exception of Pablo Neruda, who lived nearly twice as long and wrote accordingly that much more, Federico García Lorca is the Spanish-language poet most frequently translated into English. Unlike Neruda, whose voice can often be brought across fairly credibly into a North American idiom, Lorca's poetry is more resistant as an object of translation, harder to "get" as persuasive poetry in English. Partly for this reason, US translators continue year after year to attempt, with varying degrees of success and failure, new versions of Lorca.

There's an amusing anecdote in Neruda's memoirs about the Chilean poet's meeting with his Andalusian counterpart in 1933 in Buenos Aires. According to Neruda (not always a reliable narrator), one evening they were reciting poems to each other when Lorca, listening to Neruda's verse, suddenly climbed into a tree, put his hands over his ears and exclaimed, "Stop! Stop! You're influencing me!"

At the time, both were engaged in experiments with what is commonly called "Spanish surrealism"—Neruda in his *Res-*

idencia en la tierra books and Lorca in his *Poeta en Nueva York*—a compositional process (current theorists would call it a "strategy") drawing on subconscious images and intuitive musical associations that at best create surprising and revelatory juxtapositions, often dream- or nightmare-like in their sense of weirdness, mystery, ambiguity or horror. This approach to the surreal had less to do with André Breton and his rational dogma of the irrational than with the sixteenth-century prototype of Luis de Góngora (patron saint of Spain's Generation of 1927, of which García Lorca was a key member), the modernist-baroque example of Nicaraguan Rubén Darío, Freudian ideas of the unconscious, Joyce's stream-of-consciousness technique in *Ulysses*, and the technological and perceptual revelations of the dawning art of cinema. The 1920s in Spain and much of Latin America were a phenomenally fertile time for poetic experimentation, and Lorca and Neruda were among the more notable experimenters.

By the late 1950s and 60s in the United States, translations of both these poets were beginning to appear and their styles beginning to insinuate themselves into the consciousness and practice of US poets in search of alternatives to the prevailing modernist models of Eliot, Pound, Auden and Stevens, on one hand, and the more conservative formalist modes of Tate, Winters, Ransom and Lowell on the other. The Beat, Black Mountain and New York Schools of Donald Allen's seminal anthology *The New American Poetry 1945–1960* were already active and visible but well outside any existing mainstream at the time. Into these fertile fields of avant-garde poetic practice the voice of Lorca especially (as interpreted by his translators) fell like invigorating rain.

The impact of Lorca—or more precisely translations of

Lorca—on mid- to late-twentieth century US poets is the subject of Jonathan Mayhew's insightfully provocative and original cultural-critical essay *Apocryphal Lorca: Translation, Parody, Kitsch.* Mayhew examines the translation and appropriation of Lorca by an interesting range of Americans, from Langston Hughes through Ben Belitt to Robert Duncan, Robert Kelly, Robert Creeley, Robert Bly, Bob Kaufman, Jerome Rothenberg, Allen Ginsberg, Jack Spicer, Paul Blackburn, Frank O'Hara and Kenneth Koch, among others, perceptively analyzing the ways in which these writers (many of them unable to read the original) used Lorca as a point of departure for English versions of various styles and fidelities, and for inspiration and application to their own diverse poetics.

One question Mayhew addresses only glancingly, though it comes up several times in different contexts, is: Why Lorca almost exclusively, instead of other Spanish (or Latin American) contemporaries? Lorca is surely an extraordinary poet, but he happened to come of age as one of a brilliant cohort that included such comparably gifted and accomplished writers as Rafael Alberti, Vicente Aleixandre, Luis Cernuda, Jorge Guillén and Pedro Salinas, any one of whom can be said to be not only in the same league as Lorca but of equal stature. The obvious answer is that Lorca was executed by fascist forces in 1936 at age thirty-eight in the opening days of the Spanish Civil War. Emblematic martyr of the Spanish Republic and of the crushed promise of its progressive culture, Lorca is mourned not only for his prematurely extinguished creative talent but as a symbol of admired political values. For some American poets, the fact that he was also openly gay has only enhanced his allure.

Lorca's dramatic and tragic death, along with his legendary personality, his social energy and his cultural activism (he organized a touring theater company to bring the classics of Spanish drama to the provinces)—that is, his biography—has as much to do as his poetry with his elevation to such a disproportionately exalted position among his peers. When one takes a close look at his poems, and the ways they have been converted into English, one begins to realize there is both more and less to "Lorca" than meets the eye.

There is in Lorca's verse, from the early folkloric songs and ballads of his native Andalusia through the open-form "surrealism" of *Poet in New York* to the Orientalist lyrics of his final book, *Diván del Tamarit*, a truly unique and unreproducible sound—what W. S. Merwin, in his Introduction to the fiftieth anniversary edition of New Directions' 1955 *Selected Poems*, calls "the fire, the beat and snap and dance" of Lorca's language. His style is characterized by a highly distinctive set of rhythms, tones and musical moves that continue to defy adequate English translation. As much as a more deeply radical poet like Vallejo, I would argue, Lorca is "untranslatable"—and surely that's one explanation for the proliferation of Lorca versions by American poets and translators: the less translatable the original, especially when its power can be sensed even in weak translations, the more people are likely to try their hand at catching that elusive *something*.

I had to laugh a couple of years ago when I read on the back of the latest version of *Poet in New York* (by Pablo Medina and Mark Statman) John Ashbery's gushing blurb declaring this "the definitive version of Lorca's masterpiece, in language that is as alive and molten today as was the original in 1930." With all respect to Medina and Statman, who have contributed a useful addition to our cumulative reading of Lorca, Ashbery surely knows that no translation, least of all one of as singular a voice as Lorca's, is definitive. This sort of bad faith is a blatant example of promotional hype overriding critical integrity—typical perhaps, but unfair to less-sophisticated readers who may think, well, if John Ashbery says so, it must be true.

The truth is there is a Lorca industry devoted to exploiting his legend with the primary motive of selling books more than of advancing our exposure to and appreciation of the greatest poetry in Spanish. Mayhew, a scholar of more recent peninsular poetry, observes acutely that there is virtually no interest among US poets and publishers in post-Lorca Spanish poets. I would add that even among the poets of Lorca's generation, many of whom by now have been translated into English (not always with consummate skill or success, but some of them very well), none has received anywhere near the attention that Lorca has, and it isn't on account of any deficiency in their writing.

Like Frida Kahlo, a perfectly good painter turned into a marketing gimmick for t-shirts, coffee mugs and other kitschy tchotchkes, García Lorca—as Mayhew demonstrates—has been diminished and caricatured through his conversion into a domestic American icon, reduced to a *duende*-driven folksy Gypsy Negrophilic primitive hipster gay surrealist whom various factions and individuals jump to exploit at their convenience for their own sectarian and personal purposes. Lorca the actual poet and his work, meanwhile, remain unplumbed even as they are appropriated tirelessly by their admirers. While I was reading Mayhew's book a journal arrived in the mail, the *Coe Review*, a student-edited publication from Coe College in Iowa, which included a poem by Lyn Lifshin—a prolific small-press poet published widely over the last four decades—called "Sleeping with Lorca," which begins: "It's not true, he never chose women. / I ought to know. It was Grenada [sic] and / the sun falling behind the Alhambra was / flaming lava…" The poem goes on to recycle "green I want you green" and "5 o'clock in the afternoon" and various other now-cliché *Lorquismos* including "gored bull" metaphors for sex, as if to illustrate the half-baked stereotypical Lorca exploitation Mayhew spends much of his book exposing, and which, as Lifshin proves, continues.

The irony is that Lorca himself, for much of his brief career, adopted the persona of what Borges called, on seeing him in Buenos Aires where he delivered his famous lecture on the *duende*, "a professional Andalusian." His friends Luis Buñuel and Salvador Dalí titled their groundbreaking surrealist poem-film *An Andalusian Dog* as an inside joke on Lorca, who due to his winning personality and versatile genius was something of a legend even in his own time.

Writing from exile in Mexico some twenty-five years after Lorca's death, Luis Cernuda addresses his old friend in a poem called "Otra vez, con sentimiento" ("Once More, with Feeling"); he recounts the way one contemporary critic laid claim to Lorca by calling him "my prince." The poem concludes:

The appropriation of you, which you wanted
Nothing to do with when you were alive,
Is what now seems to me so utterly strange.
The prince of a toad? Isn't it enough
For your countrymen to have killed you?

And now stupidity succeeds the crime.

[my translation]

Cernuda was objecting, in the early 1960s—the same time interest in Lorca was first peaking in the US—to the exploitation of Lorca's image and memory by Spanish poets and critics who remained in Spain during the years of the Franco dictatorship, and to the "appropriation" of Lorca's angelic aura for their own self-aggrandizement. If not all American poets and/or translators have been quite so shameless in their use and abuse of Lorca, Mayhew shows convincingly the various ways in which each individual US writer has recreated the Spaniard (whether in translation or in their original poems) in his own image. If a book is a mirror, as Auden said, then Lorca's writings are a Rorschach test.

Mayhew is especially hard on Belitt and Bly for their early and influential crimes against Lorca's original Spanish. Belitt's infamously incomprehensible embellishments of Lorca's already complex yet powerful New York poems, and Bly's flattening of Lorca's style into a prosy middle-American vernacular, are taken apart by Mayhew with keen intelligence and a verve driven by personal indignation. While more respectful than Bly ever was in attacking his contemporaries, Mayhew pulls no punches in declaring the "vandalism" and damage done to Lorca and his readers by the likes of Bly and Belitt.

While there is surely justification for this critical judgment, both Bly and Belitt, each in his way, at least brought Lorca to greater public attention, so that others (provided they could read the Spanish) might look more closely at the originals and arrive at their own readings. While Bly's polemical cheerleading for "leaping poetry" unfortunately leaked into creative writing programs everywhere and infected countless MFAs with cheap "deep-image"-ry, by making such a spectacle of himself as a Lorca promoter Bly opened a number of interesting arguments about American poetry, arguments that are still going on, and of which Mayhew's excellent book is an example.

Belitt, for his part, despite his egregious violations of Lorca's verse, did *in principle* set an example for the only promising approach to Lorca translation: not an obedient adherence to the letter of the original but a re-creation of it in somehow analogous terms. While it's true that Belitt failed spectacularly to create an English comparable to Lorca's Spanish, he demonstrated—for those perceptive enough to notice—that this is *conceptually* the only method that might yield, in the hands of an imaginative and technically skilled enough poet/translator, something like the experience of the original.

In the most illuminating chapters of *Apocryphal Lorca*, the ones on Frank O'Hara and Kenneth Koch, Mayhew shows how these two New York poets, neither of whom read Spanish and both of whom were in fact more Francophile in their literary tastes, adapted Lorca somewhat irreverently, via a certain campiness in O'Hara's case and in Koch's by very witty parody, in truly creative transformations that in some essential way are truer to the spirit of Lorca than the thrift-shop spirituality of the *duende*-invokers or the fatuousness of the romantic swooners over Lorca's Gypsy soul.

While Koch, in his delightful Borgesian "Some South American Poets," dazzlingly caricatures the mystification of Hispanic poetry in US culture of the 1960s, his good-natured tone reveals that he is not ridiculing the originals but slyly critiquing the naïveté of their North American adaptors. Koch's very funny and inventive parodies are actually a greater homage to Lorca than many more earnest tributes by Koch's contemporaries. This is one of Mayhew's most astute and useful insights.

For me, however, Mayhew's identification of Frank O'Hara as perhaps the truest American avatar of Lorca—not so much in the poetry itself as in their "kinship" as charismatic, mercurial, gay, jazz-infused, risk-taking, elegiac, prematurely mortal personalities each at the center of a vibrant creative scene—is one of his shrewdest observations. This kind of intuitive leap makes for the liveliest and riskiest criticism. One of Mayhew's strengths is that he's not afraid to be wrong; he has a distinct point of view and acknowledges his personal angle of vision. For all his deeply felt conviction, he makes no Harold Bloomian or Helen Vendleroid pronouncements from the peak of Parnassus. His style is refreshingly free of intellectual pomposity or jargon. Not least important, for someone interested as I am in the subject, his book is fun to read.

My one complaint about *Apocryphal Lorca* is its unfortunately numerous annoying typos and copyediting errors, little grammatical and lexical glitches that slipped through the editors' spell-check programs and past the eyes of their proofreaders. (The poet A. R. Ammons, for example, is referred to as "A. A. Ammons," and in the title of the famous James Wright poem "Lying in a Hammock at William Duffy's Farm in Pine Island, Minnesota," the word "at" is mistakenly replaced by "in." Minor though such errors may be, one wouldn't expect them of a university press, especially one as distinguished as Chicago.) Such imperfections mar an otherwise exemplary work of creative literary and cultural criticism. Perhaps they will be fixed in future editions.

A Man Apart

[2012]

When I was twenty and just starting out as a poet, my girlfriend gave me a copy of the big Sierra Club picture book *Not Man Apart* with its gorgeous photos of the Big Sur coast by the likes of Ansel Adams and Edward Weston accompanied by lines (and some whole poems) of Robinson Jeffers. As I read the poetry alongside the pictures their combined beauty brought me to tears. I was slightly familiar with Jeffers from his ten poems in Oscar Williams's classic anthology *A Pocket Book of Modern Verse*, but by that time (1967) Jeffers's stock had fallen precipitously from its pinnacle of the 1920s and 30s, and he was seldom mentioned anymore as one of the major American poets. Eclipsed by his contemporary Modernists (T. S. Eliot, Ezra Pound, Wallace Stevens, Marianne Moore and William Carlos Williams among others) and even by more-traditional poets like Robert Frost and neo-Romantics like E. E. Cummings, Jeffers had exiled himself from both mainstream and avant-garde American culture through his geophysical isolation on the Central California coast, the unpopular and at times repugnant political attitudes openly expressed in his writings, and his indifference to current artistic and critical trends. He had carved out a singular place for himself in the literary landscape and was content to let Eternity decide what to make of him and his work.

It was only later that I was able to place him in such a historical context. What moved me about his poems, first in the Williams anthology, then in the Sierra Club book, and after that in the six-hundred-page Random House edition of his *Selected Poetry*, was the irresistible force of his voice, its muscular music, its vivid engagement with the physical world, its rhythmic power, its readily comprehensible language, its acute observation and spiritual exaltation of natural beauty. I was drawn to the shorter lyrics more than to the long narratives, but even in the latter with their disturbing stories there was a propulsive momentum in the writing that I had never encountered before except perhaps in Richmond Lattimore's Homer. The fact that Jeffers was the first great modern poet of California made him, for me as a native Californian, a predecessor to be reckoned with. Even though by then the Beat, Black Mountain, Deep Image and New York School movements were rising to replace the Southern Agrarians, the Confessionalists and the New Critics as the dominant forces in US poetic discourse, I was still reading the English Romantics and could feel intuitively the natural link between Wordsworth's *Lyrical Ballads* and the stormy dithyrambs of Jeffers in such books as *Tamar*, *Roan Stallion* and *The Women at Point Sur*.

A few years later, at the tail end of my abortive career as a graduate student in literature at UC Santa Cruz, I had the good fortune to take a seminar in the History of Consciousness program called Ideas of the Nature of Poetry with Robert

Duncan, another important California poet first associated with Kenneth Rexroth and the San Francisco Renaissance and later with Charles Olson and the Black Mountain school. Duncan, an Oakland native and one-time personal secretary to Anaïs Nin, was an inspiringly anti-academic eminence recruited briefly by Norman O. Brown to teach at UCSC (the literature faculty would have nothing to do with such a creatively unconventional mind as Duncan's). His assignment for the students in his seminar was to select one poet to study for the term and to explore "the range of consciousness" in his or her writing. I chose Jeffers.

As it turned out, Jeffers didn't have that much range—certainly not as much as Duncan, whose thinking and writing spanned centuries and cultures from prehistoric cave art to contemporary television—but rather returned again and again to a few core themes, convictions and obsessions, namely the grandeur and nobility of Nature versus the smallness and depravity of Man. Duncan helped to illuminate Jeffers's poems by explaining that many of his narratives, fraught with violence and murder and sexual transgression, were based at least in part on stories or legends of events that had actually occurred on the Big Sur coast, stories that had helped to form and to reinforce the poet's ideas about human baseness in contrast to the greatness of the rest of God's creation: ocean, mountains, trees, rocks, wild animals. Here we find hints of Jeffers's origins as the son of a Pennsylvania Presbyterian minister and theology professor who instilled in his child the notion of Original Sin. The boy was rigorously educated in the classics and languages and spent three years at schools in Europe before returning to the States to enter college in Pittsburgh at the age of fifteen.

Jeffers moved with his family to Southern California and graduated at eighteen from Occidental, followed by graduate studies at USC in forestry, medicine and the sciences. It was there, in Los Angeles, on the eve of the First World War, that he met his muse and future wife, Una, who at the time was married to someone else. After a scandalous affair and her divorce, Jeffers and his new bride planned to move to England, but the war intervened, fatefully altering their agenda. On a visit to Carmel in 1914 they found their spot on a coastal bluff and decided to settle there. While Jeffers had self-published a book of verse in 1912, it was a conventional effort in turn-of-the-century lyricism, and it wasn't until about 1919 when he started building a home that he found his own distinctive voice as a poet. Apprenticing himself to a stonemason, Jeffers physically built his own house, hauling big rocks up from the beach and setting them one upon another. Then, on his own, he constructed an adjacent four-story stone tower for Una and their twin sons. Tor House and Hawk Tower are now, a century later, surrounded by upscale homes of the Carmel elite, a popular attraction for literary tourists not far from the golf course at Pebble Beach.

Certainly the years of manual labor lifting stones and constructing buildings had a profound effect not only on Jeffers's body, soul and psyche, but on his prosody and practice as a poet. The physical quality of his verse, the muscular authority of his voice, the hardness of his vision of the universe have as much to do with his handling the materials of his family's dwelling as with his stern Protestant upbringing and the wild landscape and seascape he chose as his habitat. You can not only hear a rolling, surf-like rhythm in his lines but can feel the weight of the granite he used to build his fortress-like house. Unlike most of his modernist contemporaries Jeffers did not live primarily in his head, and his writing reveals its foundation in the physical world. Like the San Francisco-born Frost, who also resisted the modernist tide from his New Hampshire farm, Jeffers's flinty sensibility and style are informed by bodily work outdoors, away from the library and the writing desk.

While at first glance Jeffers's expansive lines may resemble those of Walt Whitman, he is in fact the anti-Whitman, marking the end of the Long Island–born poet's optimistic celebration of an America brimming with human promise and vitality, and pronouncing from the opposite end of the continent the nation's inevitable doom—a doom destined not just for the United States but for all of civilization. Gazing out at the Pacific Ocean in its immense wild splendor, observing the birds and beasts of the Santa Lucia Mountains, witnessing or imagining the terrible crimes of the puny humans living in such awesome surroundings, Jeffers took a very long view of our time on Earth and the ephemeral nuisance of society. Looking southward down the Big Sur coast rather than more immediately north to his Carmel community of privileged bohemians, artists and dilettantes, Jeffers engaged his imagination with the wild lands and their human inhabitants prone to incestuous passions, madness and violent mayhem. As he writes in the Foreword to his *Selected Poetry* of 1938, on the south coast of the Monterey Peninsula he saw "life purged of its ephemeral accretions. Men were riding after cattle, or plowing the headland, hovered by white sea gulls, as they have done for thousands of years, and will for thousands of years to come." It is these very cowboys and plowmen and their families who serve as the deranged protagonists of his narratives, not living in harmony with nature but driven mad by its savage beauty and infecting it with their own moral corruption.

This is why Jeffers is such a prophetic voice for the environmental movement: he could foresee, as early as the 1920s, the terrible damage humans would inevitably wreak on their habitat. Surely the general disillusionment following the carnage of World War I contributed to Jeffers's pessimism (and he wasn't the only one; just think of Eliot's *The Waste Land*, the emblematic poem of their generation), but his timeless perch on the edge of the Pacific with its sharp-beaked raptors and granite boulders and eternally rocking waters and cosmic weather, combined with his knowledge of the sciences, all contributed to what he came to call his philosophy of "inhumanism," his de-centering of people from the grander scheme of the universe. But Jeffers was no environmentalist as we understand the term today. He made no active attempt to save the earth and thereby save civilization from itself. He seems instead to have welcomed humanity's eventual self-destruction and to look forward to the planet's inevitable recovery of its natural equilibrium. On a scale of countless millions of years of Creation, the history of mankind is a speck of dust in a blinking eye.

As William S. Burroughs would put it later in a radically different register, Jeffers saw humanity as something like an alien virus plaguing the planet. He anticipates the Deep Ecology concept in his long view of the earth's resilience despite everything transient humans may throw at it. But like Burroughs he also flirts with nihilism in his indifference to the outcome of World War II (which he gloomily anticipated in his writings all through the 1920s and 30s), regarding Roosevelt and Churchill and Hitler and Stalin as corrupt leaders of equally evil regimes destined to lead the world into nothing but disaster. The atomic bombs over Japan in 1945 only confirmed his dire prophecies, and while his anti-political stance made him for many a persona non grata until his death in 1962, Jeffers was one of the earliest and most eloquent voices warning of the apocalyptic consequences of the century's wars. The poet once praised as the greatest of his time (his face appeared on the cover of *Time* in 1932) spent most of his later years reviled by his contemporaries as some kind of cranky reactionary so far removed from humankind as to be indifferent to the sufferings of actual people.

And it wasn't just his politics that critics objected to. Kenneth Rexroth, who shared with Jeffers an affinity for the natural terrain and skies of California and a principled objection to war of any kind, dismissed the older poet's "cowgirl tragedies" as a vulgarization of their Greek models. From Rexroth's perspective it's easy to see Jeffers's tormented narratives as melodramatic soap operas rather than dramas equal to their archetypes—a perspective possibly reinforced by Jeffers's successful translation of Euripides's *Medea* for the stage in 1946, the spare economy of the Greek text making the translator's original poems look windy and baggy by comparison.

Yvor Winters of Stanford, perhaps his most hostile critic, noted as early as 1932 that the "violent monotony of movement" in Jeffers's poetry "may have a hypnotic effect... much as does the jolting of a railroad coach over a bad roadbed." If such a nasty assessment had any effect on its subject, he didn't show it but just kept right on driving his locomotive.

And though Jeffers died before Winters did (in 1968 after a long tenure as Stanford's doctrinaire and domineering resident poet and critic), the Bard of Carmel had the last posthumous laugh when, around the turn of this century, Stanford University Press began issuing huge volumes of his collected works. Winters, who was easily as inflexible as Jeffers, is largely forgotten or ignored today as a poet *or* critic, while Jeffers, for all the insults hurled at him by irate humanists, continues to weather very well, especially in the shorter lyric poems for which he is now best known. (These are best represented in *Rock and Hawk*, the 1987 selection edited by Robert Hass on the occasion of the poet's centennial, and in the Vintage paperback *Selected Poems.*)

Randall Jarrell, another prominent mid-century critic and poet, famously observed that a poet is someone who, in a lifetime of standing out in thunderstorms, manages to be struck by lightning five or six times. As a corollary to this formula I would add that a great poet is one who is hit by lightning maybe a couple of dozen times, and by this measure Jeffers can hold his own against almost anyone else in the twentieth century. Just the ten poems in that 1954 Oscar Williams anthology (a book that holds up exceptionally well more than half a century since)—"The Eye," "To the Stone-cutters," "Night," "Boats in a Fog," "Phenomena," "Haunted Country," "Science," "Apology for Bad Dreams," "Summer Holiday" and "I Shall Laugh Purely"—are enough to establish the author's permanent place in any canon of American poetry. If he buried his best work, in these and similar poems penned through his long career, under a mountain of lesser diatribes, jeremiads, sermons, speeches and psychodramas, the fact is that most prolific poets, starting with Whitman in this country, seldom leave more than a handful of truly enduring works, and it is on these that their reputations rest.

Today there are so many canons and counter-canons, so many poets scattered all over the map thanks in large part to the "creative writing" industry and its MFA programs, so many different identities being defended, so many theories promulgated, that it's anyone's guess what or who will be remembered fifty much less one hundred years from now. Still, there is a gravity and durability in Jeffers—as in the stoutness of his hand-built house—that I think will outlast much of what passes for the finest poetry of today. Because he focused on the timelessness of what he could see and feel from his granite aerie, and at best invoked and evoked it in language that still sings to anyone open-hearted enough to hear, he can't be dismissed so easily as Rexroth and Winters tried to dismiss him, each no doubt for his own rivalrous reasons.

Even Czeslaw Milosz, transplanted from Poland to UC Berkeley for a long stay capped by a Nobel Prize in 1980, had a beef with Jeffers for his proclamation of "an inhuman thing" in the face of the real-life human tragedies that Milosz had witnessed in Europe. And more recently, the Santa Cruz transplant Adrienne Rich condemned Jeffers for his self-isolation in the face of so many social injustices and for the depiction in his poems of such unsympathetic and degraded women. There is certainly something to these complaints, and I agree that Jeffers, as represented in his writings, is not an especially likeable person and not a candidate to be the guru or role model for any aspiring humanist. Yet for all his misanthropy (he was just as contemptuous of men as of women) there is something indelible in his work—a quality of vision eloquently examined in William Everson's landmark cultural-historical study, *Archetype West: The Pacific Coast as a Literary Region*—that must be engaged with by subsequent generations, especially of California poets. Everson himself, modeling his poetry on that of Jeffers with a rogue-Catholic twist on his kinky sexual obsessions, allowed his own poetics to be overwhelmed by those of his forebear, and so became a pale shadow of his hero, his voice drowned out by Jeffers's stronger music.

Of all California poets Gary Snyder is probably the one who has most fruitfully advanced Jeffers's acute attention to wild nature into a distinctive style of his own whose human elements, while not always benevolent, at least suggest a certain compassion in the poet, and a desire to rescue civilization from its own excesses. Though Snyder has long lived on a homestead in the Sierra Nevada foothills, he has devoted his life to teaching as well as preaching, and has thus maintained his stake in some human community. Similarly Lawrence Ferlinghetti, when he writes of "freeways fifty lanes wide / on a concrete continent" where people drive "painted cars" whose engines "devour America," is echoing Jeffers but with an ironic lightness that lifts his tone beyond the merely accusatory.

Perhaps the most unlikely avatar of Jeffers is Charles Bukowski, who as a Los Angeles native and longtime chronicler of life in that sprawling city, is emblematic of the kind of squalid decadence Jeffers was above condemning, seeing all the great cities as cancers on the landscape that would consume themselves soon enough. Yet Bukowski admired Jeffers and emulated his unshakeable integrity, his hardness toward the world's cruelties, his indifference to literary opinion, and the life-and-death seriousness of his writings. Bukowski's compassion for his fellow losers in LA's human landscape and his relentlessly prolific transformation of his own experience into something more than the sum of its miserable parts make him in some way a greater soul than Jeffers, because despite people's many failings, individually and collectively, he refuses to reject the species to which he belongs. Contrary to his tough-guy persona, at heart Bukowski is a big softie, and it makes him a better writer than he would be otherwise.

Henry Miller, a California transplant from Brooklyn by way of Paris, who lived in Big Sur for many years before ending up in Pacific Palisades, found Jeffers not only "wonderful to look at" with a face like one of his beloved hawks, "a trembling rock" of a wounded soul whose presence commanded respect and sensitivity, but a writer who—with Faulkner, Twain and Whitman—in Miller's words, gives "the real American feeling." Miller too, in his groundbreaking *Tropic of Cancer* (1934, though not published in the States until 1962), both illustrates precisely the cultural decline that Jeffers held himself above, and salvages the human capacity to absorb and transform such sordid conditions into something worth celebrating—if only the human comedy itself and the potential for individual transcendence.

As a descendant of all these writers, a California native and a poet of the Central Coast, I have long since abandoned Jeffers as a model of either personal or poetic conduct. His inhumanism (which is really more like antihumanism) wielded as an ideological bludgeon diminishes much of his writing, just as Rich's genderism and Pablo Neruda's communism often compromise their imaginations with canned political formulas, rhetorical evidence of righteousness but tedious and redundant as art. Yet Jeffers, as Pound called Whitman (and like the insufferable Pound himself), is "a pigheaded father" who despite his faults has much to teach. I've learned from him to ignore current trends and hold to my own vision of what must be written, and how to write it; to trust my own voice (as Duncan advised) and to take seriously the truth of my own experience; to attend to the reality of the physical world and attempt to embody it in my writing; to have no patience with vanity and ego (including mine) and to beware of poetic presumptuousness and frivolousness alike. The words "beauty" and "beautiful" appear repeatedly in Jeffers's verse, and in their recurrence reveal that Beauty—mostly in the form of his coastal landscape and the constantly changing ocean and their creatures—is what he values above everything and what serves as evidence and embodiment of a trans-human divinity. Even for a non- or anti-religious poet, the mystery of creation is an inexhaustible subject, and Jeffers at his best opens a big window on a realm of limitless wonder.

The Colossus of North Beach

[2013]

Beard and fringe of white hair neatly trimmed for the occasion, bald dome shining in the Sunday afternoon light of his office windows above Columbus Avenue, Lawrence Ferlinghetti sat patiently at an empty desk, a mildly disconcerted look on his face, greeting a stream of well-wishers come to congratulate him on the sixtieth birthday of City Lights Books. Just outside the door in the poetry room, and downstairs on the ground floor, and spilling out onto the sidewalk and into Kerouac Alley in front of Vesuvio's where a Latin jazz band was playing, swarms of visitors were browsing and milling in and around the store. The crowd was a mix of locals, longtime friends and patrons and the usual summer tourists last June 23 when City Lights was throwing itself a party. It was, typically for this San Francisco institution and international landmark, a masterpiece of public and community relations. Ever since its founding in 1953 by visionary bookseller Ferlinghetti and his business partner at the time, Peter Martin, City Lights has distinguished itself as one of the most remarkable cultural and commercial enterprises of our time. Quite apart from his important work as a poet, publisher and painter, Ferlinghetti would be an extraordinary figure in American culture for the significance of his bookshop alone.

As a reader and writer residing in the greater Bay Area for some forty-five years, I have gotten to know the store, and its poet-founder, through a good part of its evolution from a tiny storefront with racks of paperbacks—it started out specializing in this new format for mass-market books—to its current three-story (including the basement), much-expanded emporium for all the best of what's in print, especially anything literary or political. Ferlinghetti's sensibility and signature are everywhere, from the layout of the bookcases to the historic photographs and posters on the walls to the hand-lettered signs the poet-painter posts from time to time to make his patrons feel at home and safe from the madness and distractions of the world outside—like, for example: HAVE A SEAT AND READ A BOOK; BOOKS ARE TREES MADE IMMORTAL; and, perhaps my favorite, STASH YOUR SELL-PHONE AND BE HERE NOW. Above in the windows or on the wall visible from the street are various signs or banners calling, in one form or another, for peace and justice. Seen from the outside, the building is a beacon of political dissidence; within, it is a haven of intellectual curiosity and contemplation. Although by now it has a staff of dozens, and the founder, at ninety-four, is scarcely involved in day-to-day operations, his mark on the place remains indelible.

But for someone with the publicity instincts of a P. T. Barnum and the performing instincts of a Charlie Chaplin, Ferlinghetti the person is, except perhaps to his closest friends, an enigma, a rather shy man with a detached or distracted air, as if being too friendly meant a lapse of dignity, especially with strangers, often star-struck by his fame. Like any famous person with any sense, he keeps his guard up to protect himself from celebrity-stalkers, and yet at the same time he can be seen in public all over North Beach and beyond. Besides the occasional encounter in the bookstore, over the years I've run into him reading a newspaper in the back of an out-of-the-way neighborhood café, or strolling up Columbus on the way home from work, or riding his bicycle along the Embarcadero, just another citizen going about his business. If you didn't recognize him, you would never know he is one of the most popular poets on the planet, a pioneer of independent publishing and a widely exhibited painter in addition to his accomplishment as a business owner.

Still, the glimpse I got of him that Sunday afternoon in June suggested he'd just as soon be anywhere else than politely receiving visitors in his office; this clearly was not his preferred social role. He is much more at home on a stage reading his poems, or working behind the scenes publishing books by other writers, or in his studio painting than he is meeting his admirers face to face. But such is the price of high-profile achievement over several generations in literary, political, commercial and popular culture. Icon is a terrible label to pin on anyone, and Ferlinghetti has always been and continues to be an iconoclast, but hardly anyone alive looms larger in the cultural landscape of California, or America.

Yet up close he is totally down to earth. In practically every situation where I've been with him, he is the least obtrusive person in the room, with no interest in being the center of attention. In 1983, when Nicaraguan poet and Sandinista

Minister of Culture Ernesto Cardenal came to San Francisco to read his work and represent his revolutionary government, Ferlinghetti threw a generous lunch for at least twenty poets and journalists at the New Pisa restaurant, a suitably historic venue with its checkered tablecloths and old-time baseball photo gallery. After the meal, as a group of us gathered for an interview, the host was low-key, speaking only when directly addressed, yielding the floor to his distinguished guest. In other settings, at benefits and festivals and receptions, at readings and parties and demonstrations, despite the immense respect and deference shown him by everyone, I've never seen him with an entourage or any of the trappings of celebrity. Unlike many cultural superstars, he's always just hanging out with everyone else, true to his philosophical principle of anarchism with its horizontal rather than hierarchical power relations.

But Ferlinghetti is no pushover. To have done what he has in business he must have driven a lot of hard bargains and made some shrewd deals and had the judgment to hire competent and compatible people and coordinate their working together. Certainly during its maturity City Lights benefited greatly from the savvy management of Nancy Joyce Peters, who was running the store and the publishing house for most of the time I've been going there. (Peters is now retired, and Elaine Katzenberger has stepped into the role of chief executive.) But Lawrence, as everyone calls him, even in the nineteen-nineties when he was less active than previously, was hands-on editor of his Pocket Poets Series, as I discovered when he published my translation of Julio Cortázar's selected poems, and a tough-minded negotiator of editorial decisions. In those days before either of us used email, we sent that manuscript back and forth numerous times, haggling over the selection of this or that poem, or this or that word or line, until we were both satisfied that the result was the best book possible. This kind of hardheaded give-and-take between editor and author (or in this case translator) is increasingly rare in this age of ebooks and ibooks and instant uploads and all the permutations of new media. As someone of an earlier generation of bookmen (and yes, they were mostly men), Ferlinghetti the populist and anarchist could also fairly be called a gentleman publisher.

It wasn't always so. When he published Allen Ginsberg's *Howl* in 1956 he was indicted for trafficking in obscenity, and the trial and vindication of that landmark poem was a victory for free expression that resonates to this day. Ferlinghetti's journey from literary outlaw and alleged smut peddler to his current exalted status as elder statesman proves, among other things, that if you work diligently enough and live long enough, even the most disreputable character can rise to heights of distinction never approached by your prosecutors. Without ever compromising his politics or his commitment to free speech, City Lights' poet-publisher simultaneously maintains a reputation of high distinction among the respectable (per his many lifetime achievement awards, from the American Academy of Arts and Letters, National Book Foundation, Poetry Society of America, National Book Critics Circle, and others) and of authentic rebelliousness among the marginal, the countercultural, the ostracized, the neglected. How he has managed to do this is something of a mystery, but it's also a measure of his artistic and entrepreneurial genius.

Writing in such superlative terms feels odd to me, as skeptical a critic as you will find, especially when it comes to hero worship. Yet while I have at times disagreed with his anarcho-romantic politics and had arguments with his populist poetics, Ferlinghetti's integrity as a writer, publisher and person is something I've grown to admire more and more. He has never sold out, nor been corrupted by his prominence, nor given an inch to the academics or reactionaries or war-makers or tastemakers he has opposed from the beginning, creating—under the early influence of his mentor, Kenneth Rexroth, whose poetic and political vision was instrumental in the San Francisco Renaissance of the 1940s and 50s—a dynamic alternative to the conformist ideas of his time. Through his poetry, his publishing, his bookselling, his agitating and his sheer endurance as a good-natured, lighthearted avatar of the arts, he has shown by example that it is possible both to oppose the status quo and to survive, to contest the system and yet thrive within it, to be both a lover and a fighter, all without losing your humanity. It's hard to think of many other examples of this kind of stamina in so many spheres, and it's impossible not to acknowledge as extraordinary.

And what about the poetry? His second book, *A Coney Island of the Mind* (its title taken from a chapter in Henry Miller's *Black Spring*), first published in 1958 and continuously in print since then, has sold more than a million copies in at least nine languages and ranks as one of the all-time verse bestsellers. Those poems are still fresh, even to a reader long familiar with them, but in the half-century since their appearance the author has continued at regular intervals to bring out volume after volume of new work, right up to last year's Book II of his ongoing long poem-in-progress, *Americus*, where with his usual mixture of Whitmanic expansiveness and Groucho Marxian irony, of William Carlos Williamsesque plainspokenness and Ezra Poundian authority, of high literary allusion and streetwise pop reference, of romantic earnestness and satiric irreverence, he has carried on his public chronicle of life in these States. Despite his prodigious output and sustained accomplishment as a poet, Ferlinghetti has seldom been accorded the critical attention and respect given many lesser contemporaries, perhaps because his poems are so readily comprehensible that they speak for themselves without interpretive interference. They are written not for specialists but for anyone with an open mind and heart, and their ingenuousness disarms whoever would attempt to explain or analyze them.

Maybe that's why he never takes questions after readings—believing that poetry is best left to resonate in the minds of its listeners—and why he once remarked to me that "whole books [of poetry] disappear without a sound, as if dropped into a void." (If such a renowned poet can be so widely ignored by the critical establishment, imagine the fate of more obscure authors.) Unaffected by trends and perpetually outside the mainstream when not actively going against the current of both mass culture and elitist taste, Ferlinghetti has created a body of work that can hold its own against that of virtually any American poet of the last half century. *These Are My Rivers: New & Selected Poems 1955–1993* (already twenty years old) is probably the best available introduction to this writer's work, but his more recent books *How to Paint Sunlight* (2001), *Americus, Book I* (2004) and *Time of Useful Consciousness* (*Americus, Book II,* 2012) testify that his energy is, amazingly, undiminished. The author notes that the latter title "is an aeronautical term denoting the time between when one loses oxygen and when one passes out, the brief time in which some lifesaving action is possible." This is a brilliant metaphor both for the poet's acknowledgment of his own mortality and his belief in the potential of art to rescue a civilization spiraling into catastrophe. The cumulative effect of reading these volumes over several months, as I have, is to feel a sense of awe and admiration that anyone can sustain such a life's work continuously over so long a period of time.

In the little volume of zingers and manifestos, aphorisms and exhortations, slogans and definitions titled *Poetry as Insurgent Art* (2007) Ferlinghetti spells out as directly as possible his belief in the transformative, revolutionary, magical powers of poetry to enlighten and inspire the individual who writes or reads it and to thereby change the world for the better. It is perhaps a quixotic or even naïve belief, but lived with his fervor of undiminished conviction it can feel forcefully persuasive to those who embrace it. It is this sense of courage and encouragement, of resistance to despair and to the machinations of marketing and political bad faith in all its forms that has endeared the man to his fans, even those who have read him only a little.

And so it was no surprise that when filmmaker Chris Felver brought his bio-documentary *Ferlinghetti* to Santa Cruz on October 18, 2011, that day was declared by the mayor Lawrence Ferlinghetti Day and five hundred people filled the auditorium of the art deco Del Mar Theater to have a good look at the legendary figure on film, and also to see the great man in the flesh. Onstage after the screening, Felver and Ferlinghetti took a few questions from the audience. One older gentleman toward the front of the hall asked Lawrence what advice he had for staying upbeat and productive in one's later years, and the poet replied, deadpan, "Read Samuel Beckett." That Ferlinghetti the perpetual optimist and overthrower of the powers that be should invoke Beckett, the bleak yet paradoxically hopeful bard of existential hopelessness, may have left most of the audience scratching their heads, but to me it revealed tremendous wit and self-awareness, implying that only by facing the darkest reality of what we're up against—both individual death and socio-political (not to mention ecological) disaster—do we have a chance of using it for creative purposes. Beckett's characters, like Chaplin's, are bumbling victims yet tough survivors of a world that couldn't care less. Ferlinghetti is wise enough to recognize this truth. Such spiritual resilience in the face of certain doom is a gift deserving of our deepest gratitude.

Notes on a Dirty Old Man

[1985]

My first direct encounter with Charles Bukowski occurred in 1974, in a Santa Cruz restaurant in the basement of a building that used to be the county courthouse but had been converted to a little shopping complex with lots of nice shops for the tourists. The famous writer was in town to read at a poetry festival that evening, had drunk his free meal with the literary hustlers and was looking vaguely bored and pre-obnoxious as zero hour approached. I arrived late, as the party was preparing to leave the restaurant, and my first impression of the distinguished guest (to whom I was perfunctorily introduced) was of a man profoundly indifferent to the surrounding bullshit but not really a nasty fellow. He seemed to be someone doing his job, stoically meeting professional obligations, keeping a crusty demeanor on for the sake of self-defense from the admiring vampires, not friendly but coolly tolerant of the attention. In that smallish group, which included Allen Ginsberg and Gary Snyder and a number of lesser literati, Bukowski struck me as being for real in a way that could be trusted.

Later that evening, after a marathon reading at the Civic Auditorium where Bukowski enraged the feminists and delighted the subliterary slobs by being himself onstage, reading in that unshakably murderous monotone for his allotted time, punctuated by slurps from his quart of screwdriver, then heckling his colleagues from the audience ("Read ten more!" he yelled at Snyder as the hour approached midnight and the crowd hushed reverently to receive some of Gary's Zen/environmentalist wisdom)—later, after the reading, there was a party to which the bards and their followers were invited. As one of the younger local poets, I had read that night and was honored to be in such illustrious company. At the same time I had a skeptical or even cynical feeling about the whole affair, a sour reaction to the spectacle and the sycophantic frenzy that often surrounds celebrities. Standing off to the side of the room moodily observing the goings-on, I found myself next to Bukowski, who muttered to me in a tone that seemed a mixture of distaste and weary understanding (and maybe sympathy for my unease), "I guess we have to entertain these people, don't we."

I think I just shrugged, not wanting to provoke one of the legendary brawls for which the man was famous, but in retrospect there was a gentle sincerity in his voice that was anything but hostile or aggressive. Listening to the undertone of his work before and since—seeing through the stylistic toughness of his poetry and prose—one can detect that kind of compassionate tenderness, an acceptance which softens and absorbs brutality and gives the rawness of Bukowski's voice a deep and humane resonance.

With age this compassionate quality, which was always present but masked with irony or tough-guy posturing, has risen closer to the surface of his writing and become its informing substance. The key, I believe, to understanding Bukowski's power is the 1982 novel *Ham on Rye*, where he reveals the origins of his attitude toward life and in an incredibly generous way forgives his cruel and pathetic father for all the abuse the writer withstood as a child. One can begin to comprehend how, in the relentless account of his more-sordid-than-average days and nights prolifically typed and published over the last two or three decades, the act of writing has literally saved his life. This is what makes Bukowski such an inspiration to the readers who have grown to trust him: if this guy can make it through so much misery, anybody can. His works are a reservoir of earned courage.

If he is a model for other writers, it has less to do with his style—which unfortunately has been imitated to death by a multitude of second-, third- and fourth-rate poets—than with his ability, day after day, to sit down at the machine facing a blank page and patiently put one word after another. This patience and perseverance in composition has not only tightened and clarified his language over the years, it has cultivated an increasingly persuasive truthfulness, a sense of honest simplicity which makes his books easy to read, offensive to some, sad and funny—in short, lifelike. His writing is proletarian without ever attempting to be politically uplifting; if anything, its rejection of political solutions for human plight and its embrace of such small consolations as classical music on the radio, playing the horses, drinking and whoring around is what gives it its illusionless appeal. Socially, his world is a comic wasteland where stupid jerks redeem themselves only through acts of unheroic attention.

I write this knowing that there are people who will always see Bukowski as a pig, and that the professors will want some evidence to back up any assertion of his importance. But these are notes, not a doctoral thesis (though I guarantee that the PhD's will descend one day, if they haven't already, to document meticulously the artistic achievement of this barbaric figure), and I want to be sure my subjective reading is not mistaken for scholarship. If the literary establishment has rejected Bukowski's work as beneath any decent New Yorker's dignity, it's partly because his writing resists any form of text-worship or cocktail-party appropriation, partly because he's published by a small press on the West Coast, John Martin's incomparable Black Sparrow—and has found his audience all along through funky little independent magazines and papers—and partly because (horror of horrors!) he's from Los Angeles. His presence in that city has, through no intent of his own, been instrumental in helping to generate a large and vital wave of excellent work in poetry and prose by younger writers who learned from his example that one doesn't need New York's approval to become an author on one's own power.

Despite the fact that he's been widely translated and is extremely popular in Europe, Bukowski remains a local writer in the best sense of the term, rooted in his native turf and endlessly unearthing its indigenous reality without ever pretending to speak as a public voice. More subtly and consistently than any other writer I know, Bukowski has mapped the nervous energy of LA's streets, its car culture, its architectural pathos, the truly mundane and unglamorous side of its Hollywood façade. In the novel *Women* especially, which I believe to be his masterpiece, one gets the sense of frantic desperation that permeates the City of Angels. But because he was raised in Los Angeles and knows its people—its real people, not the mosquitoes buzzing into the beams of its klieg lights, nor even the emblematic grotesques of Nathanael West's imagination—his portrayal of the city and its inhabitants lacks the bitterness and contempt so often found in the writings of outsiders taking a jaundiced peek into the dream factory. LA was never a dream for Bukowski, nor even much of a nightmare; it was and is simply a given, a landscape whose reality was never in doubt. I'm convinced that Bukowski's books will be read in the future as maps of Los Angeles in much the same way as Joyce's work is seen as a guide to Dublin.

Within the context of American literature Bukowski is sometimes compared to Henry Miller (who coincidentally also ended up in LA). In their radical rejection of mainstream social values, their survival-oriented individualism, the buffoonery of their sexual obsessions, their scatological vulgarity, the unabashedly autobiographical or nakedly personal orientation of their texts and the sheer productivity of their typewriters, Miller and Bukowski clearly share some territory in a larger egomythomaniacal American tradition. But while both are enemies of hypocrisy, Miller is deeply moralistic, often preaching to the reader or arguing for some philosophical position as if it made an important spiritual difference, where Bukowski is beneath good and evil, literally grounded in his own experience. It's not that he has no imagination—much of his earlier poetry is as richly inventive as Miller's wilder flights of lyric prose—he's just not the metaphysician or transcendentalist that Miller is. Bukowski *is* a poet, however, or an antipoet, who achieves a surprising lyricism in the midst of the most talky, typewriterly utterances. And perhaps what the two have most in common is that they're totally unafraid to make fools of themselves.

Bukowski's willingness to write badly without embarrassment, to do the same thing over and over again in poems or in stories, is one of the exasperating and endearing things about him. Exasperating because we've heard it before, endearing because it's *him*, it is the pattern out of which he has always worked, for better and for worse. He has mined deeply a relatively modest if down-and-dirty range of experience; he has not sought exotic adventures or inventions (unless being broke and drunk is exotic) because he recognizes the mundane's amazing capacity for revelation. Besides, he's lazy. He likes to be not too far from a liquor store at any time. After a lifetime of stupid jobs, he'd rather go to the racetrack than to work, to the wilderness or to a poetry reading. He does not set himself up as a model for anything, nor does he presume to be a bad example. In Bukowski's world, there's nothing even to rebel against. Life is the way it is—painful, absurd and scary—and one deals with it as best one can.

And what about alcohol, the temperate will ask; doesn't he glorify and celebrate the dubious pleasures of alcoholism? Hardly. Alcohol for Bukowski is a vice to which he admits—a crutch, a shield, a wall, a last line of defense against a world that refuses to cooperate. He no more advocates its use than he advocates driving on the freeway, but he presents it as one more element in his milieu, like any other character, circumstance or setting, however unsavory.

The misogyny of which he is often accused is also, I think, a misreading of his work. Nobody, male or female, escapes the writer's scathing gaze. The women in most of his poems and stories are real people: they come across as quirky, flawed, scarred but complete beings, eccentrically individual, not just anonymous bodies on which to exercise his funky fantasies, though they may be that as well. Fucking, as most of us know, and less-than-tender attempts at sexual intimacy, and eating and drinking and shitting are things that people actually do, and Bukowski faces these facts because they constitute life as he knows it. In his recent work he seems to be sweetening into a kindly old recluse (some of the poems in *War All the Time* show the emergence of a warmer, softer Bukowski than some readers might have anticipated) but he has earned this more kindly outlook through suffering; he didn't just decide to be nice.

Like all great writers, Bukowski is a warrior of the spirit, even in his rejection of any form of conventional heroism. He testifies to the fact that even under the worst of circumstances people can remain undefeated. My respect for his work is a personal matter, although it has more to do with his character than with his personality; that night we met in Santa Cruz was the only time we've spoken face to face. One thing about him that astonishes me is that his work continues to improve, or at least maintain a level of strength that shows he is still creating, not just going through the motions. With each new book I find myself recharged with an interest in the everyday, reminded that the life of every person counts.

What Hath Roth Wrought?

[2013]

Philip Roth's recent announcement that he is done with writing novels must have come as a great relief to all the younger writers whose air he has been sucking out of the American literary atmosphere for the last fifty-three years, especially during his extraordinary late-career surge of the 1990s. As by far the most decorated US author of his time—having bagged every major prize and critical accolade, some of them several times over, except the Nobel—and after a streak of outstanding books in his sixties followed by a string of smaller but powerful novellas in his seventies, Roth's decision to hang up his pen (revealed in a front-page interview in the Sunday *New York Times* last November 18) caught almost everyone, including me, by surprise. Admirers of his work are no doubt disappointed to be deprived of future Roth books—though plenty of the old ones are worth rereading—but what struck me was the unthinkable idea that he could even consider giving up writing, as most real writers, especially "successful" ones, are compelled to keep at it as long as their health and their wits allow. Roth, obsessed with the great unanswerable questions and still writing well, seemed the kind of person who would just carry on until he dropped. But according to what he told Charles McGrath of the *Times*, he has said everything he has to say and is tired of the daily effort to wrestle his sentences into submission.

Having read his most recent and presumably final novel, *Nemesis* (about a polio epidemic), and before that *The Humbling* (about a washed-up actor who shoots himself) and *Indignation* (about a feckless college student who winds up disemboweled on a battlefield in Korea) and *Everyman* (about the inexorable decline and demise of an average Joe) and *Exit Ghost* (about the sexual humiliation of the author's alter ego Nathan Zuckerman) and *The Dying Animal* (about a beautiful young woman doomed by breast cancer), I begin to understand that Roth as a novelist could not drive any deeper into despair. His books weren't exactly cheery in previous decades, but the narrative voice still had some fire in it, some hope, some defiance of fate, if only in the intense energy he brought to his engagement with various forms of personal tragedy.

Over the last ten or twelve years Roth appears to have surrendered to the bleakest possible view of human destiny. This gloomy vision reaches its nadir in *Nemesis*, which reads like a toxic mixture of the Book of Job, Kafka's *The Trial* and Camus's *The Plague*, a triple-whammy potent enough to subdue the novelist's formerly manic or ironic or gallows-black Jewish humor. Roth appears to be engaged, especially in *Nemesis*, in hand-to-hand combat, a fight to the death, with a God he doesn't even believe in—a God who, as he pungently puts it in the final pages of that book, is both "a sick fuck and an evil genius." How else to explain the demonic torments of World War II or a polio epidemic, except that no such God exists and people are subject to destruction by random irrational forces as well as their own mistakes. Like Jacob wrestling with the angel, the writer seems to have been looking for a blessing in the struggle with art, but ultimately he has found none forthcoming and so has decided to cry Uncle. He throws in the towel. He smashes the tablets.

At the same time he admits to McGrath that he is now "working for" his handpicked authorized biographer, Blake Bailey, by writing down thousands of pages of notes, presumably true to the best of his recollection (an always questionable presumption), on what he can recall of his life story, boxes full of notes, "so many," Bailey says, that "I won't get to read some of them for years." Roth's strategy, it appears, like Steve Jobs in his lengthy interviews with his biographer Walter Isaacson, is to control the narrative of the tome he expects to be his tombstone. Though he says he is "not Frank Sinatra," and not intending to come out of retirement like that other New Jersey prodigy, it's easy to imagine the Bailey biography as its subject's final work of fiction. He wants the last word before other, unauthorized and less-sympathetic biographers of the future perform their own investigations into his life.

While we're waiting for Bailey's book we can look back at Roth's work from a perspective more typically posthumous. I believe some of those books will endure as part of our cultural patrimony alongside the classics of Melville and Twain and Faulkner and Roth's friend and role model Saul Bellow. The first Zuckerman trilogy alone (*The Ghost Writer*, *Zuckerman Unbound* and *The Anatomy Lesson*, eventually published in one volume as *Zuckerman Bound*) is one of the most brilliant accounts of a writer's journey into catastrophic success. The earlier *Portnoy's Complaint* unleashed an ethnic id never before seen in American literature and had a profound influence, for better and worse, on subsequent generations of identity-obsessed complainers. His extraordinary novels of the nineties (*Sabbath's Theater*, *American Pastoral*, *The Human Stain* and *I Married a Communist*, possibly the greatest divorce-revenge novel ever written) contain such an intensity of perception, reflection and expression that they left this reader indelibly imprinted (or infected) with the Roth vision (or virus). Perhaps the antihero of *Nemesis*, Bucky Cantor, who attempts to escape from and ends up spreading polio, is an allegorical stand-in for his author, who has by example encouraged others to engage in the fruitless pursuit of fiction's terrible truths. The pursuit is fruitless because the greatest literature raises more questions than it answers, and is not just stellar storytelling but an attempt to tackle the unspeakable, "the dread realities of life," as Bob Dylan memorably put it. Unlike Roth, Dylan has kept his bleak deadpan humor as he slouches toward geezerhood, still writing and touring, while the older Roth, now pushing eighty, is as dependably dire as the scowl on his face in most of his author photos. Dylan may not be happy, but he's still funny.

What is bugging Roth is nothing less than The Human Condition—the existential absurdity of people being born doomed, that is, mortal, how profoundly unfair—so why keep complaining about it as to a God who isn't listening and probably doesn't exist but will smite you anyway. Yet Samuel Beckett found something to say about nothing. The popular novelist Herman Wouk is ninety-seven and has just published a novel about trying to make a movie about Moses, an up-to-date postmodernist-populist take on the archetypal lawgiver, who also happens (like Roth and Wouk) to be Jewish. And Sonny Rollins, now past eighty and in a different spiritual tradition, keeps blowing his heart out on the tenor saxophone in electrifying live performances of what he has described as "the exaltation of existence." In other words, it is not inevitable that one writes or plays or creates oneself into a spent silence. There may in fact be an inexhaustible wealth of material, however grim, to convert, transform and otherwise alchemize into art.

And yet there is an unusual integrity in having the courage to say Enough already. There's something pathetic about watching an aging artist reduced to a fading imitation of a stronger earlier self, or repeating himself ad nauseam with a once-successful shtick. For every Picasso or Elliott Carter there is a badly diminished Norman Mailer or, worse, a Jack Kerouac, who fell apart after his first great book and never equaled that original achievement and died without ever reaching maturity. The trajectory of Roth's career, from *Goodbye, Columbus* in 1959 (the first of his two National Book Awards), has been a mostly upward curve, and perhaps the gradual decline of his powers has encouraged him to exit the stage before he becomes a ghost. Despite the consoling philosophical perspective sometimes available to older artists, Roth's relentless negativity of recent years appears to have led him down a dead-end street.

The irony is, if the *Times* interview is to be believed, that his renunciation of fiction has opened a new and happier chapter in his life. He tells McGrath that he now is able to entertain guests, to enjoy meals with friends, to have time for other people, and thus be relieved of the burden of his own demons. He is no longer, as he described himself in an earlier interview, an "emergency" whose creative compulsions require constant attention. He is free at last. He has, at least for now, broken up with the bitchy muses who have been tormenting him with increasingly dark themes of human defeat.

But I wonder whether the real story of his life is sufficiently fabulous to keep his restless imagination occupied. If his earlier autobiographical writings are to be believed, Philip Roth started out as a good boy eager to please his parents (as he writes in *Nemesis*, "there's nobody less salvageable than a ruined good boy") and has spent the better part of his days parked at his desk inventing imaginary characters who have acted out variations on his life and times—counterlives, if you will, to borrow a title from one of his most vexing and inventively complicated books. But whatever disappointments and disillusionments he has found amid the glory of his own literary achievement, why such a joyless swan song? Why the unrelenting lament? Why hang up the Louisville Slugger when it may still have some homers in it?

Like any other criminal, Roth has the right to remain silent, but somehow I suspect we have not heard the last from him.

Morton Marcus, Shaman Without a Mask

[2008]

Like the Giant Dipper or Mt. Umunhum, Morton Marcus has cut such a high profile in the Santa Cruz cultural landscape over the last forty years that it's easy to take him for granted as part of the scenery. As a teacher for three decades at Cabrillo College, a poet of significant national reputation, co-host since 1986 of *The Poetry Show* on KUSP radio, movie critic and film historian, co-host of the television program *Cinema Scene*, journalist for various local and Bay Area newspapers, and all-around arts activist and literary entrepreneur, Marcus has arguably done more than anyone else in these parts to promote and cultivate a community of creative writers and critical thinkers.

In the early 1970s he all but singlehandedly created a venue for poets and developed an audience for poetry by organizing a weekly reading series out of which grew a network of friendships and a "scene" as dynamic as any I've ever witnessed. More recently his articles in the local press and public discussion of the latest films have made him a vital presence as a cultural commentator. Though officially retired from teaching for ten years now, he can't contain his pedagogical enthusiasm, describing himself in a recent conversation as "absolutely intensely engaged in everything."

But taking Marcus for granted would be a mistake, as his close friends learned last fall when he notified them that he was going in for major surgery from which he might not emerge alive. As it turned out, he survived the surgery and now, at seventy-one, is back in the game at full strength—though the first time I saw him after the operation he looked paler, weaker, wearier and thinner than I'd ever known him to be. The occasion was a memorial reading for Maude Meehan, the much-loved matriarch of Santa Cruz poetry who had died just months before. Marcus was one of more than a dozen poets to speak that afternoon, and once he was at the microphone he seemed to regain his strength, characteristically going on to read for twice as long as anyone else on the program. About halfway through his performance I leaned over to Gary Young, seated beside me, and whispered, "Well, Morty's back."

My personal history with Morton Marcus precedes our chance meeting on Pacific Avenue in 1968 when we'd both just arrived in town, he to teach at Cabrillo and I to attend graduate school at UCSC. The previous year I'd been a senior at Bard College in upstate New York, editing a little magazine called *The Lampeter Muse*; Marcus was teaching English and coaching basketball at Lick-Wilmerding High School in San Francisco, and had sent me some of his writings. I printed a prose poem of his—the first one he'd ever published.

Our paths crossed frequently in the years to follow, and

we occasionally collaborated on or clashed over one thing or another, always in a spirit of mutual respect and solidarity in the effort to integrate our passion for poetry with the public life of the community. This forty-year association culminated last month in his delivery to me of his about-to-be-published memoir, *Striking Through the Masks*. At close to six-hundred pages, the handsome volume (published by George Ow Jr.'s Capitola Books) has nearly the heft of Marcus's previous dozen books combined. Its all-embracing scope and ample size are typical of the author's maximalism, his generosity and his gift for rhetorical excess.

Defying conventional notions of the memoir, *Striking Through the Masks* is really several books in one: a coming-of-age story, an autobiography, a narrative of the author's various world travels, a collection of sketches and portraits of writers he's known, a mini-anthology of their poems, the record of an ethical and moral education, a self-portrait of the artist, and a cultural history of Santa Cruz. It's illustrated with scores of photographs, and is the kind of book you can either read from front to back, if it pulls you in, or sample selectively depending on which of its many aspects interests you most. Walt Whitman famously bragged that he was large, he contained multitudes, and that whoever touched his book was touching a man. The same can be said of Marcus and his memoir.

One of the ironies of this epic attempt to account for his own history is that Marcus has written and spoken in recent years against the trend of the memoir in American publishing. He has complained about an "all-pervasive self-absorption" that has trapped many writers in the merely personal or domestic sphere and limited the free exercise of imagination, which in turn has constrained their field of vision. Asked to elaborate on this criticism, he says, "People are too focused on themselves and family dysfunction and how they were abused; so it becomes therapeutic, you know, and we can all sit there and say, 'Oh how terrible.' Literature is much more than that."

So how does his book differ from the others? "There has been a sense from the beginning that I am not talking about myself, that I am really looking at the larger picture of the human being, and I am just another human being." He goes on: "One of the first stories I published was about a Jewish tailor, and everyone at the school said, 'How do you know about Jewish tailors?' I don't know anything about Jewish tailors, but what I did was, I put myself in his body and in his mind, and [imagined] as a human being how he would react. That's one of the things that a writer has to do."

Born in New York in 1936 and raised partly in Brooklyn, of which the faintest trace remains in his style of speech, Marcus comes from a family whose dysfunction can compete with anyone's. The only child of a mother who married six or seven times (he's still not sure), he was farmed out to thirteen boarding schools throughout his homeless boyhood, and had to find his way in the world without adult supervision. "My father I hardly ever knew; my mother had abandoned me, virtually, so I had to figure out everything myself. How to open a can, how to use a telephone, how to make out a check—this stuff and all the other stuff that we take for granted, I had no one to tell me this, so I had to figure everything out, and it was cockamamie," he says without the least hint of self-pity.

The absence of any sense of victimization is one of the most striking things about the account of his childhood in the new book. How did he manage to come through with so little bitterness or resentment? "Stupidity," he replies. "I didn't know any different. As far as I was concerned, this was normal!"

Frequently the only Jewish kid among gentiles, and feeling himself a perpetual misfit, Marcus learned to fend for himself from early on. He responded to the cruelties of his peers by physically fighting back. "The way you get the bullies off your back is by beating them," he says. "Don't let them beat you." He identified with the weaker kids, the losers, and became their defender, and he credits this awareness of others' suffering with his dawning sense of compassion and desire for justice.

He tells me he started to play what he calls his "word games" because he couldn't draw. "So I started to draw pictures in words. I spent a lot of time in these schools alone; no one wanted to be around me, they really thought I was a mad dog. Because I wouldn't join the bullies, and I didn't want to hang around these namby-pamby kids; I was just on my own.

"And I would try to describe [to myself] what the sound and the look of the wind in the trees was. I was making pictures with words, and I didn't know what I was doing. I could not read till I was almost ten years old. My mother's homicidal sixth husband—or fifth husband, depending on which calculation—taught me how to read by driving me through New York City and making me read billboards, syllable by syllable. I was just an illiterate, angry, nasty kid. But even then, I never wanted to read."

What turned him around at fourteen was a high school English teacher named Richard Martin, who lured him into his private library with an offer to lend him any book he wanted. "I went to his room," Marcus recalls, "and I said, 'I wanna read something dirty.' He didn't miss a beat, he went to the shelves and came back with a copy of James T. Farrell's *Studs Lonigan* trilogy. He said, 'I'll make you a deal: you can read all of this stuff, but you've got to talk to me about it afterwards.'"

From Farrell young Marcus proceeded to Swift and Rabelais and Joyce, and then to the school library, where he read "every damn book" at the expense of his other studies. But before failing his courses and losing all his basketball scholarships ("Basketball is great because you're moving all the time and your mind's got to move at the same speed, you can't stop to think") he was turned on to poetry by this unconventional teacher. "He tells me that poets are very sensitive to the world around them. I think he may have actually dropped the line that women are interested in poets. Well, that was the prime—I would be able to win the hearts of women—because God knows at fourteen I wanted to do that."

Having flunked out of high school, Marcus joined the air force at eighteen, served four years and then, already publishing in his early twenties, managed to get into the Iowa Writers Workshop as an undergraduate on the GI Bill, and from there he earned a Woodrow Wilson Fellowship to Stanford. How does he explain his transformation from high school failure to brilliant student and very young published writer at one of the country's elite institutions? Voracious reading, for one thing, but there was something else. "Okay, well, poetry has its own little game that it's playing with you, so that you think you're doing it to get women, but suddenly women aren't the interest at all anymore, and it's the words and what you're doing with those words," he says, that reel you in.

Marcus's prolific and varied production as a poet—in books

ranging from the spare, archetypal lyrics of *Origins* and *The Santa Cruz Mountain Poems* through the "confessional" poems of *Where the Oceans Cover Us* and the family narratives of *Pages from a Scrapbook of Immigrants* to the expansive accomplishment of his fabulist prose poems in such collections as *When People Could Fly*, *Moments Without Names* and, most recently, *Pursuing the Dream Bone*—has brought him into contact with an extraordinary assortment of other writers, and it is his portraits of them that make for some of the most engaging sections of *Striking Through the Masks*. Polish Nobel laureate Czeslaw Milosz, current US poet laureate Charles Simic, California poet laureate Al Young, master of the short story Raymond Carver, widely revered poet and blowhard guru Robert Bly, and the Transylvanian answer to Garrison Keillor, Andrei Codrescu of NPR fame, are just a few of the many literary celebrities with whom Marcus has had close personal relations and whose characters are evoked with revealing anecdotes.

Dean of Santa Cruz novelists James D. Houston, who first cajoled Marcus into moving here; Marcus's longtime friend and Cabrillo colleague Joseph Stroud, one of the best of Santa Cruz's numerous first-rate poets; master poet and printer William Everson; another fine printer and virtuoso of the prose poem, Gary Young; Aptos-based composer and musician Lou Harrison; National Book Award winner Nathaniel Mackey of UCSC—these are among the various local cultural personages whom Marcus portrays as friends and creative comrades. (Disclosure: there is included a brief sketch of me and my work.)

He credits Cabrillo in its early years, even more than UCSC, with giving Santa Cruz its first great infusion of imaginative and intellectual energy. "Cabrillo was a community college, and in those days you did things for the community, so they said, 'If any of you people have any ideas you'd like to do in the community, let us know.' And I went straight to the community services guy and said, 'You don't have a poetry series here; let's start a poetry series.'

"So the real changing of this landscape, culturally, in this county, as far as I'm concerned, was Cabrillo. We were urged to take part in the community, and it was amazing how many different things we did, and I was just a small part of that."

He notes how things have changed in the years since. "What's happened is that the poet is no longer recognized as having his job in society. The shaman had his job in the tribe—the tribe could not exist without him, you see—and I think one of the things that is going wrong is that connection of the spiritual into the social that was always part of tribal organization has now gone." One of the major themes of *Striking Through the Masks* is that the artist doesn't exist in isolation but in mutually enriching interaction with everything and everyone around him.

Marcus's appetite for life is immense, his intellectual curiosity boundless, the range of his learning vast, his accomplishments as a writer considerable, his family history tumultuous, his travels wide, his energy undiminished after a near-fatal illness, so that even in his eighth decade, his beard and what's left of his hair gone white, he radiates the ardor of an adolescent. "Really, in many ways," he admits, "I've never grown up."

Perhaps this has something to do with his sense of still learning his trade. "The learning process has gone on forever," he tells me. "I used to describe it by talking about rhythm, about imagery… and you find there are, like, twelve elements and you've got to master them all. So you start with one ball and you throw it up in the air and you catch it. You do that, and then you take two balls and you do that, and you take three balls—and it can take years. Everyone learns at a different rate of speed, and finally you have all twelve balls going in the air, the perfect juggler. But you're still not a master until you throw all twelve balls up in the air and turn around and walk away, and they stay up there."

So the poet is a kind of magician, yet also someone with an ordinary job who speaks the same language as everyone else. "I've always felt, with Wordsworth, that the poet is just another person among the people; we may have priestlike visions, but never above, always part of the crowd. But to go beyond Wordsworth," says Marcus, "I think the poet has a job as part of society: I've got to communicate to people because what I'm telling them, as far as I'm concerned, is the real vision of life itself, especially human life, which the society they come from trains out of them, and they have to be reminded of why they are on earth.

"There is a purpose, I don't know what the hell it is, but what I express, what shamans express, is part of that purpose. It reminds the tribe, it reminds the society, and it speaks in society's words. As crazy as that may sound, I really believe that."

Greg Hall, Invisible Man

[2009]

Greg Hall, whose poems have appeared in the pages of *The Redwood Coast Review* from time to time, died in June of a heart attack, on a hot day, alone in his little cottage in San José. He was sixty-two. His unexpected exit occurred just a day or two before Michael Jackson's, and the contrast couldn't have been more stark. Greg, who in his small circle of bohemian friends was known as an artistic prodigy, a self-effacing savant of poetry, was in most ways the antithesis of the King of Pop. Not exactly a recluse, but no public figure either, Greg saw himself as more like the Invisible Man of Verse. His devotion to poetry was sufficiently absolute as to make publishing beside the point.

The eldest of six brothers and one sister, he joined the Navy soon after high school only to find himself and the military incompatible. But as his brother Rusty told me, Greg's brief experience as a Navy hospital corpsman would later inform his long career working in hospitals and nursing homes—as an orderly, a technician, and eventually an administrator. His gentleness and sensitivity were traits well suited to caring for the frail and the ill.

For a while in the early 1970s he took classes at Cabrillo College near Santa Cruz and became, through no ambition of his own, a star in the small-scale poetry renaissance happening there at the time. In regular readings at local cafés and restaurants, or in intimate public venues like the attic of the YWCA, and more casually in private get-togethers or cross-town correspondence with friends and fellow poets, Greg Hall astonished us constantly with his dazzling imagination, his lyric passion, his instinctive sense of rhyme and rhythm and the formal function of the line, his eye for social absurdity, his self-deprecating wit, soft voice and gentle manner.

I first met Greg in those heady days in Santa Cruz when we were both hungry young poets, and through the sometimes volatile cycles of a long friendship we stayed in touch. Our backgrounds could hardly have been more different—he the Alabama-born working-class son of a sign-painter father, I a garment-industry entrepreneur's youngest child raised in Beverly Hills—yet we connected deeply in our commitment to poetry, and we often shared our enthusiasm or gratitude or exasperation at having been taken somehow by the ruthless muses to serve as happy slaves to their demands. He once said to me, "Anyone who wants to be a poet in the United States should beat the shit out of themselves with a fresh red snapper."

We last spoke the day before his death. He called me out of the blue, apparently just to check in after several months' silence—we routinely exchanged brief notes or postcards, but he didn't have email and I didn't even know his phone number—and we talked for maybe a half hour about nothing in particular. One thing we never stopped marveling at was the strange privilege of having sustained our respective engagements with such a marginal but indispensable creative practice as the making of poems. Greg expressed his feeling of good luck to have persisted for so long in this obscure enterprise. And he said he was saving up to buy a motorcycle.

He had continued since those Santa Cruz years, through various detours and spiritual conversions when he would destroy his work or even renounce poetry, to write more or less continuously for the next four decades, evolving in his poetics from a maximalism incorporating the cacophony of popular culture to a more refined focus on the pure economy of the lyric utterance, a desire to boil the song down to essentials. He managed to mix both aspects all through his writing life, and there were times, especially in his "Dirty Greggie" poems, when he exercised an earthy vulgarity. He went through periods when it seemed to me he was just goofing around—adopting a Clint Eastwood or Bob Dylan or Jean Genet or Alberto Giacometti persona, typing out little western movies or faux Hank Williams songs or mock crime stories or goofy existentialist riffs—but always continuing the work, unafraid to play the fool, or even the jerk, simply setting the lines down as they came to him.

Greg Hall's best poems can hold their own, as far as I'm concerned, against those of any other contemporary. The fact that he published so little—a couple of slim chapbooks, *Flame People* (Green Horse Press, 1977) and *Inamorata* (Tollbooth Press, 2002), over forty years, and a few poems scattered in magazines, almost always because editor friends, including this one, asked permission—was for him almost a badge of honor, and to me a measure of his integrity. After a few early and unsuccessful attempts to break into poetry journals, he lost patience for the political machinations of publishing, the career-cultivation of the Masters of Fine Arts, the self-promotion and the networking demanded of anyone who would become "known" (a word he used with disdain) in that world of small-time fame and vanity.

Discovered in the 70s by Robert Bly, who wrote the introduction to *Flame People* and included one of Greg's poems in his anthology *News of the Universe*, Greg never tried to play that connection to his advantage. He would sometimes send his poems to Allen Ginsberg and would receive from the master a postcard in reply with a brief comment and a grade of "A." Michael McClure once advised Greg, for the sake of his poetry: "Go swimming." But despite the admiring attentions of such bardic demigods, he remained, by choice, in the shadows.

He looked to the great artistic misfits and radical outsiders—Dostoyevsky, Miles Davis, van Gogh, Beckett, Muddy Waters, Poe, Baudelaire, Robert Johnson, Vallejo—as his models, uncompromising devotees of go-for-broke, truth-or-consequences, live-or-die creation. Greg used alcohol and cigarettes to enable, emancipate and stimulate his angelic demons, the psychic forces that drove his soul to poetry. He knew he was doomed (he had a bad heart) and that he was hastening his end, but he surrendered, for better or worse, to what he felt was his destiny. "Poets are born to lose—and lose big," he told his friend the poet Robert Pesich, and he accepted that possibly self-fulfilling prophecy with the equanimity of a holy man. As he wrote to poet and translator Walter Martin: "I know literature cannot save us—it is water, mercifully, moistening the lips of an accident victim, before the blackout."

For a while there in the late 70s, around the same time Dylan got religion, Greg embraced a quasi-evangelical Christianity ("Do you know your God?" he asked me once in a letter. "You are of his chosen people."), but he got over that phase soon enough—just as he evolved through the World War II military history phase, the Holocaust phase, the keep-a-gun-by-the-bed phase (his lover had been murdered by her husband, who shot his wife "while cleaning his gun"), the Gurdjieff phase, the Samurai phase, the Proust or Chairman Mao or Yeats or Camus or Neruda or Robert Graves phase. He constantly recycled his books and music at the appropriate shops in Santa Cruz or the Santa Clara Valley, and gave away his other stuff to friends or left it at the Goodwill. Like a good Buddhist, he practiced both nonattachment and compassion, taking things in stride, comforting hospital patients with quiet sympathy, or counseling friends with pithy, ambiguous non-sequiturs.

To be in a room with Greg and a few friends was always to be on the verge of overhearing, as the evening wore on and Greg grew looser under the influence of his latest brew, his subtly hilarious one-line observations and gnomic commentary. These mutterings, addressed to no one in particular, had a tone of sly bemusement, as if even he wasn't sure exactly what he was saying. It was this sense of what Keats called "negative capability," the ability to live in uncertainty essential to a poet's disposition, that often came across in Greg's writings as a humble respect for the mystery of existence and for the bleak joke of human self-consciousness. Mortality was always the implicit punch line. And Greg's laugh was always wistful and laced with rue.

With his shifting moods, his periods of self-doubt, his alcohol-fueled reversals of attitude, Greg Hall was not an easy person to know. His friends, his wives (he was married and divorced four times), his family would surely testify to the difficulty of dealing with his unpredictable changes. But at his memorial gathering in San José, which drew about forty people to a downtown art gallery, every such testimony was suffused with affection and respect for Greg's unswerving commitment to art, music, love, beauty, kindness, humor, and to their blended presence in his writing. Though he sometimes seemed to reject his friends, we knew that if we waited a while the connection would return in the form of a phone call, a letter, a new poem in the mail.

In the weeks after his death I went through my files and was struck not only by the volume of pages his poems and letters amounted to—some five hundred—but by how well those texts that blew my stoned young mind in the 70s have held up over time, so that even now they ring with the truth of wildly imaginative yet down-to-earth revelation. The deeply authentic tenor of his voice, from his early experiments in Beat and Surrealist rhetoric to his more recent plainspoken aphoristic simplicity, his variations on the lyric, the comic and the philosophical, the high fidelity of his tone to his own spiritual center of gravity—all these qualities put to shame so many poseurs and hustlers who pass for successful poets in our current verse-glutted culture. In the democratized landscape where anyone with a laptop can "workshop" a poem into existence, and maybe even into publication, Greg was the humblest of workingman elitists, tapping away at his keyboard well above or below the fray, and ultimately covering his tracks. There were no poems found in his computer after his death, just one draft scribbled on paper—everything else he had long since deleted, or printed and sent to friends, either for safekeeping or disposal, it hardly seemed to matter.

Greg Hall proved you could live a full life as a poet with none of the trappings and corruptions of a career. You could share your work with a self-selected circle of like-minded souls, and thus avoid the vortex of solipsism—the involuntary solitude of isolation—while staying true to your muses, come what may.

F. A. Nettelbeck, Outlaw Poet

[2010]

F. A. Nettelbeck, who died January 20 in Bend, Oregon, at age sixty, is probably the most important avant-garde poet you've never heard of. Through his twenty-three books and chapbooks, countless magazine (and more recently online) publications, quite a few infamous readings, and for me personally a friendship and correspondence spanning nearly four decades, Nettelbeck since 1970 established himself more than anyone else I've known as a truly outside-the-law literatus, a man who, if not for poetry, very likely would have ended up in prison. His genius as a writer was to echo or reflect back through a fractured idiom some of the deepest pathologies of our culture, and through anger and outrage and an irrepressible need to offer some cry of defiance, to create a formally meticulous, visually musical, highly personal yet counter-lyrical poetry.

Aggressively urban, angular as the cacophonous media din we live in, often obscene, occasionally sexy and tender, ruthlessly perceptive, precise in its indictments, full of combative energy like the bar-fighter he was, Nettelbeck's poetry is not fit for most mainstream tastes, and that was fine with him. But for those readers to whom it spoke with electrifying vividness—cognoscenti of the poetry underground and more lately many of the younger rebels of the Internet—his voice resonates with great authority and authenticity and is a bracing antidote to the "well-crafted" workshop poem and to the cerebral obscurities of some of the more refined postmodernists.

I first discovered Nettelbeck in Santa Cruz in the mid-1970s when he was publishing poems in little magazines and working as a janitor at San Lorenzo Valley High. He had finished high school, but he had no use for higher education and had lived by his wits since leaving LA not long before. He was the kind of hustling entrepreneur who would dive into Goodwill boxes, appropriate whatever merchandise he could use and sell it that weekend at the flea market. It's hard to figure out how he made that kind of improvisational lifestyle work for some forty years, but even recently, out in central Oregon, he was organizing swap meets and supporting a family of five on virtually no visible income.

Though Nettelbeck was nothing like me—quite the opposite in most ways—and his poetics miles from my own, I recognized something real and forceful and highly skilled and inspired in his writing, and by 1979 I had the privilege of publishing, under my Alcatraz Editions imprint, what many still consider his magnum opus, the epic poem *Bug Death.* Only five hundred copies of *Bug Death* were ever printed (up to now, anyway) but I and some others remain convinced that it's one of the key poetic documents of our time, a *Waste Land* or Watts Towers that collects and recombines fragments of ruins into a soaring testimony of societal breakdown and human suffering and creative transformation.

Fred, as Nettelbeck was known to his friends, was a loyal comrade and a no-nonsense partner in conversation, but I can't say he was easy to get along with. Born in Chicago in 1950, he came to LA with his family as a boy and grew up in Inglewood, gravitating to the bohemian shores of Hermosa Beach and to the sun-baked streets of Watts for his cultural education. At twenty, during what's now called "the mimeo revolution," when hundreds of little journals were springing up across the United States, he started his own magazine, *Throb*, which featured writings by and interviews with such then low-on-the-totem-pole and under-the-radar bards as Charles Bukowski, Gerald Locklin and Susan Fromberg Schaeffer. In the later years of his career as a publisher he put out a series of tiny folded pamphlets called *This Is Important* with a half-dozen or so texts by distinguished renegades like William S. Burroughs, Tom Clark and Wanda Coleman, among others. Fred would photocopy a few hundred of these little poem-bombs and place them like evangelical propaganda in unlikely places like Laundromats and public rest rooms—a guerrilla assault on a-literate complacency.

For nearly forty years he published a steady series of his own books from very small presses—books with titles like *No Place Fast*, *Americruiser* (remarkable notebook of a cross-country journey by Greyhound), *Hands on a Mirror*, *Bar Napkin Poems*, *Everything Written Exists*, *Drinking & Thinking*, *Pesticide Drift*, *The Used Future*, *Don't Say a Word*, *Ecosystems Collapsing* and *Happy Hour*, handsome books in editions of a few hundred epitomizing the best of low-budget independent publishing. As some of these titles suggest, Fred was a serious drinker—a habit or genetic disorder inherited from his abusive alcoholic father—and while he was sometimes violence-prone (fueled by the rage he felt at the way things are and the hand he'd been dealt), he managed to channel much of his urge for destruction into verbally devastating works of literature. His formal experimentation sometimes extended to readings, like the one I witnessed at a Santa Cruz restaurant where he set up a half dozen tape recorders with his and other voices and cranked up the volume until the scandalized host, responding to complaints from the adjacent dining room, literally pulled the plugs.

When we read together in Palo Alto a few years ago, he was so pornographically aggressive toward the audience—not my preferred strategy for winning readers—that we lost a few customers before my turn at the mike. Last time I saw him, at a reading a couple of years ago in Santa Cruz, he was so drunk and so obnoxiously uncool and out of control that I fled the scene as soon as possible. I couldn't abide that kind of behavior—by now it is so passé and cliché, no longer amusing nor the sign of some Bukowskioid or Kerouackian genius. Alcoholism may be an illness, but so what.

Yet within a matter of weeks our correspondence resumed as if nothing had happened. He would report with dry stoicism on the struggle to get through the winter in his trailer in the boondocks with his family, and I would send whatever news I had along with selected clips from *The New York Times*, and we would exchange whatever new books we were bringing out. It was a strange friendship, in some way purely "literary" except that Fred was among the least literary—though most accomplished—of my writer friends. Between our common Southern California backgrounds (though from very different parts of the LA basin), our respective efforts as small publishers and our highly distinct yet parallel paths as poets, somehow we sustained a strong connection across the years.

What I saw in him, beyond the belligerent drunk, was an artistic brilliance and drive to create that nothing could stop. I found a lot of his writing to be too harsh and hardboiled and vulgar for my taste, but it was also powerful, unique and honest, formally inventive and tight and true to his experience, so I couldn't escape its integrity. Like the music of Howlin' Wolf or Albert Ayler, the novels of Louis-Ferdinand Céline or Hubert Selby Jr., the funky assemblages of Ed Kienholz or Robert Rauschenberg, Nettelbeck's verse might at first puzzle or repel, but you could, if you paid attention, feel its soul and its peculiar beauty. Unsentimental yet sensitive as hell, his lines were a conduit for an unruly current of discontent and chaos barely contained beneath the surface of civil society. His alienation was both intelligent and visceral, and his ear for the tones of contemporary American speech impeccable.

Because of his solid reputation and long history in the avant-garde, Nettelbeck's papers have been collected for several years now by the Ohio State University Library in its archive of experimental literature. It's a relief to know that, disreputable though he may have been to the tastemakers, his documents will be saved for any future scholars or publishers who may eventually wish to unearth and possibly reissue his works. More than an intensely personal record of a life lived on the edge and in service of the word, Nettelbeck's writings are a vivid if not a very pretty picture of our world, and testimony to the toughness and wit of a human being determined to survive and even thrive under the most unforgiving conditions.

At the end he was brought down not by his liver, as I expected, but by a spinal infection that surgery could not repair. He was left paralyzed but clearheaded enough to ask to be taken off life support, a decision that seemed to me both reasonable and courageous. He died on the fiftieth anniversary of JFK's inaugural address. Fred never asked what he could do for his country, but he sometimes wondered aloud what his country had done to him and other similar hard-luck, sub-working-class, godforsaken, seemingly good-for-nothing citizens—the kind one sees on the streets of any American city, and in poverty-stricken parts of the countryside, too.

"Not much news here, kind of hitting the wall," he wrote to me in a fairly typical letter dated June 4, 2008 (the fortieth anniversary of Robert Kennedy's assassination), shortly after Obama had clinched the Democratic presidential nomination. "The flea market is dead, no one has money, gas is $4.50 a gal. Blah blah, everything is fucked up. I'm too old to get a job, if there was any. Can't even sell weed anymore. Too many of these 'medical marijuana' growers now. So I sit waiting for 'change' and 'hope' to set us all free. It's not even summer-like here yet, I got a fire going this morning! A long, long winter. And that's about it. Kids are doing good. So that's all that matters. I don't hear from anyone in the poetry world...Maybe I'll get picked for the vice president spot, I'll keep the phone lines open...I ain't quite beaten *yet*."

I'll miss those letters.

Wanda Coleman's Last Laugh

[2014]

Wanda Coleman was a big woman. Physically, for sure—she was built like a linebacker, and she liked to fight. But far larger than her imposing physical presence was her prodigious accomplishment as a poet and performer. Wanda, a good friend of mine for thirty-five years who died last November 22 after a series of serious health problems, was for my money one of the major voices, in any language, of our generation. A frequently featured guest at international poetry festivals, winner of various prestigious national awards, prolific author of verse and prose who traveled widely for readings, she was first of all a Los Angeles writer who reigned as Queen of Poets in that city, a Watts-born native who stuck around to claim her turf as a vast resource for imaginative transformation. Her writing was both intensely personal and explicitly political, and LA was her ruthless yet generous muse.

At a packed memorial reading in January at the downtown branch of the LA Public Library, a diverse assortment of poets, most of them residents of Southern California, praised and thanked Wanda for inspiring them and for demonstrating by example that even such a seemingly antipoetic environment can offer great riches of resonant material to a writer with the presence of mind and the stamina to pay sustained attention. In this she had much in common with Charles Bukowski, the other, older, LA monster poet with whom she hated to be compared. But both were published by John Martin's pioneering independent Black Sparrow Press, in beautiful editions designed by Barbara Martin, and each unleashed a different kind of LA-inflected American vernacular that took the Walt Whitman–William Carlos Williams–Frank O'Hara legacy of common, conversational yet lyrical speech in liberating new directions.

Wanda was of course both black and female, as well as much angrier than Bukowski. At her best she synthesized the most diverse traditions, from the ancient Greeks and Shakespeare to the funky earthiness of the blues and the snappy hooks of pop music, with the rhythms of freeway traffic, colloquial black English, an advanced modernist poetics and a highly sophisticated personal prosody that made optimum use of space on the page as a musical score for her carefully wrought "free" verse. Her formal control is extraordinary in the way she is able to combine what sounds like natural speech with extremely subtle poetic technique to deliver her scorching torch songs and hair-curling narratives of life and death in a very tough cityscape of racial and class conflict, sexual clashes, economic struggle and automotive aggravation, all in an atmosphere of sweet-smelling semitropical menace laced with intoxicating traces of noxious smog.

I've lost a lot of writer friends in recent years, but none has left as large a hole in my personal universe as Wanda Coleman. Her nonexistence seems impossible. It wasn't just her physical size and the scale of her personality but the magnitude of her genius and her furious determination to make her mark with maximum ambition that set her apart from most of her contemporaries. Wanda's enormous energy and talent were deployed not only (as with so many writers) in the service of her own ego—though that, too—but as a defiant refusal to be defeated by circumstance and as a model of creative resistance. Even in the most intimate expressions of personal experience she felt herself representative of an oppressed minority determined to overcome its disadvantages. While the hardness of her life surely contributed to the health crises that finally felled her, her work is a powerfully impressive record of artistic victory and spiritual transcendence.

That's why so many other writers, in LA and beyond, regarded her with such admiration and found her to be such an encouraging, if sometimes intimidating, figure. Her live performances were incomparable ("electrifying" was the adjective most often used to describe them) in the way she dramatized her poems with virtuoso operatic passion. Her alternately and sometimes simultaneously ferocious and tender, enraged and erotic, frightening and funny readings made a huge impression on anyone who witnessed them. She overshadowed practically anyone else on any stage where she appeared, not because she was a scenery-chewer but because the natural force of her personality and the authenticity of her art just blew them out of the picture.

Because of her constant struggles to survive and to raise three kids mostly as a single mom in her twenties and thirties (before she met her third husband, the artist and poet Austin Straus, to whom she was married for more than thirty years), the fact of her tremendous literary production was even more remarkable. Working various jobs—as a men's magazine editor, a soap opera writer (she won an Emmy for *Days of Our Lives*), a medical secretary, a journalist, a university professor (a job she was doomed to lose because she was fearlessly herself in all she did and took no shit from anyone, whether student, faculty or administrator)—she somehow found the time and strength to take care of her kids, read tons of books, listen to a vast range of music, watch countless movies and remember them, stay conversant with old and new art, maintain a voluminous correspondence, and still write more and better poems than pretty much anyone else I know.

With her huge dangling earrings, her fingers decked out in big rings, her colorful wardrobe inspired by and often composed of African fabrics, her big natural 'do or cornrows or dreadlocks meticulously groomed, her enthusiastic enjoyment of every sensory pleasure from food and sex (it's in her writing) to watching tennis on television or sharing a joint with a friend, she relished life's fleeting delights like someone who knew her days were numbered. She had a swagger and a chip on her shoulder—a persona as the baddest bitch in the hood, someone not to be messed with—yet also an enormous warmth.

Wanda's mother had worked as a housekeeper on the Westside (Ronald Reagan was one of her employers, she told me; he loved Lewana's macaroni and cheese) and I had been raised by such women from South Central who worked for my family in the 1950s while my folks were out building their business, and these polar opposite upbringings on different sides of town created a curious bond between us, as we were also almost exactly the same age (she was two months older). Although we were born in different hospitals, she died at Cedars-Sinai, like my dad, in her case of a pulmonary embolism after a series of ailments exacerbated by years of economic insecurity, anxiety and stress. Somehow despite our radically different backgrounds we had an effortless connection, perhaps in part because we both so valued honesty in personal relations. She wasn't afraid to tell you anything if that's what she really thought, and this is such an unusual (and dangerous) trait that I was refreshed (if sometimes exasperated) by her candor. She was hypersensitive and easily provoked, but you always knew where you stood.

Wanda often confided in and consulted with me about her problems—domestic, professional, economic, medical, automotive—in long letters or phone calls punctuated by black humor and parenthetical laughter at her own expense. That unforgettable laugh—a high cackle, a crazed wail, a wild howl just this side of sobs—was, I'm certain, one of the things that kept her alive for sixty-seven years despite the hardships perpetually besetting her. She had a strong sense of the pathos and absurdity of her situation combined with pride that nothing could stop her, and the tension between those attitudes seemed to trigger a wickedly ironic wit. A glance at her sweeping signature at the end of a letter revealed a forceful, confident personality; the big *W* in the shape of an inverted heart was a graphic representation of her bravura.

Three years ago she wrote to me, in the middle of a litany of her latest troubles, "I'm counting on you to write my obituary (hahaha)." That wasn't necessary, as it turned out, because the *Los Angeles Times*, on the front page of its Sunday paper of November 24, 2013, published a long obit celebrating her as one of that city's premier writers, its "unofficial poet laureate," a fallen hero of local culture, an artistic warrior and a star whose light still shines. And as if to confirm her own certainty that the triple-whammy of being black, female and from LA had relegated her to the margins of mainstream literary respectability, *The New York Times*, which routinely publishes an obit for the most obscure TV actor, completely blacked out, so to speak, any news of her death. It was the kind of insult-by-omission she would have understood, and perhaps predicted (a scathing review she wrote of Maya Angelou some years ago had even gotten her blackballed by much of the African-American literary establishment), but it still astonishes me that the most literate newspaper in the country could be so myopic as to ignore the loss of such an important writer.

I am confident that in the years ahead, as her absence is felt in the cultural landscape and her books take their place in the historical record as the huge contributions they are to the literature of our time (the *African American Review*, a journal published by Johns Hopkins University, dedicated its recent issue to "Wanda Coleman and Nelson Mandela," in that order, which gives some idea of her stature), Wanda will be remembered with awe and gratitude for generations to come. Even now, on YouTube, you can see evidence of her enduring afterlife, and her works in print will surely outlast those of most other contemporaries. Like Mandela, Wanda Coleman is one for the ages, and she will have the last laugh.

Do We Need a Poet Laureate?

[2009]

When I first received the call from the Cultural Council informing me that I'd been nominated for the newly created post of Santa Cruz County Poet Laureate, naturally I was flattered—honored, even, to be among the candidates in this community crawling with accomplished poets. On reflection, though, I wonder what it means to be poet laureate, and whether Santa Cruz really needs one.

The idea of a poet laureate was invented by the British (and named for the Greek and Roman custom of crowning a winning athlete with laurel leaves) as a position of patronage in the royal court. The monarch accorded the honor to his chosen bard and in exchange the poet would compose appropriate odes for state occasions—like for example the king's birthday. While the custom has evolved, even in England, beyond such courtly duties, the role of laureate carries about it a whiff of Official Respectability at odds with the American tradition, beginning with the radical Walt Whitman (and the reclusive Emily Dickinson), of the poet as democratic wild man (or antisocial eccentric).

Only since 1986, when Robert Penn Warren was named poetry consultant to the Library of Congress, has the United States had a poet laureate. The PL's job has since become one of chief pitchman for poetry's presumably salubrious pleasures—a Garrison Keilloresque promoter of verse as an "accessible" and edifying ingredient in the cultural life of the nation. Like eating your vegetables, reading poetry is supposedly good for you.

Actually, in my experience some poems may be good for you and some not so good. Like vegetables, poems can be over- or undercooked, fresh or soggy, delicious or disgusting, green or moldy. There is no inherent virtue in poetry. Perhaps the "obscurity" and "elitism" that once gave poetry a bad name with the masses are no worse than the blandness and mediocrity that have lately made it somewhat more popular.

Shelley called poets "the *unacknowledged* legislators of the world" (my emphasis), and Julio Cortázar once said that the writer in our time is a bit like the medieval fool, "who between two jokes would tell the king four truths."

I'm not sure, in any case, what exactly a poet laureate would do around here. The energetic folks of Poetry Santa Cruz do an excellent job of making poetry available to anyone who may be interested. But I remember when poetry was a secret vice, an intimate indulgence, and while I confess to having done my share over the years to spread the dangerous virus of poetry, I still favor the idea of the poet as someone beyond or beneath the law—someone in the margins, where he or she is truly free to say whatever the muses dictate, even if it should prove impolitic—rather than as a literary equivalent to the surgeon general.

So, public venues for poetry? Absolutely. Poems for any and all people and occasions? Sure, if you can find the inspiration. A crown of laurels? Bring it on—and don't forget the olive oil. But maybe a guerrilla theater of poetry is a more enriching concept of the art, and the art's role in society, than is the wholesome notion of laureateship.

Poetry Month: Proceed with Caution

[2014]

April is a foolish month—T. S. Eliot might have said that, had he lived to see the domestication and professionalization of American poetry we've witnessed in recent years. With more poets than ever publishing and teaching creative writing, and still very few readers, Old Possum might wonder whatever happened to poetry as a disreputable art practiced mostly by effete eggheads and drunken bohemians. Poetry in his lifetime (1888–1965) was the dangerous and possibly fatal vocation of those who could not resist the siren call of the muses—tyrannical imaginary beings whose demands could never be met by any normal, well-adjusted person.

The deadly allure of poetry was in its seductive illusion that the true poet might someday join the company of immortals, those poets whose work the nascent bard read feverishly, admired extravagantly, and aspired to emulate; that one's best poems, and one's name, might be remembered for generations, centuries even. But in order to pursue this phantom fame you had to risk everything. No wonder hardly anyone with any common sense wanted to be a poet.

Today poetry is a harmless pastime democratized by organizations like Poets House and the Poetry Society of America. Poetry, like leafy green vegetables, is advertised as good for you. Open mikes and poetry slams pop up in virtually any community with the least literary or performance culture. All over the country people write poetry in workshops and informal support groups. Garrison Keillor reads verses every day on the radio, like a benevolent weather report. Masters of the fine art of poetry are manufactured by the thousands every year by the creative-writing industrial complex.

And the Academy of American Poets promotes National Poetry Month in an effort to persuade otherwise uninterested consumers to please buy a book of verse and thereby help support the publishing industry and its starving bards, a disadvantaged minority who require their own special month for commercial and professional survival. Like children with some disabling affliction, poets and poetry need your help. So give generously.

Some of my best friends are poets, and some of the nicest people I know write poetry, and I wish them only good fortune. But I confess to feeling nostalgic for those ancient times (circa 1966) when poetry first took possession of me. It was exhilarating because there was no social support or approval for such a reckless passion—I was barely nineteen, and it felt like a leap not of faith but folly to embark on a path more likely to lead to ruin than to glory. Yet when the muses deploy their whips, one must obey.

A month for poetry? It was a lifetime or nothing.

So by all means take a poet to lunch; buy a good book of poems and read it, and take a chance that you may be drawn further and deeper into poetry's mysteries—including perhaps the temptation, the infection, the compulsion to write your own. But know that it's a slippery slope that can plunge you into depths of pleasure and torment and realms of awareness from which you may never again return as the same person.

Know that it may open a door into a world with nothing to offer but the enchantment of language at its most intensive and no practical application beyond a heightened sense of reality. And ask yourself whether a month is enough to even begin to explore such a vast and perilous universe. And also ask whether most of what passes for poetry today begins to measure up to this transcendent standard.

Confessions of a Heteroformalist

[2013]

My writing comes in many different forms. It started when I was little, imitating my brother Rick, eight years my senior, who would compose funny parodies of poems from Palgrave's *Golden Treasury* (Oscar Williams edition), classic English lyrics of rhyming metrical verse that awakened in me some innate musical-verbal sense of the strange magic of language raised beyond its routine function of communication into a realm of fun and wonder. Whether I understood the poems was secondary; I liked the sounds and rhythms of the words, much as I liked pop music on the radio—it stayed with me, the tunes stuck in my head. Even now, decades later, just through primal and repeated readings and listenings, I am a walking jukebox of songs and poems.

Borges writes of hearing, in early childhood, his father read aloud to him, in English, Keats's "Ode to a Nightingale," and feeling an enchantment that infused him forever after with a love of poetry. I suppose what I experienced in reading the poems in Palgrave's anthology was more pedestrian, like the joy I felt in hitting a baseball, an ineffable excitement of connecting sounds and sensations—the solid crack of the bat vibrating with the sweet strength of my wrists receiving the impact of the pitched ball was like the way the words fell just so on the page to link the lines together as in some harmony sung on the air by the Andrews Sisters. Whatever it was, it hooked me on the sounds of words and on the patterns lines and stanzas made on the page.

This must have been when I first discovered Wordsworth, whose poems later moved me in a way that made me realize poetry was more than a game and could in fact express things that couldn't be said in any other way. In high school, reading him and the other English Romantics, I started writing what I felt were more serious poems, still in regular rhyme and meter, but trying to get at some of the confusions and agonies of adolescence. The poems were no good, anachronistic, full of clichés and recycled sentiments, but the exercise of writing formal verse served to train my ear in listening for the echoes, the rhymes and rhythms and resonances of the language, so that eventually, when my prosody opened into more contemporary modes, I retained what had by then become a second-nature formal and musical sense of a poem's structure.

This may sound merely technical, but technique is an essential means to an end; it is a servant of style, without which there is no individuality in writing, no virtuosity in music, no grace in dance, no visual harmony in art. From experimenting with formal verse through attempts to sound more up to date in what Denise Levertov called "organic form"—a stylistic flexibility increased and expanded in my translation of different Spanish-language poets, having to impersonate them to reliably represent their diverse voices—gradually, over many years, with many digressions into various kinds of prose, I've come to subscribe to what I call heteroformalism, or writing in a variety of forms and styles and genres.

This range of formal variations derives in part from a desire to surprise myself, and I hope the reader, with unpredictable alterations of mode and mood and tone from page to page in any particular book yet with a voice that is recognizably mine, a personal sound that's been synthesized over several decades of echoing and emulating, mimicking and appropriating the work of other writers I admire.

In the early 1970s, on top of translation, I started writing journalism and criticism—once my brain had been detoxified of what I'd been taught in grad school—and since then the essay has become one of my favorite forms, partly because it too is flexible with plenty of room for variation. Composing newspaper columns, interviews, features, satire, reviews, cultural commentary, poetic riffs on current events, imaginary memoirs, political analysis, polemics about whatever was bugging me, obituaries, cryptic journalistic love songs to elusive muses—all this was fantastic exercise for extending my range as a writer. Though I still thought of myself primarily as a poet, it was through the regular practice of prose that I discovered my writing did not have to limit itself to the marginal place of poetry in the culture and could speak to nonspecialists in a language they could understand, and in the newspaper, no less.

In the early 1990s I wrote a novel, *The Mental Traveler*, based on a watershed episode in my personal history, a book conceived as fiction rather than memoir because that was how I felt I could reach a deeper subjective truth. I believe all memoirs (including this one) are a form of fiction because they are the creation, or reconstruction, of one person with a particular point of view and selective memory and incomplete research, and the past, despite the efforts of Proust and lesser searchers since, can never be recaptured. But subjectivity is another thing, and if it's deep enough it reaches the universal, and that is one of the specialties of fiction.

Over the last few years, egged on by then-editor Traci Hukill of the *Santa Cruz Weekly* for a column of local color she called Street Signs, I've been writing short texts of around 350 words that I call prosems (a word I confess to have stolen from Julio Cortázar, who called some of his writings *prosemas*), which I like to think of as a hybrid of the personal essay, local reporting, memoir, lyric poetry, amateur philosophy and "creative nonfiction"—whatever the individual prosem (often based on or inspired by or invoking a specific place) demands.

Since 1999 I've also been working with the prose of other writers in the quarterly literary newspaper I edit, *The Redwood Coast Review*. I try to clean up sentences, if necessary, to help the authors sound more like themselves. I write headlines, house ads for the publisher, solicitations for letters to the editor, corrections, subscription pitches, library propaganda, whatever's needed.

So what began as a fascination with poetic form has, over more than half a century, expanded to embrace a range of genres, each best suited to a particular kind of writing intended to fit a particular kind of experience or assignment. And within those forms—verse, translation, the essay, fiction, editing—the streams keep branching, and thus enriching the palette, broadening the canvas, widening the screen on which I write. I feel freer to experiment and to explore when I have at hand such an assortment of polygraphic possibilities. Formal and "free" verse (which is also formal, in a different way), journalism, personal narrative, cultural and literary criticism, each has its role and is a means to diverse creative ends; each is a tool with a different purpose, an instrument with a different sound.

The pleasure I find in writing is perhaps in part a result of having cultivated this array of distinct yet integrated formal resources. A heteroformalist practice keeps me engaged in an ongoing process of discovery, and keeps me interested in what comes next.

A Note on the Author

Stephen Kessler is a poet, prose writer, translator and editor. Born in Los Angeles in 1947, he received his BA in languages and literature from Bard College and an MA in literature from the University of California, Santa Cruz. He published his first essays and criticism in the early 1970s, and his reviews, columns, articles, features and interviews have appeared steadily since then in dozens of magazines and newspapers, chiefly in Northern California. He was the founding editor and publisher of the international journal *Alcatraz* (1979–1985) and of the Santa Cruz newsweekly *The Sun* (1986–1989). He has received a National Endowment for the Arts Fellowship, a Lambda Literary Award, and the Harold Morton Landon Translation Award from the Academy of American Poets for his translations of Luis Cernuda, and is the editor and principal translator of *The Sonnets* by Jorge Luis Borges. From 1999 through 2014 he was the editor of the award-winning literary newspaper *The Redwood Coast Review*. He lives in Santa Cruz. For more about Stephen Kessler, visit www.stephenkessler.com.